Psychotherapy
with Older Men

The Routledge Series on Counseling and Psychotherapy With Boys and Men

SERIES EDITOR

Mark S. Kiselica
The College of New Jersey

ADVISORY BOARD

Deryl Bailey
University of Georgia

Chris Blazina
Tennessee State University

J. Manuel Casas
University of California–Santa Barbara

Matt Englar-Carlson
California State University–Fullerton

Ann Fischer
Southern Illinois University–Carbondale

David Lisak
University of Massachusetts–Boston

William M. Liu
University of Iowa

James O'Neil
University of Connecticut

Steve Wester
University of Wisconsin–Milwaukee

VOLUMES IN THIS SERIES

FORTHCOMING

Psychotherapy
with Older Men

Tammi Vacha-Haase,
Stephen R. Wester, and
Heidi Fowell Christianson

Routledge
Taylor & Francis Group
New York   London

Routledge
Taylor & Francis Group
270 Madison Avenue
New York, NY 10016

Routledge
Taylor & Francis Group
27 Church Road
Hove, East Sussex BN3 2FA

International Standard Book Number: 978-0-415-99862-8 (Hardback) 978-0-415-99863-5 (Paperback)

Library of Congress Cataloging-in-Publication Data

Vacha-Haase, Tammi.
Psychotherapy with older men / Tammi Vacha-Haase, Stephen R. Wester, and Heidi Fowell Christianson.
p. ; cm.
Includes bibliographical references and index.
ISBN 978-0-415-99862-8 (hardcover : alk. paper) -- ISBN 978-0-415-99863-5 (pbk. : alk. paper)
1. Older men--Mental health. 2. Psychotherapy for older people. I. Wester, Stephen R. II. Christianson, Heidi Fowell. III. Title.
[DNLM: 1. Aged--psychology. 2. Mental Disorders--therapy. 3. Men--psychology. 4. Psychotherapy--methods. WT 150 V118p 2010]

RC480.54V33 2010
616.890081--dc22   2010004640

Visit the Taylor & Francis Web site at
http://www.taylorandfrancis.com

and the Routledge Web site at
http://www.routledgementalhealth.com

We dedicate this book to those older men who have sought our services and, through that, taught us so very much about themselves, their needs, and their lives.

—TVH, SRW, HFC

Contents

Series Foreword

Getting old can be a vexing experience for men, especially men who have been raised with very traditional notions of what it means to be a man. According to traditional gender roles, men are supposed to be protectors and providers—tough, strong, and virile (Levant, 1995). Consequently, how traditional men feel about themselves is determined to a great degree by their ability to live up to these perceptions regarding manhood (O'Neil, 2008). Aging, however, gradually limits the extent to which a man can live his life according to these traditional expectations. Inevitably, a man's physical strength and sexual prowess will decline, and the older a man gets, the more likely he is to experience health problems that can further limit his abilities, if not cause him to suffer considerable pain and anguish. In addition, at some point in his later years, he will choose to retire or he will be forced to do so, which can alter his identity and self-worth. He may also endure significant personal losses as close friends and family members die. The experience of these changes can be a source of considerable distress (National Institute of Mental Health, 2009), and older men who believe that it is unacceptable to talk about or seek help for their concerns—that it is unmanly to do so—are likely to bear their burdens alone.

But the golden years can also be a time of great joy and satisfaction for men. An elderly man who has invested in loving his spouse or partner and their children and serving his community and his country can know that his life has meaning because he gave of himself to others in selfless ways, caring for the next generation and helping to make his world a better place (Snarey, 1993). He can look back on his career with a sense of pride, knowing that he worked hard, and as a result was a good provider (Heppner & Heppner, 2001). He can slow down the pace of his life and take advantage of new opportunities for leisure, hobbies, and the exploration of his spiritual life (Herr, 1999). The shift away from work duties can give him more time to be with his family and solidify his role as a teacher, mentor, nurturer, and source of wisdom for his family members (Taylor, 2007).

Recognizing that the later stages of life can be filled with both significant adjustment difficulties and tremendous opportunities for growth
and fulfillment for men, I was determined to add a book on older men
to the *Routledge Series on Counseling and Psychotherapy with Boys and
Men*. Gradually, that wish became a reality after I learned that three
colleagues, Drs. Tammi Vacha-Haase of the Colorado State University,
Stephen Wester of the University of Wisconsin–Milwaukee, and Heidi
Fowell Christianson of the Wisconsin Medical School, were interested
in writing a book on addressing the needs of older men. During several conversations with the authors, I was excited to discover that they
shared my view that mental health professionals tended to lack knowledge about the lives of older men and how to help them. We agreed
that adding a book on the subject would be an excellent addition to
this series, and I am pleased and honored to say that Drs. Vacha-Haase,
Wester, and Christianson have weaved their rich, clinical experiences
counseling older men with their sophisticated research expertise on the
psychology of men and masculinity in this much-needed and timely
volume, *Psychotherapy with Older Men*.

In this sensitively written and scholarly book, Drs. Vacha-Haase,
Wester, and Christianson take us into the world of older men, helping
us to understand the eras in which they were raised, how they view the
world, the gender role conflicts they experience, and the physical, mental, and emotional challenges and problems they face during their later
stages of development. The authors explain in clear, accessible language
how to engage older men in psychotherapy, earn their trust, and join
them on their journey during their twilight years. Every practitioner
will find their work to be an illuminating guide to working with older
men, which is a process that can not only enhance the lives of elderly
male clients, but also be a fulfilling endeavor for the practitioner.

I thank Drs. Vacha-Haase, Wester, and Christianson for their fine
work, and I am proud and grateful to say that they are my colleagues.

Mark S. Kiselica, Series Editor
*The Routledge Series on Counseling and
Psychotherapy with Boys and Men
The College of New Jersey
April 2, 2010*

REFERENCES

Heppner, M. J., & Heppner, P. Pl (2001). Addressing the implications of male socialization for career counseling. In G. R. Brooks & G. E. Good (Eds.), *The new handbook of psychotherapy and counseling with men* (pp. 369–386). San Francisco: Jossey-Bass.

Herr, E. L. (1999). *Counseling in a dynamic society: Contexts and practices for the 21st century* (2nd ed.). Alexandria, VA: American Counseling Association.

Levant, R. F. (1995). Toward a reconstruction of masculinity. In R. F. Levant & W. S. Pollack (Eds.), *A new psychology of men* (pp. 280–333). New York: Basic Books.

National Institute of Mental Health (2009). *Depression in elderly men.* Retrieved online on April 2, 2010 at http://www.nimh.nih.gov/health/publications/ men-and-depression/depression-in-elderly-men.shtml

O'Neil, J.M. (2008). Summarizing twenty-five years of research on men's gender role conflict using the Gender Role Conflict Scale: New research paradigms and clinical implications. *The Counseling Psychologist, 36,* 358–445.

Snarey, J. (1993). *How fathers care for the next generation: A four-decade study.* Cambridge, MA: Harvard University Press.

Taylor, A. C. (2007). Grandfathers: Rediscovering America's forgotten resource. In S. E. Brotherson & J. M. White (Eds.), *Why fathers count: The importance of fathers and their involvement with children* (pp. 91–103). Harriman, TN: Men's Studies Press.

Preface

It was Tuesday; a day that he should have been golfing with his buddies. But instead, John Russell sat looking out the window of his private room in the rehabilitation unit of a skilled nursing facility. Having suffered a stroke two months ago, John realized not only would he not be golfing today but most likely would never be on the golf course again; in fact, according to his physician, there was a high probability he would never walk. How could that be? He was only 68 years old. John had golfed all his life; he was an avid skier and horseman. But not being able to walk was only part of the current challenges in his life. His right hand still didn't work, so eating and writing were difficult; even getting dressed in the morning was a chore. He had no privacy and little independence. For the first time in their 50-year marriage, his wife was managing their finances. His children were doing the yard work at his home. A military veteran who had survived battle and earned a purple heart, a successful businessman, and an elder of the church—and he couldn't even get out of his wheelchair into bed by himself. How would he ever be Mr. John Russell?

As a therapist, how would you approach psychotherapy with Mr. Russell? Would you begin by focusing on his health problems? The recent changes in his life? His past? Or the more traditional approach of directly addressing psychological symptoms?

Should focus be given to his age, his gender, or his medical diagnosis? How much, if at all, should you consider his changing roles or relationship with his wife and family? What other health care professionals are currently part of his care, and to what extent should they be included in your treatment plan?

Turning to the existing resources on psychotherapy with older adults might be a practical first step; unfortunately, you would soon realize that little guidance for psychotherapy with an older man was offered. Although core concepts in the clinical geropsychology literature would be applicable, a more thorough understanding of the psychology of men would be necessary. For you to best work with Mr. Russell, you need an integrated understanding of how the masculinity literature applies to older men, that is, Mr. Russell and his cohorts and their life issues.

Men are socialized to have a set of specific attitudes, beliefs, and behaviors based on societal views of masculinity. Although men are influenced by the historical experience of their cohort, the traditional male role emphasizes independence, control over one's destiny, physical prowess, and restriction of emotions. The extent of Mr. Russell's internalizing the traditional male role of his cohort and masculine values is apparent in the case example at the beginning of this chapter. And, to some degree because of his acceptance of this role, Mr. Russell has accomplished much and lived successfully as a result. However, as can be noted in Mr. Russell's current situation and his struggles, this socialization can be a disadvantage when men are experiencing life changes that occur with age.

UNDERSTANDING OLDER MEN THROUGH RECOGNIZING MALE SOCIALIZATION

Masculinity is often understood as a social construction (see O'Neil, Good, & Holmes, 1995, for review), as society reinforces boys to be aggressive, dominant, competitive, and self-sufficient (Pollack & Levant, 1998). As a result, many boys internalize these traditional notions of masculinity as they grow into manhood, regardless of the interpersonal and intrapersonal consequences. Brooks (2001), for example, described how the developmental "male chorus" (p. 207), consisting of a young boy's family members, peers, and cultural models, teach him a confusing combination of characteristics and skills (e.g., strength, independence, achievement) that may be adaptive in one situation (e.g., work, school) while at the same time maladaptive in another (e.g., relationships, collaborative efforts, and health care), with little consideration of how these values will be of consequence in later life.

The extant literature has identified several accepted concepts of traditional masculine traits including dominance, emotional restriction, competition, and sexual prowess. Career success and the ability to provide and care for one's family are imperative to achieve acceptable levels of masculinity. But what about men, such as Mr. Russell, who because of their advancing age or medical issues can no longer meet gender role standards?

CHANGES OVER THE LIFE SPAN

There are concrete changes that men experience as they age: Children leave home, parents die, and the awareness of the passing of years can turn the focus from time since birth to the direction of time until death.

Many men may struggle with the recognition that options for their future are decreasing and that in fact they may have already achieved their greatest accomplishments in the form of family success, career promotion, and physical strength. Older men, many of whom for much of their life have wanted to appear strong, independent, and in control, may struggle to continue this facade, perhaps even more so when they encounter situations of retirement or declining health, where they have virtually no control, such as in Mr. Russell's case. When older men are unable to take charge of the situation or be self-reliant, both of which are socialized expectations of men, many of them may identify suicide as the only option. Indeed, men commit 84% of the total suicides among older people, with White men over the age of 85 being at the greatest risk of all age, gender, and race groups. Could it be that the need to be masculine during the later stages of life is simply too much of a burden and that rather than fall short of society's dictate to be a man, some men would rather die?

But death by his own hand does not have to be the answer for the older man experiencing male role conflict. By definition, reaching older adulthood symbolizes a certain resiliency, with the proverbial "many lessons learned along the way." There are endless amounts of events and experiences, both good and bad, that men nearing a century of life have incorporated as part of their being. As Rabinowitz and Cochran (2002) proposed, some aspects of the traditionally socialized male gender role provide survival value; older men won World War II, served their country in other conflicts, raised families, and built their country's economy to be the envy of the world. Thus, older men such as Mr. Russell who are experiencing change and distress benefit by being placed in the context of their strengths and finessing personal resources to the best of their capabilities in the current situation (e.g., see Brim, Ryff, & Kessler 2004). Ultimately, the goal is to help the older man capitalize on his past experiences and masculine socialization, applying the best of these to his current place in life.

FOCUSING ON OLDER MEN

Prior to the women's movement culminating in the 1960s, men's experiences, and by extension socialized masculinity, were assumed to be the normative point of view in mental health. One of the consequences of the subsequent social change triggered by the women's movement was the beginning of a critical exploration of men, their power, their social role, and the effects of their socialization process. However, it was not until Pleck's (1981) book *The Myth of Masculinity* that mainstream scholars began investigating "masculinity not as a normative construct, but rather as a complex and problematic construct ... [and] question[ed] traditional norms of the male role" (Levant, 1996, p. 259). The years since have brought notable texts such as *A New Psychology of Men* (Levant & Pollack, 1995), both volumes of *The New Handbook of Psychotherapy and Counseling With Men* (Brooks & Good, 2001a, 2001b), the *Handbook of Counseling Boys and Adolescent Males* (Horne & Kiselica, 1999), *A New Psychotherapy for Traditional Men* (Brooks, 1998), and *New Psychotherapy for Men* (Pollack & Levant, 1998). Furthermore, empirical work on the socialized male gender role has increasingly been represented in academic journals such as *Professional Psychology: Research and Practice*, the *Journal of Counseling and Development*, the *Journal of Counseling Psychology*, and *The Counseling Psychologist*.

However, in regard to older men, the literature has not kept pace with the need. There remains, on both a research and an applied level, what Applegate (1997) called "a blind spot" (p. 2); that is, men in the later stages of their life, middle-aged and older, are largely ignored. Although dated, Applegate (1997) captured a significant omission: Older men are invisible (Thompson, 1994), even though there were over 15 million men in the United States age 65 or older in the year 2000.

PSYCHOTHERAPY WITH OLDER MEN

The purpose of this book is to extend the literature on the psychology of men to those men in their later years, offering guidance for therapists who provide psychotherapy to older male clients. Focus is given to aspects of aging in the 21st century, integrating both gender role conflict and strain for older men, with focus on their cohort as well as challenges intrinsic to aging. This book highlights the social stigmas older men face through exploring the context of their life and the obstacles with which they must cope. The conceptualization of older men's experience is through a lens identifying a lifetime of socialized demands and incongruent situations, neither pathologizing nor overtly blaming them for their problems.

There are inherent complications in melding two relatively unrelated bodies of literature. When available, the most recent research focusing on older men and psychotherapy was included, as was the latest research in the areas of aging and the psychology of men. However, the reader will surely notice that the empirical support falls behind current theories and contemporary thinking about psychotherapy with older men.

Although the time is right for the psychology of men to address the needs of those in late life, the extant literature has only begun to make the first strides into understanding how gender role socialization effects men of color, men of differing sexual orientations, and men of various socioeconomic and sociopolitical statuses. The nature of these initial developments, as well as what they might mean for older men, is covered in a later chapter. However, the reader should be aware that the application of the approaches presented throughout the book will require adjustment when working with men outside the majority group.

This book begins by setting the stage to support the reader in appreciation of the older man in the context of masculinity, society, cohort, and family. Gender theories, as well as theories of aging, are described and integrated to provide a theoretical foundation for further understanding. A basic model of psychotherapy, organized around issues that surface with older men during the psychotherapeutic process, is described. Focus is then directed toward clinical issues common in psychotherapy with older men, with discussion about symptoms, screening and assessment, differential diagnosis, and best-practice interventions.

EXPECTATIONS OF THE READER

This book is intended for the experienced therapist, in that it presumes a degree of competence in the practice of professional psychology. The audience is intended to include both those who are new to working with older adults and those who have experience with older adults in psychotherapy. Expectations include familiarity with the American Psychological Association's "Guidelines for Psychological Practice With Older Adults" (APA, 2004) and competence in the delivery of mental health services to older adults as defined by the Pikes Peak model of professional geropsychology (Knight, Karel, Hinrichsen, Qualls, & Duffy, 2009), with additional focus on the unique gender role experiences of male clients.

Acknowledgments

As I compose this section, I realize that this is my final writing for the book. I am the last of the authors to finish my acknowledgments, and am overwhelmed thinking about all those individuals whom I want to thank. There are so many amazing people, personally and professionally, clients and family and friends, students and colleagues, who have been a part of my reaching this very moment. I could not have done it without them, and I am not able to give them the gratitude they so greatly deserve. Every day I strive to live in a way in which they are aware of the significance they hold in my life and how much I cherish our relationship.

Reading the next few pages you will note that my two coauthors recognize the value of working with one another; my own sentiments could not have been echoed more accurately. This book truly was a collaborative effort, one I will always value and treasure. My hope is that the readers of this book benefit even a part of what I have gained throughout this process.

I have been rather single-minded over the past few years and determinedly spent many hours at my computer; however, I always leave the day's writing to join in the family evening meal. It is during this time that I am able to laugh, listen to stories, ask about their day, and truly enjoy my family, reenergizing for more hours of work ahead. So thank you, David, Colten, and Conner: When the four of us are together, it is as if nothing else exists or matters. The magic that appears when we gather is indescribable, something I revel in and will continue to seek my entire life.

In closing, I want to acknowledge my father, husband, and son—the men in my life.

—Tammi Vacha-Haase, PhD
Fort Collins, Colorado

Little that I have professionally accomplished, including this book, is solely the result of my efforts. Certainly I owe my coauthors a debt of gratitude; without the tireless efforts of both Tammi and Heidi, both who are better than I at turning a phrase, this book would have never seen the light of day. My students at the University of Wisconsin–Milwaukee need to be honored as well. Graduated though many of them may be—and you know who you are—during their matriculation through the program they held me to a standard that in the end reignited my passion for the writing as well as the science. As nice as I am, I am not the easiest person to write with, so those connections that do develop have that much more meaning.

It is also very important to note that the Great Bird of the Galaxy has seen fit to truly bless me with many powerful mentors—Jedi Masters, all of them, who have guided me as my career (I hope) continues to unfold. Nadya Fouad (University of Wisconsin–Milwaukee), David Vogel (Iowa State University), Jim O'Neil (University of Connecticut), Marty Heesacker (University of Florida), and of course Mark Kiselica (The College of New Jersey) have influenced me for the good lo these many years, and it is not hyperbole when I say that I am grateful beyond measure for their support, encouragement, and friendship.

Of course, all of these professional relationships occur under the umbrella of a family that is, in many ways, better than I deserve. My parents, of course, Tom and Karan Wester, got me started on understanding, and behaving in accordance with, the very multifaceted meaning of being a man (and every holiday season my brothers have a go at refining that meaning) while also providing me the space in which to actualize toward that meaning. My wife, Dawn, who knows better than anyone how difficult I am to be around when writing, has offered her unconditional love for 17 years now (despite periodically losing me to the word processor), and throughout that time she has sought to bring a sense of art and grace to my life. I owe her more than I can say, especially because it has been her voice these almost two decades now reassuring me that I can, indeed, be a counseling psychologist.

Both of my children, my daughter Shelby Paige and my son Nathan Lafayette, make me more proud than I ever thought it was possible to be. Shelby always has a smile and as such brings a sense of joy to my life that is inspirational and also is patient as I learn to parent a teenage girl. Nathan never quits, even when things get challenging, and even better he has fun; the mischievous glint in his eye as he goes through his day makes me want to be 10 again.

To all of these individuals, as well as to those whom I lacked the space to mention, I express my heartfelt gratitude for your presence in my life. The word "thanks" does not convey it well, but I shall say it anyway: Thanks!

—**Stephen R. Wester, PhD, LP**
South Milwaukee, Wisconsin

This book was born from the boundless energy and dedication of my coauthors, Tammi and Stephen. It was a pleasure to work collaboratively with both of you, and I cannot express in words my respect for you both.

I would like to acknowledge the influential mentors with whom I have had the honor to work. Dr. Nadya Fouad provided supportive yet challenging mentorship when I needed guidance. She demonstrated how a strong woman survives, thrives, and leads without excuses or apologies. Dr. Jo Weis took me under her wings and showed me what it means to be a psychologist, therapist, academic, researcher, colleague, and friend. I cannot thank her enough, and I look forward to years of collaboration and friendship. Dr. Stephen Wester showed me that the path to success is through fortitude and hard work. He provided the empathy and genuineness that allowed me to ask difficult questions, express differing opinions, and ultimately develop a personal sense of efficacy as a researcher and psychologist.

I would also like to acknowledge my supportive colleagues at the Medical College of Wisconsin, Department of Psychiatry and Behavioral Medicine. Dr. Laura Roberts, my department chair, has given me the support to develop my clinical and academic career in a burgeoning and innovative area within the medical school. Dr. Tom Heinrich, chair of the Division of Psychosomatic Medicine, has invested his time, mentorship, energy, and advocacy to help guide my career. I look forward to a proliferative academic and clinical career at the Medical College of Wisconsin.

Last and most important, I would like to acknowledge the support and energy provided by my loving husband, Andrew Christianson. Andy stood by me throughout this writing process, as he has for all challenges in my life. He never failed to provide me the space to write and humor to enjoy as I undertook this endeavor. His love, humor, friendship, companionship, and support make all of my professional activities possible and fulfilling experiences. I love you and look forward to a lifetime of mutual learning, challenge, and enjoyment.

I would also like to acknowledge my family, who taught me to strive for the best and be pleased with myself regardless of the outcome. I would especially like to thank my father, Edward Fowell, who instilled in me a tenacious work ethic and sense of determination, as well as the empathy, kindness, and compassion that is reflected in all that I do. To the rest of my family, including my mother, Dawn Kidd; sisters, Heather Harper and Kim Hicks; stepmother, Sue Fowell; stepfather, Frank Mowery; in-laws, Meg and Pete Christianson; and the rest of my family, I thank you from the bottom of my heart for your kind words, understanding, and support throughout my professional endeavors. Without your humorous comments, understanding words of support, and encouraging cheers, this would have not been possible.

—Heidi Fowell Christianson, PhD
Wauwatosa, Wisconsin

1

Life as an Older Man

Richard Donovan, age 70, was the older of two children. His sister, age 55, now lived in a different state, and his parents had recently died. Mr. Donovan never married, instead devoting 45 years of service to the local high school, first as an English teacher and later as the principal. Described by his colleagues as gentlemanly and civil, Principal Donovan valued rules and procedures that served him well in his academic roles. He could be a perfectionist at times, based on his belief that high standards were needed to mold children into proper adults. Colleagues, as well as parents of students, often noted he could be rigid and controlling. To fill his days after retirement, Mr. Donovan decided to volunteer at the high school where he had served so long. However, this experience did not go well; he often tried to take over projects and was described by other volunteers as bossy and domineering. Mr. Donovan became easily offended by what he called the inefficiency of the other volunteers. This would be followed by a ranting discourse on how the younger generation had deteriorated, exhibiting behaviors that would not have been tolerated while he was principal. Mr. Donovan had long been accustomed to having people serve him in his personal life; being unmarried, he hired people to clean and cook for him. Interested in academic pursuits, he retained a handyman and a mechanic to complete lawn care and car repair. However, as his health deteriorated, Mr. Donovan began to demand the same servile treatment from professionals in the health care system. He was often frustrated, as he believed the health care providers did not "put forth their best efforts" and were "unresponsive" to his needs. When confronted, Mr. Donovan became more demanding of those around him, which led to many health care workers avoiding him in response to his sharp criticism.

How would Mr. Donovan best be understood and his behavior described? Is he simply a demanding, grouchy old man who wants his own way? Is his behavior reflective of outdated standards and a sense of patriarchal entitlement? Or are his actions somehow related to a values system, stemming from both his gender and the time period in which he was born?

Growing up and growing old in the United States involve expected rites of passage and unique challenges that provide an important context for understanding, conceptualizing, and ultimately providing psychotherapy for older men. Thus, to conceptualize older male clients, the therapist must be aware of the multitude of factors involved in the individual man's development, both historically and in more recent events.

Mr. Donovan learned what society expected of him as a man during a very specific time in this country's history. That is, Mr. Donovan was born into World War II, experiencing his teenage years and early adulthood during those postwar years. The zeitgeist of that time shaped his attitudes and values, as well as his expectations for himself as a man and the world around him. During his adulthood, Mr. Donovan was able to build a successful life and career around those expectations. However, these same values and "rules of behavior" now seem to be interfering with his current functioning; he appears to be unaware that the behaviors that were once valuable to him and adaptive to many situations throughout his life are no longer allowing him to be successful in his current stage of development and life circumstances.

Thus, the life of an older man can be understood only through an integration of gender, age, cohort, and individual personality characteristics. Not doing so, conversely, runs the risk of dismissing both a lifetime of experience and a rich history. Psychotherapy with older men such as Mr. Donovan should begin with an integration of basic knowledge of masculinity, including masculine scripts and male socialization, as well as the aging process, such as normal versus pathological aging, fact versus fiction, and stereotypes. Contextualization of older men's experiences is a necessary requirement for understanding the complex clinical presentation of older men and a key to providing gender, cultural, and generationally appropriate care.

MASCULINE SCRIPTS

Mahalik, Good, and Englar-Carlson (2003) detailed seven "masculine scripts" (p. 124) that often arise during the course of psychotherapy with male clients. The "strong and silent" (p. 124) script stresses the importance of being stoic and unemotional, lest men be labeled as less manly than their peers. The "tough-guy" (p. 124) builds on this idealized script, stressing the suppression of emotions so as to be called "tough in the face of pain" while also responding to situations through physical prowess. The "give-'em-hell" (p. 125) script, conversely, downplays emotions and instead focuses on the importance of physical action or violence as a method of achieving goals. For example, from early in childhood, boys are often taught that fighting with others is a means to an end, required to build character that is critical to successful manhood. Emotions in this context are acceptable, as long as they do not convey vulnerability. The outcome of following these scripts for decades is commonly exhibited in older men; a lower range of emotional expression, with the exception of anger or aggression, becomes the preferred mode of communication.

Consider the time frame in which Mr. Donovan came of age. He was born in 1940, and his early childhood was characterized by World War II and the sacrifices made during that campaign. He may have had a family member serving in the war, or perhaps he had family contributing on the home front, through the USO or other volunteer organizations. Certainly the civilian population cut back on many things to support the troops, including having rubber drives and recycling campaigns and rationing, and also lived with lower incomes because of family members serving. This environment would likely instill many values consistent with the strong and silent and tough guy scripts. Complaining, for example, would be seen as inappropriate, and the expression of any disappointment or sadness would be stifled, as one would quickly be reminded that those fighting overseas had it much worse. These views would continue to be reinforced even after the war ended, as soldiers returned home, many of them burying their experiences. The societal norm indicated that war experiences were not to be talked about, and everyone was to move on with life (Winters, 2006). In sum, Mr. Donovan, like the other boys and men, was taught not to demonstrate sensitivity or express tender emotions; signs of weakness or presentation of vulnerability were not acceptable.

Two additional male scripts center on the importance of sexuality, and specifically heterosexuality, in a young boy's life. The "playboy" and "homophobic" scripts refer to the expectation that so-called real men are sexually active, often in a nonrelational fashion. Virility is associated with masculinity and of greater value than tender relationships focused on feelings other than those of a physical nature. Building on the implications of the playboy script, the "homophobic" script (Mahalik et al., 2003, p. 125) stresses the absolute nature of relationships with others, especially men. From the playboy perspective, close and caring relationships are not important and exist only as a means to obtain physical pleasure. Between men, therefore, such intimate relationships cannot develop because of potential appearances of homosexual intentions. The expression of love for siblings, friends, and even fathers becomes difficult if not impossible. Early learning of these scripts can cause older men considerable challenges given physical sexual changes in later life, when sexual relations become less of a central feature in their lives. In addition, with age, the father and son relationships may evolve, as do peer interactions, leaving questions about how to approach such change within the context of previously embraced masculine scripts.

Another two scripts draw on the importance of success and achievement in a man's life. The "winner" and "independent" scripts (Mahalik et al., 2003, p. 126) describe how messages regarding masculinity across the life span associate being male with victory over adversity and obstacles in life; this also includes defeating other men, formal competition or not. Men are generally expected to achieve victories independently, without the need of assistance from others. Indeed, the image of John Wayne as Shane and Clint Eastwood as The Man With No Name each riding out to face their fate alone is etched into the fabric of modern Euro-American culture. These images communicate the importance of individual accomplishments, with men being encouraged to be independent, focusing on hard work, physical strength, and emotional restraint to attain success in life.

Mahalik and his colleagues stressed that many of these scripts are adaptive to men, either when they are enacted flexibly or when they are considered contextually valid. For example, men who are able to switch between a tough guy script on the job and a deeper emotional availability at home are far less likely to encounter difficulties. How men experience the world, as well as their ultimate social scripts and roles, is intertwined with the social, political, and cultural advances of their time. Addis and Mahalik (2003) offered a social constructionist perspective to understand this process. In brief, a man's contexts are an environment in which he constructs the scripts that guide his understanding of what it means to be a man. Thus, for some men and under some conditions, certain behaviors are adaptive and appropriate; however, under different conditions or for different men, those same behaviors interfere with functioning. Consider Mr. Donovan. His value system and the behaviors it promoted were contextually understandable and adaptive during his adult life. However, at a later stage of life, when he was no longer employed and in charge and was beginning to experience a decline in his health, those same behaviors actually interfered with his functioning and ability to be successful in his environment.

Thus, when working with older men, therapists will find it particularly important to assess and identify their cohort-related experiences and belief systems, not as pathology but as a sign of socialization. The process of psychotherapy involves understanding older men through their eyes, gaining a sense of their needs from their lived experiences and the scripts they embrace. Older men are individuals who have been shaped by distinct social and cultural movements and who are experiencing age-related, developmental aspects of the life span.

Older men, for example, undergo physical changes and increasing health issues related to aging and the cumulative effect of chronic illness, psychological challenges, social stereotypes (e.g., ageism, devaluation), and cohort-related socialization. Mr. Donovan is merely one example of this interaction of cohort-specific expectations and deteriorating health conflicting with the belief systems of those around him. His inability to switch from male scripts that most likely helped him to succeed in his professional career is now hindering his forming positive relationships in his retirement, as well as the ability to obtain medical care.

DISENGAGEMENT THEORY

Disengagement theory (e.g., Cummings, Henry, & Damianopoulos, 1961) is well positioned to explain the experiences of older men. In one example, Cummings and Henry argued that men have an instrumental role in society that is primarily associated with their employment; a point that Mahalik and colleagues would have agreed with given their narrative on both the winner and the independent scripts. When the job ends, often in the form of retirement, older men transition to a period of life associated with less participatory involvement. This results in a circular process, in that less involvement means fewer interactions that might also contradict the push to disengage.

Older men may be prone to the disengagement process given their socialized tendency to avoid the expression of tender emotions (e.g., the tough guy and the strong and silent scripts) required to form the close interpersonal ties that might resist disengagement. Consider that Mr. Donovan's interpersonal difficulties did not become readily apparent until after he retired and decided to return to the school system as a volunteer.

Admittedly, disengagement theory is not without its critics (e.g., Hill, 2005), and the use of such a pessimistic theory to explain the experiences of older men might seem anathema. However, in many ways societal views regarding older men reinforce the idea that disengagement not only occurs but is both expected and encouraged. Cultural images attribute expectations of strength, intelligence, and status to younger men while suggesting that older men are incompetent, infirm, and an undesirable distraction on the busy lives of their adult children. Such ageism is a widely accepted phenomenon that broadly explains a series of inappropriate evaluations, stereotypes, and implicit social messages negatively characterizing men in their later years of life.

SOCIAL STEREOTYPES: AGEISM AND DEVALUATION

Many people in advancing age may resist identification with the older adult identity or change their physical appearance (Jones & Pugh, 2005) in an attempt to maintain a sense of culturally relevant personal identity and competence. Katz and Marshall (2003, 2004) argued that older adults, both men and women, experienced pressure from a culture driven by pharmaceutical products encouraging hormone replacement and revitalized sexual functioning. Unfortunately, a side effect of pharmacological marketing interventions targeted at maintaining sexual virility in older men can have the negative impact of reinforcing gender-specific expectations throughout late life where men are expected to continue to be strong, powerful, and sexually driven (Marshall & Katz, 2006).

The Healthy Aging Movement

The healthy aging movement, for all of its positive encouragement of healthy behavior and positive physical and cognitive activity, has also been strongly criticized as an ageist conceptualization of later life. Advertisements encouraging sexual virility, unwrinkled skin, mountain biking in late life, and keeping active regardless of circumstances provide implicit cues to younger and older people that one must actively prevent the determents of aging. This image is to support active aging, in contrast to becoming a feeble, frail, dependent, helpless older adult. Unfortunately, these subtle social messages do not account for the likelihood that growing old can sometimes result in the occurrence of illness and disability in the absence of amoral behavior, leaving much room for older and younger individuals alike to negatively evaluate and subsequently dismiss physically, cognitively, and emotionally ill elders.

Scholars have also criticized the current social construction of aging. Katz and Marshall (2003) argued that the healthy aging movement, encouraging individuals to combat decreases in functioning, changes in physical appearance, and changes in lifestyle to "successfully age," is blaming and negative toward older adults. Specifically, if one has an illness or lives with a functional impairment or disability, the healthy aging movement subtly indicates that this is due to a character flaw of the individual rather than to a natural decline associated with aging. Within the healthy aging movement, older adults are personally responsible to maintain a risk-averse lifestyle, and if they do happen to experience illness or disability, there must be a personal flaw worthy of significant blame. Marketing targeted toward sustaining youth, physical, functional, sexual, and cognitive, provides the implicit message that one has the tools to maintain health and not age. As a result, older adults may engage in behaviors, activities, and attitudes to preserve their gender and age-related social status (Calasanti & King, 2007).

Social Messages to Men

In an analysis of the differential representation of men and women in anti-aging discourse, Calasanti and King (2007) found current social messages men receive about aging suggest that masculinity is biologically and hormonally based, with more testosterone being less feminine and elderly. Loss of testosterone and an increase in estrogen level is readily equated with both the aging process and the subsequent loss of manhood, a term coined "male menopause" (Calasanti & King, 2007).

Social gerontologists argue that implicit messages provided to men suggest that loss of testosterone is equated with poor sexual vitality and performance, indecisiveness, weakness, lack of purpose and direction, low self-confidence, being unworthy of competition, and apathy, whereas maintenance of male hormones protects men from the "dangers" of aging (e.g., depression, decreased sex drive, muscle atrophy, depression, weakness, fatigue, and motivation). These changes correlate with elements of male gender role socialization, the playboy script specifically, suggesting that as a man ages, and barring any intervention, he loses his manhood. Thus men are subtly taught, through anti-aging marketing, that without a static level of testosterone, which does not occur with unimpeded aging, they will become impotent, effeminate individuals on par with women (which is interpreted as negative).

In addition to threatening basic identity and social privilege awarded to men, living in a society implicitly producing such messages restricts the ability of men to experience a range of behaviors outside of a rigidly socialized male gender role. The homophobic script is a prime example of this; even as men age, their ability to express love and affection for the men in their lives is severely curtailed. Unfortunately, the anti-aging material targeted toward men strongly and negatively attacks deviation from a traditional gender role, prompting many men to staunchly defend their masculine identities to the determent of their relationships, health, and psychological well-being. This is a hallmark of disengagement theory; the restriction in feedback results in a retrenchment, rather than a reexamination, of socialized expectations. Indeed, the impact of this conceptualization of aging for older men has several potential consequences, including self-blame and psychological distress secondary to physical disability, which may be contradictory to one's view of how one "should" age. In addition, older men may fail to fully embrace some of the potential freedoms associated with aging with an attempt to maintain a strong gender role identity. Although it is possible that older men may be free to conform less to gender role expectations as they age, it is also likely that older men would continue to view themselves from a set of potentially unrealistic standards related to both gender and age.

COHORT PHENOMENON

Although subject to similar developmental processes, members of each generation are given the context in which they age. For example, the cohort born in the late 1930s through early 1940s was shaped by the experience of knowing both extremely limited resources (i.e., the Great Depression) and global conflict (i.e., World War II). Many people from this generation continue to keep leftover or newly expired food and save most everything they can because of the indelible mark left on them from living through extreme poverty. Furthermore, they tend to have specific perspectives on concepts such as freedom, sacrifice, and responsibility given the efforts made by America from 1939 to 1945. Mr. Donovan is in many ways an example of this; his perfectionist tendencies and somewhat ridged teaching and leadership style can be contributed to an outgrowth of this era.

The cohort of Americans born in the 1950s to 1960s, conversely, did not know, until recently, economic hardship stemming from a global recession. The messages sent from that experience, including the drops in property values, loss of wealth when the stock market dropped, and subsequent governmental response, is shaping their outlook, with the ultimate outcome to be determined. As another example, the cohort of Americans born in the 2000s will never have known a world without the technological advances of the Internet. Outdated processes such as registering for classes in person, writing letters by hand, or physically going to the library to complete research will have become largely foreign concepts because of the social learning that occurs in reaction to a known environment.

This process has been referred to as the "cohort phenomenon" because although the characteristics of older adults are constantly evolving as generations of people age and develop, each cohort embodies its own unique identity. Labels such as the Greatest Generation, the baby boomers, Generation X, and Generation Y are examples of how society categorizes the nature of that distinctive character. The nature and expression of gender is a part of this process. For example, social and cultural changes associated with the feminist movement have moved the bar for women; what society found acceptable for women in the 1940s is far different from what society considers acceptable in 2010. Masculinity, conversely, has only just begun to be examined. Accordingly, many of the culturally held beliefs about men, specifically that they should be powerful and successful in their career, show limited emotional expression, and place work above leisure time with family, retain strong ties to earlier centuries.

For the past many years, men have typically assumed the responsibility of financially supporting the family and presiding over the household. Work during earlier time periods, especially as the Industrial Revolution occurred, was extremely physical and deadly to the worker. This is an example of what Mahalik et al. (2003) referred to as contextual validity. Complaining about the environment, having concern about one's conditions or one's health, or showing any weakness meant that men would be replaced and lose their livelihood. Thus, men in this cohort were raised with circumscribed cultural and social scripts and are more likely to exhibit the behavioral and psychological signs of the socialization of the times.

As alluded to previously, continuing to adhere strictly to traditional gender role socialization and masculine scripts allows for advantages in some domains (e.g., success at work, healthy competition with others, etc.) but disadvantages in others (e.g., difficulty establishing intimacy with family and children, accepting increased disability and subsequent limited functional ability, and transitioning to the world of retirement, help seeking, and limited social support). Mr. Donovan's interpersonal style seemed to provide him the ability to serve his school successfully for 45 years, but later as a volunteer he was described by those around him as rigid and domineering. This is known as a generational stamp, as current events make certain practices obsolete; those same cultural practices are taught (in this case to boys) and expected by society. Therefore, as men from earlier cohorts approach their later years of life, they may find themselves faced with changing environmental demands (i.e., physical and/or psychological disorders, retirement, more time with family members) and an increased need for treatment (i.e., traditional medicine and psychological services), many that are to varying degrees incongruent with their gender role expectations for themselves and how to act in society.

Mr. Donovan's interactions with the health care system exemplify this; when the medical providers did not act in the way to which he was accustomed, he responded by becoming more demanding, which in turn pushed the workers further away while also leading them to label Mr. Donovan based on a stereotype. Eventually, Mr. Donovan may give up, as he in effect would run out of learned behaviors. Baltes (1996) explained this as a process through which observable behavioral changes of disengagement are the result of increasing disconnects between an individual's learned behavioral pattern and societal expectations. In essence, the distance between how one *knows* to behave and the norms of a society grows larger as one goes from early adulthood, to adulthood, and to the years of later life. Men such as Mr. Donovan who have been successful in their lives leading others through specific behavioral patterns may find that those patterns do not translate well either to life outside the workplace or to life outside the generational context.

DEVELOPMENTAL ASPECTS OF AGING

Physical

Older men often face a series of physical changes associated with aging that impact their physical ability, expression of masculinity, and body image. Normal biological changes associated with aging occur across anatomical and functional domains. Although these changes are conceptualized as normal parts of the aging process, the functional changes associated with them, such as decreased strength, physical endurance, and physical tone, can have a large impact on the body image and self-identity of older adults. This is especially the case for men who have a history of valuing the physical aspects of themselves, through work and career, for example, or perhaps through hobbies or extracurricular activities. An individual who labored as a carpenter and house builder may struggle more with these physical limitations than a man who was employed as a librarian.

Physical changes occur across organ systems and functional domains as part of the aging process. Older men will likely find changes in their sexual response time, taking longer to achieve an erection and requiring a longer rest time between erections. Muscle mass, although slowly deteriorating over adulthood through a process known as sarcopenia, typically decreases to half of what it was in early adulthood by the age of 75, related to multifactorial causes including slight inactivity and decreases in testosterone levels. Eyesight changes in later life make dim environments, fine details, and shadows more difficult to accurately perceive. Presbycusis, or age-related hearing loss, also occurs, making high-pitched sounds more difficult to discern and hear. Because the senses allow connection with other people and the environment, these changes can be challenging. Sensory deficits can limit an older man's ability to interact socially and perhaps cause an accelerated process of withdrawal and isolation.

Although there are more systemic physical changes associated with aging ranging from normal to pathological, these physical changes can have a major impact on the body image of men. Research supports body image issues coinciding with male gender role expression (Cohane & Pope, 2001; McCreary & Sasse, 2000). Social images of ideal men portrayed primarily in the media, but implicitly reinforced in social interactions (e.g., Thompson, 1994; van den Berg, Thompson, Obremski-Brandon, & Coovert, 2002), suggest that attractive men are muscular, strong, and lean (Leit, Pope, & Gray, 2001; Spitzer, Henderson, & Zivian, 1999), characteristics needed to fulfill the tough guy script. In addition to cultural messages regarding masculinity and attractiveness, older men are constantly exposed to images of the healthy aging movement, which suggests that older men should be able to maintain a healthy and functional state well into the later years of life. The decrease in physical function, strength, stamina, and activity can be internalized as a loss of masculinity among older men (Gerschick & Miller, 1995).

Appearance

Physical appearance may be the most concrete indication of aging. The first outward signs of aging are typically seen in the skin, as aging skin becomes drier, thinner, less elastic, and more easily torn. Changes in body shape and musculature also occur with age as men become shorter in late life because of settling of the vertebrae. Body shape changes as body fat redistributes and collects in the torso, abdomen, and lower face. Regardless of the fat redistributed, there can be an overall weight loss occurring with age, due to loss of muscle and even bone, leading older men to be at risk for falls.

Sexual

Changes in physical appearance and sensory acuity may feed the stereotype of the older man as asexual. However, research indicates that intimacy and sexuality are an important part of healthy relationships throughout the life span. One age-related physiological change is that of the slowing of the sex response cycle, as it may take a man longer to attain an erection; an erection may not be as firm as it was at a younger age. It may also become more difficult for men to achieve orgasm. However, contrary to popular belief, these changes do not signal the end of a satisfying sex life, and many older men enjoy intimacy and physical contact throughout the life span. The key to this outcome seems to be the flexible adherence to the male gender role norm; if an older man accepts and prepares for these changes, the odds are greater that he will have a rewarding sex life as he ages. However, if he holds himself to the standard of his 20s or the playboy script without taking his advancing age into account, he sets the stage for increased disconnect between his socialized behavioral expectation and the demands of his current situation.

Researchers have established that sexual desire, expression, and function, as with other physical changes associated with aging, also change as a function of aging. Men are vulnerable to several physiological changes that can impair sexual functioning, including degeneration of vascular supply affecting vasodilatation, decrease in sex hormones associated with decreased sexual desire, increased incidence of chronic disease, and polypharmacy associated with impairment in sexual function. Although abstaining from sex in the later years of life is not necessarily aberrant or unhealthy for older men, an imbalance in functioning, desire, or expectation can lead to relationship problems in older adulthood. Many older men, in the face of physical, psychological, and illness-related factors, experience sexual dissatisfaction in the later years of life. Even more troubling, however, is the stigma associated with discussing sexuality in current culture, especially with regard to sexuality in older adults, leaving many older men who may be experiencing sexual function, desire, or relationship problems with little avenues for treatment.

Ability

Although the above are normal developmental changes in a man's body over the life span, men may tend to focus more on their physical abilities rather than appearance. This is consistent with social stereotypes of older men, as it is presumed, for example, and even expected that older men will be heavier, have less hair, and often pay less attention to their physical appearance. In interviews with 10 men aged 68 to 88 that explored older adults' perceptions of their bodies, half of the men denied dissatisfaction with their body image but instead expressed "the importance of strength, autonomy, and the need for gratitude for what they were still able to do" and "described management techniques that included the downplaying of their symptoms so as to retain an impression of healthiness and autonomy" (Clarke & Griffin, 2008, p. 1092). This may be thought of as an adaptive attempt by older men to hold on to those aspects of masculinity that are meaningful and obtainable, consistent with male gender role socialization. Men who in the past defined themselves as physically capable, strong, and commanding may now interpret the normal physical changes associated with aging as a sign of weakness and disability. Men adhering strongly to the success, power, and competition gender role socialization who are faced with the normal physical changes associated with aging may find themselves ineffective according to their previous standards or may engage in unsafe behaviors rather than accepting new, adaptive ways to perform physical tasks.

Psychological

Research suggests that although many older adults have an increased incidence of physical illness and pain, the majority do not develop psychological disorders (Scott et al., 2008). In addition to normal, developmental psychological changes that occur in older men, there are several abnormal psychological processes that older men are vulnerable to, including anxiety and depression. Although not indicative of normal aging, stressors contributing to the vulnerability for anxiety include an increased incidence of health-related concerns and poor health, existential issues related to loss and death, and perceived or real loss of control.

Older males experience multiple causes for increased symptoms of depression, typically related to loss in function or ability, and increased isolation. Depression can often masquerade as cognitive impairment or other physical problems. Older men who adhere to stringent male gender role socialization may be at higher risk of developing depressive symptoms but the least likely to seek treatment. Disengagement theory suggests that this is a normative process, a consequence of an ever-decreasing cycle of positive reinforcement based on decreasing interpersonal interactions. However, do not mistake the concept of normative with safety; older men are at a significant suicide risk, having the highest rate of completed suicide and being more likely to make more serious attempts that result in death.

Older men are also vulnerable to increased substance abuse in later years of life, including exasperation of long-standing substance abuse problems and the development of problematic drinking late in life. Men have been socialized to use alcohol as a social outlet and a way to cope with stress. However, in the earlier years of life, many circumstances prevent men with problematic drinking from escalating their behavior, including the need to maintain employment. Drinking behavior can therefore increase in later years for men who drank socially in the past, those with alcohol abuse problems, and those with alcohol addiction due to the interplay between increased unmonitored time, fewer external responsibilities, increased life stressors, and increased isolation.

CONCLUSION

The unique experience of an older man can be best understood through recognition of the broad social and gendered context in which he lives, as well as the time in society in which he grew up. Older men must contend with implicit messages about the aging process and their societal value, adapting and buffering sense of self from the views of older adults as frail and dependent. The social construction and lived experience of aging and masculinity interact dynamically to produce a host of issues specific to older men. In psychotherapy with older men, therapists must be cognizant of the unique issues older men experience regarding physical changes and psychological functioning, placed within the context of the complex relationship between gender role socialization and the biopsychosocial experience of aging.

2

Gender and Aging

Robert Acrann did not understand. He felt as if the world was shifting, and he knew in his heart that he did not like where it was going. Born in 1934, he watched his older brother go off to fight the Germans in 1943 and not return. He himself served in the Army; he enlisted right out of high school and built a career until his retirement in 1982. He started a business soon after, providing security services to those who felt they needed protection. He could not help shaking his head when he watched his employees go through their day. The attitudes of the kids today; they protested everything and were angry at the world but also expected those around them to take care of all their problems. Did they not understand responsibility? What about the mistakes they were making? Mr. Acrann knew how things should be; his father had taught him, and his brother had showed him, how men were supposed to think, act, and serve. Yet the boys today had no sense of right or wrong, let alone honor and courage. Wanting to work only their 40 hours per week, yet complaining when they were not promoted and suing him when they were fired for their own incompetence. They laughed at his standards and called him old-fashioned for his expectations. He was confused; his sense of morals had kept his nose to the grindstone for over 60 years and provided him with a good living. How could they not see the value in that? Most of his friends were gone; some had retired and moved south, and others had died. The majority of days, Mr. Acrann woke up, went to work, and then returned home for dinner and bed. He tried watching television, but it scandalized him, and music had ended the day Frank Sinatra died. Not much of a reader, and never one for hobbies, Mr. Acrann found his life revolving around his business and nothing else.

Theories abound regarding the gendered experience of men (see Smiler, 2004, for a recent review). Many have speculated, for example, that men are the way they are because of genetics or evolution (see Buss, 1995). However, most researchers agree that *masculinity* is a social construction (see O'Neil, Good, & Holmes, 1995, for review) related to, but distinct from, biological sex (i.e., Lips, 2007). Specifically, society teaches boys to adopt a set of culturally embedded standards of appropriate masculine behavior (Levant, 1995, 2001). Consider Mr. Acrann in the case example; he "knew how things were supposed to be" because men in his life, his father and brother, had impressed on him the value of working hard, not complaining, and serving others as a way of honoring himself. However, the extreme end of such teaching causes boys to "suffer under a code of masculinity that requires them to be: aggressive, dominant, achievement-oriented competitive, [and] rigidly self-sufficient" (Pollack & Levant, 1998, p. 1). Indeed, characteristics such as "problem-solving, risk-taking, staying calm in the face of danger, assertion, and aggression" (Levant, 1995, p. 229) are expected of boys if they are to be perceived as manly. "Big boys don't cry" (Good & Sherrod, 2001, p. 24) becomes the standard, and boys are subsequently punished for expressing "weakness and vulnerability" (Good & Sherrod, 2001, p. 24). For example, how would Mr. Acrann's father and brother have reacted if as a teenager Mr. Acrann had cried about or protested the standards he was living under? Could that predicted response be part of the explanation for why Mr. Acrann is now disgusted with the "kids" of today?

MASCULINITY AND LATER LIFE

To what extent can the extant literature on the psychology of men be generalized to older men? For example, being virile, especially with regard to sexuality, has been long seen as a significant component of masculinity (e.g., Levant & Brooks, 1997), the essence of Mahalik, Good, and Englar-Carlson's (2003) playboy script. What happens, however, when an older man suffers from physical limitation that restricts his sexual ability? In addition, men's roles within a family have changed dramatically in the past decade (Shapiro, 2001). Merely being a tough guy, successful on the job, is no longer sufficient, as men are expected to contribute to family relationships, particularly in their roles as spouse, father, and grandfather. Such involvement, although not noted as an aspect of traditionally socialized masculinity, is a reality facing older men.

Many older men seem able to successfully adapt to such shifting demands; unfortunately, some men in later life experience more negative consequences, typically conflict and confusion regarding the differences between their identities and their socialized male role. As noted in the first chapter, disengagement theory (Cummings, Henry, & Damianopoulos, 1961) suggests that some older men might respond to such confusion by pulling back from social interactions while increasing their engagement in stereotypically masculine behaviors in an effort to hold on to their gender role ideal. Mr. Acrann, although appearing to continue to function at a successful level, exhibits some characteristics of disengagement, as his days revolve around his business and little else. He seems to have few friends and few if any interests outside of his work.

Huyck and Gutmann (1999) would term Mr. Acrann's daily routine as "dystonic dependence," a state characterized by submergence in behaviors considered consistent with the male gender role designed to avoid the public suggestion of vulnerability stemming from the changes imposed by the shifting gender role demands associated with aging. In essence, such men are unsure about how to balance what they view as being masculine with the behaviors their current situation requires, and it is possible that they feel ashamed of their seeming inability to cope with such changes (Levant, 2001a).

A more positive outcome, however, is the possibility that the socially proscribed gender role expectations change as a man ages (e.g., Collison, 1987; Sternbach, 2001). "Systonic dependence," as described by Huyck and Gutmann (1999), is characterized by a more passive behavioral style and the overreliance on others for their caregiving and support. Although this may or may not be an adaptive condition, many older men are given more latitude by society in their expressions of masculinity. Indeed, in the seminal text *The Seasons of a Man's Life*, Levinson (1978), drawing heavily on Eriksonian (e.g., 1959) theory, described a process by which aging brings with it freedom from gender-role-related constraints such that a man develops

> a greater capacity for intimacy and integrates more fully the tender, feminine aspects of his self. He has the possibility of becoming a more tender friend to men as well as to women. He can be a more facilitating parent to his adolescent and young offspring as he recognizes that they are no longer children and that he is no longer the youthful controlling father. He can become a more caring son to his aging parents (for whom he increasingly assumes parental responsibilities), and a more compassionate authority and teacher to young adults. (p. 25)

Transitions to later life continue this process, such that older men might evolve a new balance between societal demands and their sense of self. Retirement, for example, might bring a sense of having earned the right to self-determine one's lifestyle regardless of what attitudes, behaviors, and habits are considered by the world to be masculine or feminine. As a man's children have children themselves, he might take on the role of a nurturing grandfather and therefore allow himself to enjoy the relationship without the perceived burdens of parenthood and with the broader range of emotional expression allowed by that role. Unfortunately, in addition to societal changes regarding behaviors that are acceptable for older men, this also requires both that he give himself permission and that he have opportunities in the form of friends or family to engage in such behaviors.

THEORIES OF MASCULINITY

The theories of gender role strain (Pleck, 1981, 1995) and gender role conflict (O'Neil, 1981a, 1981b) were among the first to examine the construct of masculinity in a more critical light. This appraisal review identified several assumptions that seem to indicate that there are a number of dysfunctional aspects to masculinity. Those assumptions include the following: (a) Power, dominance, and control are necessary features in proving one's masculinity. (b) Emotions, and the expression of vulnerability, are considered feminine weaknesses and therefore should be avoided. (c) Cognitive, as opposed to affective, communication is superior. Interpersonal interactions that emphasize human emotions, physical contact, and feelings are feminine and should be avoided. (d) Work and career successes are measures of one's masculinity and self-worth. (e) One should be competitive with other males. Thus, intimacy, and by extension the expression of vulnerability, between males should be avoided. (f) Sexual prowess, not intimacy, is the primary means through which a man proves his masculinity. (g) Men are different and superior to women in career abilities. Therefore, men's primary career responsibility is that of economic provider, and women's primary role is that of homemaker.

Gender Role Strain

Pleck's *The Myth of Masculinity* (1981) deviated from earlier notions that masculinity was a given, normative process. As such, he is often considered a forerunner in thinking critically about masculinity and often credited with steering the field toward recognizing masculinity as a constellation of social constructions. He coined the phrase "gender role strain" (GRS; Pleck, 1995) to describe the conundrum society places on men. Specifically, men must adhere to the male gender role regardless of the personal, psychological, or societal consequences. Euro-American society, for example, traditionally teaches boys to focus on (a) independence and self-reliance, to the exclusion of collaborative efforts (e.g., Kiselica, 2001); (b) the restriction of emotional expression, despite the fact that their emotional experience is just as intense (e.g., Heesacker et al., 1999; Kiselica, 2001; Wester, Vogel, Pressly, & Heesacker, 2002); and (c) toughness and aggression, in absence of other coping styles (e.g., Levant, 1995). Boys "suffer under [an unattainable] code of masculinity that requires them to be: aggressive, dominant, achievement-oriented competitive, [and] rigidly self-sufficient" (Pollack & Levant, 1998, p. 1).

Pleck (1981) identified that overadherence to the traditional assumptions surrounding the concept of masculinity furthered the patriarchal nature of society, as well as precipitated the emotional and physical problems faced by, and also denied by, men. Mr. Acrann's value system, as well as his overt behaviors toward what he called the "kids" of today, as well as others around him, might be considered a manifestation of this phenomenon. Furthermore, Pleck believed the constraints placed on men by these assumptions led to many of the problems experienced by both men and women into adolescence and adulthood; for example, Mr. Acrann's lack of interpersonal opportunities and interests. Pleck (1981, 1995) concluded that the historical culturally defined role of masculinity was not positive for men in contemporary society, as it was (a) defined more by gender stereotypes than by physical sex, (b) inconsistent and contradictory, and (c) violated by many men because of the demands of specific environmental requirements. In applying these constructs to older men, Pleck's work would be consistent with the ideas put forth by Applegate (1997), who suggested that masculinity, with age, might be defined in part by the "contradictory experiences of power" (p. 9), referring to the fact that gender-role-related benefits reaped by men during their youth lead to corresponding losses in privilege and abilities, as well as increased isolation, later in life. Indeed, Mr. Acrann was able to construct a successful life for himself, serving in the military and later building a thriving business. From Pleck's perspective, however, this came at the cost of interpersonal connections, as those same behaviors he used to succeed in the military and chosen career were incompatible with developing close, loving interpersonal relationships.

Gender Role Discrepancy, Trauma, and Dysfunction

Three aspects of Pleck's (1981, 1995) theory of GRS have been identified, and although Mr. Acrann may at first glance seem to exhibit some of these characteristics, further assessment of his upbringing and the nature of those experiences would be needed prior to any final conclusions. In Pleck's theory, *gender role discrepancy* refers to the idea that a significant portion of males will fail to fulfill the expectations of the traditional male role. Research exploring this concept assumes that all males experience some degree of gender role discrepancy (e.g., Eisler, 1995). For example, Deutsch and Gilbert (1976) found that the degree of discrepancy between one's description of oneself and a description of an "ideal man" was negatively correlated with measures of self-esteem. As the degree of discrepancy increased, feelings of self-esteem plummeted. In addition, men reporting higher levels of gender role discrepancy were more prone to anger and anxiety (Eisler, Skidmore, & Ward, 1988). Overall, Pleck concluded that those increased levels of psychological distress were the result of the perceived differences between the defined male role and one's actual self (Goffman, 1963; Pleck, 1981, 1995).

The second major concept underlying GRS is *gender role trauma*. According to Pleck (1981, 1995), even if one is successful in meeting the expectations a majority of the time, the very process by which those expectations are socialized is traumatic. Young boys are often shamed into behaving aggressively, denying their emotionality, and avoiding anything remotely feminine (Brooks, 1990; Levant & Brooks, 1997; Levant & Pollack, 1995; Lips, 1997; Pleck, 1995; Pollack, 1992) for fear of being labeled queer or gay (e.g., Best, 2010). Mahalik and his colleagues (2003) captured this idea with their homophobic script; the expression of tender emotions, especially toward other men, is taboo because of the potential for being shamed as a homosexual. Such humiliation would account for the fact that some males seem overcommitted to their masculinity (e.g., Bem, 1981) and therefore are unable to adapt their behaviors to the demands of specific situations. With older men, this can be identified in the emotional disconnect often experienced between father and son. Being socialized under the same gender role standards, albeit in a cohort-specific manner, many older fathers and their adult sons have difficulty expressing their love for each other even at critical times such as the end of life.

The third major subtype of GRS is *gender role dysfunction*. In this case, fulfillment of the male gender role expectations can have negative consequences for everyone, as the socialized behaviors themselves are inherently problematic. In some ways, this is the aspect of Pleck's work most applicable to Mr. Acrann; living up to the socialized male gender role, for all it was adaptive early in life, has come at a cost. For example, according to Pleck (1981, 1995), men often deny their own emotionality, compete against other men, engage in aggressive behaviors, separate sex from emotions, distance themselves from their spouses and their children, place their career above all else, and assume that they are above feeling pain in their rush to meet the expectations set before them by the construct known as masculinity (e.g., Brooks, 1990; Levant & Pollack, 1995; Lips, 1997; Pollack, 1992). Older men often exhibit this in the form of physiological consequences of a youth spent striving for a masculine ideal. The consequences of a tough guy lifestyle or the long-term impact of living life in a strong and silent fashion can be seen in the form of psychical injuries, heart and liver problems, and potential difficulties with alcohol.

Gender Role Conflict

One of the more recent advances in the study of men and masculinity, gender role conflict (GRC) theory differs from GRS in that it stresses an understanding of how situational demands potentially conflict with traditionally socialized male gender role characteristics (e.g., Wester, 2008; Wester & Vogel, 2002). Although the study of GRS focuses on the impossibility of adhering to the male gender role, and the consequences of attempting to do so, GRC incorporates the role of specific situational demands (see O'Neil, 2008, for review) and the degree to which they conflict with socialized abilities. Some men's learned tendency to restrict the public expression of emotion, for example, may be adaptive in situations such as work, school, or interpersonal interactions requiring quick action and response (see Brooks, 1998, 2001; Wester & Pick-Lyubelsky, 2005). As mentioned, Mr. Acrann was able to build a life around characteristics his father and brother taught him, including the value of hard work, individual achievement, and the need to avoid any appearance of complaining. At the same time, however, this tendency toward emotional restriction may conflict with the situational demands associated with returning home and being emotionally available to spouses and children. This is another example of contextual validity (Mahalik et al., 2003), as well as of the consequences that stem from an inability to be flexible in the enactment of that gender role.

Certainly, many men are able to adapt to such fluidic situation demands, in effect switching between being tough, stoic, and independent in one context and being warm and affectionate in another context. Still other men, however, experience confusion about how best to respond. They appear ill prepared to adapt what they understand as masculinity, behaviors, and ideas society demands of them that allow them to succeed in certain situations to fit with the differing demands of external situations. This state of confusion is the crux of what concerns those involved in studying the construct of GRC. However, at the same time, GRC should be considered a "multidimensional and complex concept" (O'Neil et al., 1995, p. 167), as the methods by which male gender roles are learned and experienced throughout the life span are very individualized. Such individualization becomes even more pronounced when issues of race, class, ethnicity, and sexual orientation are considered (e.g., see Horne & Kiselica, 1999). Therefore, therapists should be aware of potential within-group variations among men, just as theories of development in general, and identity development specifically (e.g., Cross, 1995; Helms, 1990), have accounted for variations among women and people of color.

The advantage of GRC theory is that it defines the issues older men experience as the result of incongruent situational- and socialization-related demands rather than blaming them, or their gender role, for their own problems. For example, Mr. Acrann may not have experienced difficulties until he was in a situation that required him to be flexible in his behaviors; the potential for conflicts with his employees may represent one example of how this might manifest in an older male client. Given the variability introduced into a man's life based on the interaction of his gender role and developmental changes of aging, along with physical concerns as well as issues stemming from socioeconomic status, race, ethnicity, and interpersonal relationships, GRC seems uniquely suited to capture the experience of older men. For example, male gender role socialization produces psychological distress only under specific conditions: (a) Men are unable to adapt their socialization to a current life situation, for example, interpersonal or family demands, and (b) the situation is unable to recognize and validate their socialized method of expression, for example, instrumental or action oriented (see Heesacker & Bradley, 1997). In the absence of such conditions, however, gender-role-related conflict and any accompanying psychological distress potentially decreases (see Wester & Vogel, 2002). At minimum, this variability could be used to explain why some older men seem to embrace the changes associated with aging while other men have tremendous difficulty with such adjustment. Ideally, "it is precisely this sort of within-person and across-situation variability that needs to be understood if [therapists] are to adequately understand and facilitate adaptive [coping]" (Addis & Mahalik, 2003, p. 9).

Gender Role Conflict Patterns

Four overall patterns of male GRC have been identified (O'Neil et al., 1995), measured by the Gender Role Conflict Scale (O'Neil, Helms, Gable, David, & Wrightsman, 1986), and linked to many types of men's psychological distress (see Brooks & Good, 2001a, 2001b, for reviews). As with GRS, Mr. Acrann may seem to evidence some of these characteristics, but further assessment would be required. Each GRC pattern gives voice to those specific aspects of the socialized traditional male role deemed problematic for some men in certain situations. Success, Power, and Competition (SPC), the first GRC pattern, examines the degree to which men are socialized to focus on "personal achievement ... obtaining authority ... or comparing themselves to others" (O'Neil et al., 1995, p. 174). Some men's desire to excel competitively as opposed to collaboratively is an example of this concept.

The second pattern, Restricted Emotionality (RE), discusses the degree to which men are taught to "fear feelings" (O'Neil et al., 1995, p. 176). An example includes the male tendency to avoid the public expression of emotion, despite the fact that their emotional experience is just as intense as that of women (e.g., Wester et al., 2002). The problem for older men is that although they may attempt to meet these expectations as they age, they do so in the face of a distinct possibility that, because of age-related declines, they are no longer able to be successful.

The third pattern, Restricted Affectionate Behavior Between Men (RABBM), explores how men are socialized to have difficulties "expressing [their] feelings and thoughts with other men" (O'Neil et al., 1995, p. 176). A man who tends to avoid verbally expressing his tender feelings for other men demonstrates this aspect of GRC.

The fourth pattern, Conflict Between Work and Family Relationships (CBWFR), identifies the degree to which men struggle with "balancing work, school, and family relations" (O'Neil et al., 1995, p. 176) because of the competing socialized roles. Behaviorally, this is identified in some men's tendency to place their career ahead of their family (Heppner & Heppner, 2001). The challenge facing older men is how they cope when they no longer need to place their career ahead of their family; perhaps they retire, or their career is no longer a priority because of age-related health declines.

THEORIES OF AGING

The challenge in offering a summary of aging theories is multifaceted, including the diverse nature of the extant literature in this area, compounded by the length of time aging has been a topic of interest. Unlike the critical study of masculinity, which is a relatively new area of research, the study of aging as a process has been represented in the medical, psychological, anthropological, and social sciences literature for well into the past century. Adding to the complexity is the fact that each of these areas seeks to predict, understand, or explain different outcomes of the aging process (Birren, 1999). Biologists seek to explain physical changes associated with aging, with intention to predict and perhaps prolong length of life. Some specializations in psychology focus on understanding changes in behavioral or cognitive capacity; other social scientists are concerned with contextual variables such as socioeconomic status and political advocacy. Constructivists explore the meaning of aging, and philosophers attempt to ground such meaning into broader belief systems. In each of these areas, differences exist between formal theoretical frameworks designed to explain a process and individual models designed to explain specific theoretical data.

Unfortunately, as Birren (1999) noted, much of the early twentieth-century research into aging consisted largely of what he termed "dust bowl empiricism" (p. 463): researchers collecting large amounts of data on what variables correlated with aging without looking at the underlying explanations for that relationship. Models may have been developed, but efforts to advance an underlying theory to systematize the process were absent. This is similar to what many multicultural researchers (e.g., Quintana, Troyano, & Taylor, 2001) labeled as one of using proxy variables rather than actual psychological constructs to explain findings. Age could become the explanation for any demonstrated effect, rather than variables associated with age but more directly related to, in the case of this work, masculinity. To avoid this, the following section will summarize those theories that have a direct relevance to the psychology of men.

Biological Theories

Biological theories of aging seem to fall into two distinct categories, postulating that aging is due to either the result of random damage to the organism or the result of genetically determined processes of obsolesces; for example, that growing old is merely a set of biological processes and that older individuals need to stay active to successfully cope with such changes. Continuity theory (e.g., Atchley, 1989, 1999) suggests that people should fall back on the more successful social frameworks they have built over their life and as a result be better positioned to handle the changes associated with aging. Other popular examples include the free radical theory, which holds that reactive oxygen metabolites can cause cumulative physiological damage, or the theory of somatic muta- tion, which explains aging as the result of genetic damage stemming from background radiation. However, potentially most relevant for older men is the stress theory, which argues that excessive physiological activation has pathological consequences. In this case, the neuroendo- crine activity, which results from the autonomic activity consequential to physical and psychological stress, produces increased risk to disease and disability. The stress of either living up to or failing to live up to the socialized male gender role could be an important factor. Overall, chal- lenges such as being in control of one's life and situation, for example, or succeeding in one's life regardless of the intrapersonal consequences might place some men at risk. Men's coping styles, dangerous activities, and substance use increase this phenomenon. In the case of Mr. Acrann, the impact of living up to the socialized male gender role is more subtle but no less negative. As mentioned, his apparent focus was building a career, which may have precluded the development of interpersonal relationships. Without support systems and outlets other than work, changes in neuroendocrine activity may occur, which would in turn put him at risk for disease and disability.

Many of these consequences are more likely to be found in men who have spent their lives trying to live by the strong and silent, the tough guy, or the give-'em-hell scripts. The internalization of emotions, essentially keeping things bottled up, has long been linked to signifi- cant distress, and if one sees physicality as the way to solve all of one's problems, then one is likely to suffer the physical consequences. Of course, it should be noted this is not only referring to physical violence and the injuries that stem from that behavior. Injuries incurred through trying to live up to these scripts via healthy aging ideal are common, as men engage in behaviors that their aging bodies can no longer tolerate. Although healthy behavior is to be encouraged, gym injuries, as well as other sport-related difficulties, often are seen when men pursue certain athletic endeavors far beyond the age at which they should.

Sociological Theories

Current thinking from this perspective considers the context in which older men are living as a key component to understanding the aging process. Although many models have been developed to understand the nature of specifics such as age and socioeconomic status, or age, race, and gender, there are few hierarchical theories that allow for additional synthesis. This seems to be the result of semantics, in that sociologists differentiate between the study of age and the study of aging. Age refers to merely one of many factors that guide a person's interactions through life. The predominant theme in this case is one of generational principles; generations serve to organize social lives, and although they have little to do with chronological time, they designate relationships between people, events, and both internal and external events. Consider Mr. Acrann; born in 1934, he likely experienced hardship associated with both the Great Depression and the Second World War, including the loss of a brother to that conflict. Out of these life events came the values of hard work, service, and an overall disdain for those who would rather complain than work for a living. Differences in the gender role message, as well as the gender role expectations, experienced by men potentially as a consequence of age could instead, from this perspective, be classified as the result of generational change.

Although related to age, aging is distinctly different, referring to the changes experienced to these relationships during the life course. Indeed, life-course theories focus specifically on changes in the context of the society in which the person exists and under the presumption that this context exerts regular influence on the individual throughout the life span. Those who study this process do so at three levels, each of them important to understanding the older man. First, they examine the events across an individual person's life through to death; that is, they examine the experiences of an individual man in order to understand how he defines himself and how that definition was shaped by his experiences. Second, researchers examine the collective patterns of individual lives within a population, looking collectively so as to explore how a man's definition fits, or does not fit, within the broader social context. And third, individuals from this perspective examine the life course in terms of the socially shared knowledge and the boundaries between life events and lived roles. This means they examine how a man's relationship with himself, his history, and those around him has changed. Has he gone from a person who, based on gendered expectations, leads from the front of the line to someone who advises and mentors members of the next generation? Furthermore, has society given him that permission?

Implicit to the sociological theories is the cohort phenomenon, as the characteristics of older adults are constantly evolving as generations of people age, and each cohort forms its unique identity. Although certain behaviors and ideals of older men may seem out of place today, they served a purpose both for the man and for the society at large. For example, in earlier years, Mr. Acrann was most likely considered a pillar of his neighborhood, as a man who served his country and came from a family that had given a son to defeat America's enemies. He built a successful business, never complaining about loss or what his life might have lacked, such as interpersonal contacts or after-work pleasurable activities such as hobbies or travel for entertainment. This behavior was originally adaptive for him, as well as for the society in which he existed; however, it may be only now, as society has changed and Mr. Acrann is at a later stage in his life, that these values and ideals have become maladaptive.

Psychological Theories

Similar to sociological theories, psychological theories of aging seek to understand the behavior of individuals as a function of social process. Although many models blend the sociological with the psychological, unlike sociological theories that focus to a larger degree on the social context of the individual, social psychology focuses on the role of the person and the sense of agency within a situation. Examples include coping theories that delineate between accommodative and assimilative coping, attribution theories, or theories of personal control that explore the difference between primary and secondary controls. Shapiro, Schwartz, and Astin (1996) argued that although control is one of the most crucial variables for psychological health and well-being, normally functioning individuals are also likely to drastically overestimate the amount of control they have in a situation, as well as be more optimistic about their ability to gain control in the future. This is critical to consider when working with older men who might have been used to being in control and indeed achieved significant success with such behavior.

Selection, Optimization, and Compensation

One theorist has emerged whose work bears special implications for older men. Baltes (e.g., 1996, 1997; Baltes & Baltes, 1990) argued that there are psychological gains and psychological losses at every stage of development, but for the older individual the losses exceed the gains because societal supports are no longer sufficient to compensate. This theory, called one of selection, optimization, and compensation (SOC), argues that the lack of opportunities available to older individuals contributes to a sense of loss experienced by those in their later years of life. Older men, for example, can no longer engage in the behaviors of their youth, with few outlets to replace these losses. This leads to a condition Baltes (1996) referred to as learned dependency in later life; dependency should be considered not an automatic consequence of aging and decline but instead an outcome of social conditions. Said another way, and with consideration to the theories of gender-role-related outcomes, the dependency observed in older men should not be presumed either as a given or as a correlate with old age. Rather, it may be the result of the long-term outcome of social learning; a man who relied on his spouse to care for the house, the children, and him, in the form of meal preparation and laundry, never learned to complete those tasks on his own. So impairment is not the result of age per se but the result of learning that did not take place earlier in life, a hallmark of GRS theory. This impairment is partially reinforced by society through a confusing mix of messages aimed at the older man; independence and self-reliance are valued in the abstract but either decried in person or allowed to wither because of lack of resources. This confusion is in turn a feature of GRC theory.

Theories of Cognitive Aging

Theories of cognitive aging can be understood as falling into one of two categories. Proximal theories explore the role played by concurrent influence, which might determine age-related changes in cognitions. Information processing efficacy, for example, or strategy-based age interventions would be considered based on proximal theories. Distal theories, conversely, attribute aging related changes to influences that occurred at earlier periods in life but contribute to concurrent levels of performance. Said another way, just as in utero exposure to teratogens has been linked to cognitive delays in some children, exposure to toxins, on the job, perhaps, or associated with coping or lifestyle choices might result in cognitive declines later in life. Social changes across the life span are important as well, but in the end advocates of distal explanations to cognitive functioning in later life presume cumulative cohort effects that lead to individualized patterns of obsolescence in older men.

Theories of everyday competence explore the degree to which an individual can function effectively within a situation characterized by everyday experiences. These are partly related to theories of cognition because they assume the underlying cognitive processes individuals might use to organize their environment. In the absence of such organization, for example, certain forms of dementia, functioning in the tasks of daily living becomes very difficult. Three patterns have emerged in the extant literature. First, everyday competence is seen as the result of reliance on latent constructs explainable through models of basic cognition, information processing currently being a popular example. An older man is able to function in everyday life in part because his cognitive functions allow him to do so; the more efficient he is in the latter, the better he will be in the former. Second, everyday competence involves domain-specific knowledge called on and employed in response to situational demands. Finally, everyday competence is seen as the result of person–environment fit, or the degree to which a person's cognitive competence fits the environmental demands. For an older man, the loss of a spouse, especially one who handled the household tasks such as finance or social interaction, may produce a decrease in everyday functioning. At the same time, it is possible that with the changes in a man's environmental demands, he develops new areas of cognitive competence that his gender role did not allow earlier in life.

AGING AND GENDER

Baltes's (e.g., 1996, 1997; Baltes & Baltes, 1990) theory of SOC has specific applications to the psychology of men. First, it suggests that changes traditionally associated with aging are more the result of increasing disconnects between an individual's learned behavioral pattern and societal expectations. In essence, the distance between how one *knows* to behave and the norms of a society grows larger as one grows from early adulthood, to adulthood, and beyond. As in the case example at the beginning of the chapter, Mr. Acrann believed that he knew how to behave; it was everyone else who had problems. This is consistent with GRC theory, such that learned dependency is directly the result of conflicts between socialized gender role behaviors and contextual opportunities. Living as a playboy might be advantageous when a man is younger, as it is both expected and reinforced by society and possibly lead to meeting women and the potential for a long-term relationship. However, that same behavior becomes increasingly disconnected on two fronts as a man ages. First, men who have grown up associating their masculinity with sexual conquest may no longer be able to avail themselves of such activities as they age, due perhaps to physical challenges but also to both declining available partners and changes in the preferences of those potential partners from physical activity to companionship. Second, older men who engage in playboy behavior often run headlong into the social stereotype of the "dirty old man."

The role of the cohort phenomena in developing this disconnect cannot be overstated. Addis and Mahalik's (2003) social constructionist perspective, for example, suggested that a man's cohort might dictate his context, and from there he will develop a template that will guide his interpretation of life. The developmental experience of boys is rooted in their generational experiences; as those boys grow into men, they act according to those experiences for the betterment of themselves and society. It is fairly easy to envision a young Mr. Acrann, the strong and silent 18 year old, circa 1952, heading off to basic training to earn a living and continue his brother's legacy of military service. However, each subsequent generation of boys undergoes a potentially different experience based on their generational context. The boys of the 1930s learned a very specific set of messages rooted in the experiences of the Great Depression, which in turn served society well as they grew into men during World War II. However, the events of the late 1940s and early 1950s produced a different set of developmental experiences, which set the stage for young boys to serve themselves and their society during the late 1950s and 1960s. Thus, the older generation's behavioral patterns become somewhat less relevant as society moves forward, supplemented by those of the younger generation.

From this process a sense of disconnect can develop. Older men may feel estranged from their society and report that "things are moving too fast"; Mr. Acrann used the phrase "as if the world was shifting" to describe his experience. Eventually, disengagement occurs as the disconnect between learned behaviors and the demands of current situations grows to the point of outright conflict.

One prominent example of this can be exemplified in the GRC pattern of SPC. As a man ages, the SPC becomes less adaptive, given that the man may spend more time with his family and less time at work. An older man may also fall into the role of caregiver as his spouse ages or his children have children. Fear then develops; fear that he will not be up to the task, as well as fear about what his peers would say if they saw him engaging in these behaviors. Disconnect, therefore, as well as GRC and subsequent psychological distress, develops when men fail to recognize a need for flexibility.

From a GRS perspective, furthermore, the manner in which many older men respond to this situation causes multiple levels of psychological difficulties. Inflexibly adhering to the gender role ideal of SPC would produce an increase in the very behaviors that started the problem in the first place. In essence, men feel that if they are not successful at home, as perhaps their wife or their children are unhappy, it is because they are not working hard enough to accumulate the trappings of success society considers acceptable. So, they spend even more time at work and become more and more competitive rather than ask for help from those around them. This process is unfortunately compounded by the degree to which many men did not learn additional coping strategies, although they aged, because of the social proscriptions against them. Older men, then, do not ask for help because they do not know how, as they did not develop this ability as a boy or younger man. From a sociological perspective, generational change, although a natural part of any society, carries with it the possibility that many behavioral patterns learned in one's youth become obsolete in late life.

Another example of this disconnect is the general expression of emotions, specifically tender emotions. As a rule, society tends to wrongly criticize men for being hypoemotional (e.g., Heesacker et al., 1999) while at the same time actively discouraging men from openly expressing their emotions (e.g., Wester et al., 2002). In essence, society is critical of those men who exhibit a more stoic, instrumental orientation to their lives. This "double-edge sword" (Heesacker et al., 1999) leads to the conflicted sensibilities captured by the GRC constructs of RE and RABBM. As young boys, many older men developed an acute sense of specific situational demands and learned to present an emotional face to the world reflective of the context. In grade school, they learned not to cry in front of their peers; in high school, boys, present with a tough, instrumental orientation because they sense that this is what their peer group, females in particular, will reward (e.g., Buss, 1995). It is not until the older man's sense of the context changes, perhaps during a 50-year marriage, that he learns he can trust a female not to tease him or take advantage of his emotional expression of vulnerability.

Older men may specifically experience this as their relationships change. For example, it is often the case that the role of grandfather imparts an increased sense of contextual freedom to express tender emotions such as love and affection. However, at the same time there might remain a sense of fear regarding potential reprisal based on a gender role violation. For example, should a grandfather hug his teenage grandson or offer him a firm handshake? In essence, conflict stems from the concern that violating the gender role proscriptions against expressing love for one's male grandchild may communicate homosexuality. The disconnect between the socialized gender role and the demands of the current situation in turn develops as both the internal need demands that expression of emotion and the external role allows it. The key, therefore, is for older men to give themselves permission to accept those feelings as part of their new role.

At this point, it is important to note that context also plays a significant role in the development and experience of disconnect for older men. Therapists need to consider a four-dimensional universe in which the enactment of gender role expectations is influenced by the biological reality of aging while also being strongly influenced by one's generational cohort and one's specific context. The above-mentioned situations of disconnect and distress stemming from inflexible adherence to the ideals of SPC do not develop if a man's specific situation requires those same SPC values. One example of this might be a man who because of his financial situation cannot retire and instead has to work well into his older years. Being competitive might allow him to succeed in a workplace that stresses such behaviors and often attributes them to youth rather than the aged. Military and law enforcement are prominent examples (e.g., Brooks, 1998; Wester, Arndt, Arndt, & Sedivy, 2010). Another example might be a man who never married, or a widower who can devote himself to furthering his own success and achievement. Presuming that men's physical situation does not preclude their engaging in such behaviors, the odds of developing any disconnect are lower because they are freer to determine their situational demands.

CONCLUSION

Melding the body of work from the extant literature on aging and that from the psychology of men presents unique challenges. However, the similarity between the psychology of men and perspectives on aging within the sociological and psychological disciplines is quite striking. All of these areas suggest that the psychotherapeutic process involve the role played by an individual man's unique history and context. Furthermore, agreement seems apparent regarding the potential for negative outcomes for men stemming from the degree to which socialized behavioral patterns are not consistent with the demands of both specific situations and broader cultural norms. In essence, behaviors, values, and ideals taught to boys or young men may have served a purpose at one point but become obsolete as both the demands of a situation change and social expectations shift. Adaptive functioning in this case, as well as living up to the shifting expectations society has for older men, requires flexibility as well as support as society continues to evolve.

3

Therapeutic Considerations in Working With Older Men

"Why am I being pushed to retire," wondered Captain Lawrence Montgomery, an officer in the U.S. Naval Reserve. He felt like he was still 25 years old; he had turned 60 only just this past week. They said "too old" to command the ship's crew and no longer able to "handle" the requirements of the position. The captain had always been willing to follow his superior's orders. But being directed to participate in psychotherapy? That was for people who were crazy and those who were too weak to handle their own problems. I've been through the Naval Academy; I have the education, training, and experience—I would know best what is right. There's nothing wrong with me; I'm as good as ever. Show no weakness—that's what the old navy was about. Of course, things had changed. This was the new fleet, warm and fuzzy, worried about how people felt. Touchy-feely. OK; so maybe he hadn't quite been himself lately. He had been drinking more often, enjoying his whiskey late into the night, and maybe he lost his temper a couple of times, or at least more than usual. Sure, going through another divorce had been difficult. Just like the first Mrs. Montgomery, his second wife didn't appreciate his sense of drive and career ambitions; then again, they were women, how could they ever understand? Sometimes he was lonely and maybe even had a few regrets about his choices over the years to put the navy first, family second. But that didn't mean he had to spend endless hours in some therapist's office mulling over his feelings—what good would that do? What was done was done; he had done what he had to do. Therapy was definitely not for him. More action, less talk; that was the answer. No touchy-feely business; instead focus on showing no weakness. He was a leader, a man's man, a naval officer. No time for talking; just man up and get the job done.

There is no question; older adults can, and do, benefit from psychotherapy (Scogin & McElreath, 1994). Although no single modality of psychological intervention has proved to be most effective (Scogin & McElreath, 1994), a number of individual psychotherapeutic interventions have been offered for treating older adults, including interpersonal psychotherapy (Hinrichsen, 2008), cognitive-behavioral treatments (e.g., Satre, Knight, & Steven, 2006; Stanley, Beck, & Glassco, 1996), and reminiscence therapy (Fielden, 1992). Significant progress is being made regarding empirically supported treatments or evidence-based practice, still in their infancy, for older clients. A noteworthy contribution on evidence-based psychological treatment for older adults was provided as Scogin (2007) and his colleagues provided reviews of psychological treatment for anxiety (Ayers, Sorrell, Thorp, & Wetherell, 2007), insomnia (McCurry, Logsdon, Teri, & Vitiello, 2007), and behavior disturbances among older adults suffering from dementia (Logsdon, McCurry, & Teri, 2007). An additional article (Gallagher-Thompson & Coon, 2007) reviewed treatment strategies for family caregivers of older adults.

Although the knowledge base of psychotherapy with older adults has not yet established which psychological interventions for mental disorders faced by clients in later years of life provide optimal success, it is evident that side effects, that is, negative consequences brought about by psychotherapy, are limited (Sperry, 1995). This is particularly true in comparison to psychopharmacological interventions, such as antidepressant medications, which have the potential to exasperate physical symptoms or cause medication reactions. Given that on average those over the age of 60 years fill more than a dozen prescriptions per year (American Society of Consultant Pharmacists, 2003), pharmacological intervention for mental disorders significantly increases the risk for adverse interactions. Research has demonstrated that with patients with mild clinical depression, psychotherapy is as effective as chemical intervention, without the high potential for adverse side effects (Sperry, 1995). When there is indication for the need for pharmacological intervention, such as in severe depression, treatment is most successful if psychotherapy is utilized in addition to medication, as this can drastically reduce the noncompliance rate of medication use as well as contribute to longer lasting change (Little et al., 1998; Reynolds et al., 1999).

RELUCTANCE TO SEEK HELP
THROUGH PSYCHOTHERAPY

Research has suggested that in general, older adults find psychological intervention to be an acceptable treatment (Lebowitz et al., 1997), despite identifiable barriers such as physical access, financial resources, cognitive limitations, and attitudinal issues (Yang & Jackson, 1998). However, in an older male population, psychological suffering often remains undetected and not treated because older men mistakenly blame symptoms on the aging process or have a negative view of psychotherapy, much like Captain Montgomery in the example at the beginning of the chapter. When compared to women, men report more negative attitudes toward seeking psychological help (Fischer & Farina, 1995; Kessler, Brown, & Broman, 1981; Mackenzie, Gekoski, & Knox, 2006). A primary explanation may be that for the older man, admitting he should seek help suggests weakness and failure, which is counter to the socialized male gender role (Addis & Mahalik, 2003) and a potential source of tremendous stigma (Pederson & Vogel, 2007; Vogel, Wade, & Haake, 2006).

Thus, an unsettling paradox emerges; despite the nature and severity of such consequences, as well as the fact that seeking psychological services can often be helpful (Bergin & Garfield, 1994), men are far more likely to stigmatize, and therefore avoid, seeking mental health treatment (e.g., Addis & Mahalik, 2003; O'Neil, 2008). Pederson and Vogel (2007), for example, demonstrated that the stigma associated with psychotherapy partially mediated the link between male gender role conflict and attitudes toward both therapy and willingness to seek therapy.

Therapists should be aware of the implications of cognitive dissonance theory (e.g., Festinger, 1957, 1964; see also Cialdini & Trost, 1998, for review) in relationship to the understanding of men and their help-seeking behaviors. According to this approach, a state of dissonance exists when there is an inconsistency in thoughts or beliefs. An older man may be intellectually aware that he should seek psychotherapy, as he has been encouraged by those important in his life and reminded that he could benefit from treatment. However, he may continue to view entering psychotherapy as a stigma given his socialized concerns for the potential negative aspersions that would be cast upon his masculinity. Indeed, dissonance is most powerful when the cognitions in question refer to self-image, and it increases with both the importance of the decision and the difficulty of reversal (Festinger, 1964). From an older man's perspective, the decision to move beyond the socialized male gender role expectations by beginning psychotherapy could be considered as addressing one's self-image, and once such a decision was found out by peers, it would be difficult to reverse. The subsequent feelings of

shame, fear, and even gender role conflict could be considered dissonance in action. This phenomenon can be thought of as a specific case
of what Addis and Mahalik (2003) labeled "What can I lose if I ask for
help?" (p. 11), or better known as the "psychological cost of seeking
psychological services."

Thus, older men who traditionally avoid asking for help, no matter
what the circumstances, are at higher risk to not only ignore symptoms
but also refuse recommended treatment. "Real men are not in psychotherapy" becomes the mind-set; a view exacerbated by the perception
that the older man will be seen as incompetent or perhaps loses some
aspect of his masculinity, both of which are crucial in his eyes to his
adaptive functioning should he participate in talk therapy.

Unfortunately, little is known about the numbers of older men
whose distress is muted by their beliefs of masculinity and their need
for psychotherapy ignored. According to the cover story in *Newsweek*
in February of 2007, "Six million American men will be diagnosed with
depression this year. But millions more suffer silently." Even above and
beyond these millions mentioned are the older men who will report
their emotional distress through physical symptoms, such as stom-
achaches, headaches, and just generally feeling poorly. Because these
older males may express problems through vague medical problems,
the likelihood of accurate detection of emotional distress is small. For
example, how would Captain Montgomery, the naval officer presented
at the beginning of this chapter, respond to being asked how well he
was coping with his current situation? Would Captain Montgomery
be willing to share his feelings of hopelessness, apathy, frustration,
and sadness? Or would he be more likely to deny any problems, only
recognizing physical symptoms when the emotional distress became
unbearable?

BEGIN WITH A STRONG FOUNDATION
OF BASIC CLINICAL SKILLS

Psychotherapy with older men is centered on awareness and sensitivity to issues arising from both aging and the male gender role, allowing
for adaptation to the therapist's individual theoretical orientation. At
the core of effectively working with older adults in psychotherapy is
a strong foundation of basic clinical skills (Duffy, 1999), with modifications to meet the unique complexity of needs in the male client in
later life (Knight, Karel, Hinrichsen, Qualls, & Duffy, 2009). Thus, the
implementation of an age and gender sensitive model is the fundamental
element to effective psychotherapy with older men. No matter the preferred therapeutic orientation of the therapist, the psychotherapeutic
process must encompass responsiveness to the interaction of situational
demands, aging, and the male gender role.

Modifications of the Basics

Perhaps one of the most concrete variations of providing psychother-apy services to an older male clientele is the potential for inclusion of family members and other professionals in the client's care. In some situations, spouses, adult children, siblings, and other involved family members can serve as a beneficial aspect of the older man's psycho-therapy process. Whether through collateral interviews or by joining a therapy session, recognition of the potential for contributions from others is advantageous. Of course, any interaction with other individu-als must not only be approved by the client but also be soundly agreed to, with clarity of the purpose for the outside or additional involvement. Therapists should be aware that even well-meaning family members can be so devoted to the older client, or at times so concerned about his well-being, that without intention they cross boundaries or fail to recognize the harm rather than aid in the psychotherapeutic process. For example, an attentive, outgoing, talkative wife who is so frightened by the change in her husband's personality since his diagnosis of can-cer provides so many details for the therapist that they run the risk of her views dominating the initial session. Given the couple's 55 years of marriage, her input would be helpful in providing pertinent histori-cal information as well as a context for the current situation, and she may eventually play a significant role in the therapy process. However, valuable information is obtained by meeting individually with the older man. Having spent many years with his wife being responsible for verbal descriptions of any medical or relational concerns, the older male client may tend to follow her lead or even encourage her to answer the ques-tions posed, unwittingly continuing in the strong and silent masculine script. However, once she is no longer available to respond, he will more likely be willing (or perhaps compelled) to provide his own opinions, thus engaging in the exploration process of psychotherapy.

In addition, integrated service delivery is essential, as therapists work-ing with older clients are likely to operate within a multidisciplinary approach, collaborating with other care providers, such as the primary care physician, medical specialist, or case manager. Skills should include having the ability to communicate psychological conceptualizations in a concise and useful manner to medical and other professionals, as well as having knowledge of aging services in the local community (e.g., day care, transportation, residential) and how to refer older male clients to these services.

Older male clients, perhaps more than any other population, may respond positively to being addressed as "Mr." rather than their first name. The advantage of using "Mr." in addressing older male clients goes beyond manners. It shows respect for the older man and his accomplish-ments, and recognizes an integral part of the traditional male gender role socialization (e.g., Brooks, 1998; Brooks & Good, 2001a, 2001b).

Older men can best be acknowledged within the context of their independence, dominance, success, power, and competition scripts. The majority of older men will exhibit a sense of having earned their title, be it "Mr.," "Dr.," "Judge," "Reverend," or "Colonel," by virtue of their age and their status. The older man may later invite the therapist to address him by his first name, but starting with the title is congruent with what the older man may prefer and expect based on socialization and also empowers him to control an aspect of the psychotherapeutic relationship from the first contact. Offering the older man your business card upon introduction may also be advantageous, as it sets the norm of respect of the older man, framed within a businesslike manner.

Because some older men may be at risk for physical and mental decline, with potential problems of vision, hearing, mobility, or cognitive slowing, modifications are required based on client need. For example, if the client's hearing is a challenge, the therapist may want to speak slightly lower, louder, and slower, remembering that maintaining eye contact is vital. Materials printed in a larger font are often useful, as well as particular attention to lighting, temperature control, appropriate seating (too low and difficult to get up), and ease of accessibility (with a walker, cane, or wheelchair). These modifications are implemented with the idea of allowing the older man, regardless of his limitations, to maintain his dignity; that is, a sensitivity to providing measures of required assistance, prior to the older man having to request them or without a direct offer.

At times, interactions with an older male client may be somewhat informal, with a conversational quality. In response to clinical questions, some older men may offer additional information, sometimes within a storytelling framework. For example, a specific question about appetite may solicit a response that includes comments about his wife's cooking or his increased stomach problems and associated bowel problems, with a summary "I just don't have an appetite anymore." A willingness to engage in storytelling can ultimately nurture the development of an adaptive therapeutic relationship. Older men in particular may be prone to describing events or what occurred, rather than their emotions or reactions to the situation, given the degree to which their socialized gender role has led them to avoid self-disclosure and reluctance in expressing deeper emotions. This pattern is likely to be evidenced in older men who more strongly identify with scripts such as the strong and silent type and the tough guy ideal.

Working Alliance

The ability to relate empathetically and effectively connect with older men and their families is critical in establishing a therapeutic working relationship. During the early stages of psychotherapy, developing rapport often involves the therapist making an increased effort to understand the thoughts, behaviors, and ideas of men in general, and older men specifically, within the broader context of masculine culture. Duffy (1999) identified the idea of complementarity, referring to the flexible, interactive manner in which control is negotiated within the therapist–client relationship. A give-and-take approach, where the therapist and client trade control and power depending on mutual goals and trust, is at the core of this concept. Older men, the majority who have a long history of being in control of their lives and socialized to value such dominance, are more likely to respond within a complementarity relationship in comparison to one in which the therapist dictates outcomes and therapeutic directions.

Although the concept of working alliance has traditionally been associated with the psychodynamic orientation, research has begun to extend the concept (e.g., Bordin, 1979) across all theoretical orientations given its importance to therapeutic outcome (e.g., Horvath & Greenberg, 1994). Duffy (1999) was among the first to assert the importance of a working alliance in counseling older clients. In the seminal book *Psychotherapy With Older Adults*, Knight (2004) dedicated an entire chapter to the discussion of establishing rapport with older clients. He highlighted the need for understanding older clients within their contextual cohort and integrating this with an educational approach about psychotherapy, suggesting awareness of the historical influences affecting particular cohorts, as the understanding of the broad historical timeline of events that may have influenced an older man's perspective on life is paramount. A general awareness of the social impact of wars, the Great Depression, and other historical events may help an older man to recognize that the therapist is interested in understanding his stage in life within an overarching context.

Consistent with this, the task facing older men is one that empowers a man to be situationally adaptive and flexible, similar in outcome to the gender role journey process articulated by James O'Neil and his colleagues (e.g., O'Neil, Good, & Holmes, 1995). The working alliance underlies the gender role journey. It is in a nonjudgmental approach, characterized by mutual respect and shared goals, in which older men give themselves permission to move beyond those aspects of the socialized male gender role that are contributing to their difficulties. Thus, therapists seeking to cultivate a strong working relationship with an older male client will allot time for this metamorphic process, as well as develop a sense of their own comfort relinquishing the control they might prefer within the therapeutic context. Hindering an older man's developmental progression of recognizing and initiating acceptance of the traditional male values that have come to interfere with his functioning runs the risk of stimulating those socialized male gender role behaviors of avoidance, anger, and defensiveness.

Language Considerations

In general, attention to vocabulary and use of specific words during psychotherapy with older men is crucial. Many current, commonly used words may have little meaning for older adults (e.g., "hooking up," "awesome," or "hanging out"). Use of general mental health terms such as "depression," "anxiety," "cognitive impairment," and "dementia" may cause unnecessary concern for the older man and his family and on occasion increase denial of symptoms. Using terms more acceptable to them, older men may state they have been "feeling blue" or "down in the dumps" or summarize with "I just haven't been myself lately." More anxious clients may indicate they have "felt more on edge," have "been tensed up," "can't stop thinking," are "shook up," or have experienced a "hard time relaxing." Many older men may use descriptive words such as "tough" to explain their current situation. Client reaction to terminology is determined not only by age but also by education level, cohort, religious preference, culture, and geographical surroundings. Listen carefully to the words the older male client uses when he speaks and integrate his vocabulary or phrases into your own when appropriate.

It is also important to avoid "elder speak" when working with older men; that is, speaking too loudly or slowly to an older man who does not having a hearing impairment, treating him like a child, or using a term of endearment such as "sweetie," "honey," or "dear." Although perhaps meant in a positive way, research indicates that elder speak is more likely to be experienced as an insult, continuing negative views of aging and possibly even increasing negative health consequences (Ryan, Giles, Bartolucci, & Henwood, 1986; Ryan, Hummert, & Boich, 1995). Often being in a position of respect throughout their life, many older men may become offended by such communication.

One resource offering further guidance communicating with older adults is "Talking With Your Older Patient: A Clinician's Handbook" (National Institute of Aging, 2009). On the basis of the premise that good communication is a part of the healing process, this booklet offers practical techniques and approaches to help with diagnosis, promote treatment adherence, make more efficient use of the therapist's time, and increase client satisfaction. Focus is given to specific skills essential in communicating with older adults and to guidance when approaching particular situations, such as talking about sensitive topics of terminal illness, loss of driving privileges, or change in living arrangements and communicating with older clients experiencing confusion or memory loss.

In addition to adhering to the above recommendations, those involved in providing services to older male clients should be fluent in what Heesacker and Prichard (1992) referred to as the "masculine voice" (p. 274), that is, the contextually unique way in which men may behave and communicate (see also Wester & Vogel, 2002). Increased awareness of the masculine voice involves developing an appreciation for focusing on, and when appropriate using, therapeutic examples during the session that incorporate the older man's tendency to (a) be action oriented, (b) value honor and loyalty, and (c) focus on solutions.

Furthermore, this includes the therapist finding "a way to get behind aversive features of the male client's pretherapy behavior and highlight the client's positive or enabling characteristics" (Brooks, 2001, p. 214). The recognition that in many ways traditional masculine behaviors served the older male when he was younger through increased job success, stress management, and overall survival recognizes the value of such styles and allows the therapist to see where and when they interfere with the client's adaptive functioning. Using an analogy from the man's former workplace to illustrate a certain behavior or psychological concept may increase understanding. For example, with an older male client having difficulty in relating to his adult daughters, helping him to remember that as a salesman all of his life, he most likely was required to modify his interpersonal approach depending on his client and the specifics of the situation will focus on how he could use his previous skills to help him adjust and improve his interactions with his daughters. Behaviorally, this presents an opportunity for the therapist to engage the older male client in a manner that is known to him, with the goal of increasing therapeutic rapport and increasing comfort with the therapeutic process while at the same time bringing about learning and possible change. Accordingly, therapists should consider recognizing and valuing possible differences while not overemphasizing gender- and sex-stereotypical ways of being (e.g., Heesacker & Prichard, 1992; Heesacker, Prichard, & Socherman, 1994; Heesacker et al., 1999).

MULTICULTURAL MASCULINITY

In discussing the interaction of race, ethnicity, and masculinity, Kimmel and Messner (1992) noted that male gender roles usually vary according to one's race and culture, whereas Wade (1996) described how "societal forces affecting men's [gender role] experiences will be differentially salient for men of different [backgrounds]" (p. 18). More recently, Brooks and Good (2001a) acknowledged that "there are many masculinit[ies], depending on a man's ethnicity" (p. 16). Not only does masculinity evolve as one ages, but race and ethnic background adds another level of complexity within the psychotherapeutic process.

Inclusion

Robertson and Fitzgerald (1992) were among the first to articulate how therapists must make an extra effort to "sell" men on the prospect of psychotherapy and provide reframes such as coaching, consulting, or a concept more sensitive to the male identity (see also Brooks, 1998). With men of color, however, therapists need to go farther to make psychotherapy available. Outreach advertisements should be developed that involve older men of color speaking about the issues they face as men. They should be in the native language and aired or placed where they are likely to be seen by the target population.

An area that requires special attention for psychotherapy with older men of color is that of accessibility. Accessibility involves more than making adjustments to where and when clients are seen; it also includes making the setting as available, inviting, and comfortable as possible for the older man. For example, men need to be represented on the professional staff, decorations should be reflective of masculinity as well as of multiple cultures, and efforts should be made to ensure that therapists and staff are aware of and educated in not only the issues faced by older men of color but their habits, their hobbies, and how they spend their lives.

Although the issue is complex, as it involves an awareness of race as well as gender- and cohort-based values and ideals, time should be given to educate older men of color on what therapy means, what is expected of them as well as of the therapist, and how the process unfolds. Therapists may need to adopt a more solution-focused approach early in the psychotherapeutic process in order to overcome some men's socialized reluctance to engage in deeper work in unknown settings (e.g., Kiselica, 2001).

Caveats and Cautions

At the same time, there are several cautions. First, despite the recent advances in how a man's race and/or ethnicity effects his overall experience of masculinity and its socialized gender roles (e.g., see O'Neil, 2008; Wester, 2008), much more empirical evidence is needed to fully understand how the myriad cultural, racial, ethnic, and other identity variables intersect with masculinity and age. Second, each of the groups discussed next in reality represent a wide range of ethnic backgrounds that have been collapsed into distinct racial categories. "Asian American," for example, is a term used to describe individuals from backgrounds as diverse as Asian Pacific, Pacific Islanders, and Orientals. "Hispanic American" encompasses Mexico, South America, Cuba, and Spain. Even sexual orientation, often considered a bipolar category, encompasses a continuum ranging from exclusively heterosexual, to bisexual, to exclusively homosexual, and even to transgendered. Although the classifications discussed in this chapter are distinct for purposes of review, in reality therapists attempting to work with older men of color, just as with age or cohort groups, should be aware of the unique nature of their individual client's background.

A Multidimensional Phenomenon

Although individual men are affected differently based on their cohort and their own construction of masculinity, the overall challenge for older men of color is that they seem to be dealing with what might be considered a multidimensional phenomenon. They face numerous sets of conflicting gender role messages (e.g., Harris, Torres, & Allender, 1994; see Wester, 2008, for review); one of these stems from their culture of origin whereas the other stems from Euro-American culture. At the same time they are living with the impact of their aging, and the potential shifting of those gender role expectations as a result, they are a part of a society that often prevents them from meeting either set of expectations (Canales, 2000). To illustrate, consider that one socialized aspect of Euro-American masculinity is that of individual success and economic achievement, typically to the exclusion of collaborative efforts. However, adhering to this standard may conflict with an older man's culture of origin, which stresses cooperation and the promotion of the collective good. Racism and ageism further complicate this process (Clatterbaugh, 2001) in that men of color often encounter barriers to their economic success because of racist attitudes, although the realities of aging may be that they are not able to achieve success in a manner to which they are accustomed.

African American Men

Franklin (1997, 1999) defined the concept of invisibility as an inner struggle with the recognition that "one's talents, abilities, personality and worth are not valued or recognized because of prejudice and racism" (p. 761). In effect, it is a developmental process by which older African American men define themselves within the larger context of an essentially racist society and its skewed construction of race. For African American men of any age to navigate this process, according to Franklin (1999), they must decode the meaning of other people's behavior toward them and respond in a manner consistent with their evolving sense of themselves. Their goal is to gain a sense of visibility and through that attain a victory over the racism that invalidates their talents, abilities, and sense of self.

A vital component to this process is feedback from the African American community at large because it offers a set of rules and values with regard to race contrary to that of the dominant culture. The sense of belongingness, validation, and respect provided by the larger African American community, as well as the traditions and institutions, serves to give many older African American men a sense of visibility. In effect, this sense of belongingness serves to balance the racism experienced in the dominant community. Unfortunately, the experience of invisibility, especially in cross-cultural contexts, reminds many African American men that their characteristics have led to racism and prejudice. Thus, the possibility of a paradox exists; increased connection with the African American community, despite its many benefits, increases the likelihood of violating rules posed by the dominant society. Such confusion is potentially exacerbated when an older African American man's construction of masculinity is defined *exclusively* by using the dominant culture as his primary reference group. If that group consists solely of the dominant (i.e., Euro-American) culture, the potential for experienced gender-role-related distress increases, especially as the man moves farther away from his culture of origin's version of masculinity. This movement potentially increases as men age, to the extent that it might resemble the disengagement theorized to affect older men (e.g., Cummings, Henry, & Damianopoulos, 1961), again further violating the tenets of the more traditional African culture.

Asian American Men

Liu (2003) seems to have captured the status of men of Asian descent when he wrote how they must strive to occupy a "middle ground ... [in that] they may need to simultaneously accept and repudiate the White masculine norm in search of alternative definitions of masculinity" (p. 108; see also Chin, 1998). For example, older Asian men do not tend to see their masculinity in opposition to femininity. Rather, they are willing to engage in domestic tasks, their interpersonal style is polite and obedient, and they are less prone to confrontation. Adherence to the family name and success of the group over the individual are prized. The dominant culture may reject these concepts, however, and as such many Asian men find themselves trapped between the opposites. In essence, if they behave according to their culture of origin's values, they are defined as less masculine by the dominant culture. Indeed, many of the historic portrayals of Asian men in classic film, television, and advertising are based on this phenomenon of Asian men as subservient and therefore less masculine. But if they adhere to the dominant culture's definition of masculinity, they run the risk of rejecting their culture of origin.

Age plays a significant role given that society seems to be somewhat more tolerant of gender role violations, such as emotional expression, when exhibited by older men of color (e.g., Kim, O'Neil, & Owen, 1996). At the same time, older Asian men may face significant adversity in their attempts to define a middle ground for themselves, given that many of the expectations held for older Asians have their basis in racist and ageist points of view. For example, Asian men have historically provided the dominant culture with a source of cheap, effective labor while their subservience contributed to the assumptions that they were happy, healthy, and not interested in advancing their status above that held by members of the dominant culture. Asians were therefore seen as better than other groups of color because their subservience was misconstrued as a desire to assimilate and not threaten the status of the dominant culture. It may be the case that much of what constitutes older Asian men's reactions to their gender role is accounted for by their cultural identity, in effect, the context in which they developed their social construction of masculinity (e.g., Addis & Mahalik, 2003).

Hispanic and Latino Men

One of the most common assumptions about Latino culture, more than other cultural backgrounds, is that it tends to value traditional beliefs and behaviors associated with masculinity. Indeed, this perception permeates the profession to the extent that the term "machismo," a description of men who strongly adhere to traditional masculinity, has become synonymous with Hispanic and Latino men (e.g., Casas, Turner, & de Esparza, 2001). At the same time, however, a number of theorists contend that this construct "plays a less determining role in defining the culture than previously thought" (Casas et al., 2001, p. 759). Some even assert that it has become a stereotype that denies the tremendous diversity within groups of Latino men. They point to research demonstrating how factors such as population growth, socioeconomic status, religious background, and historical context seem to impact the engagement of this behavioral set (Baca-Zinn, 1982; de la Cancela, 1986). However, research has demonstrated that for many Latino men, traditional masculinity and a sense of control are tied to their self-esteem, and as such they might avoid situations that make them appear weak or vulnerable, one being psychological services.

The degree to which Latino men, like other older men of color, experience tension between the gender role of the dominant culture and the gender role of their culture of origin tends to be the strongest predictor of psychological distress. For example, although many espouse traditional values, at home they tend to share the duties with their wives, and there tends to be greater opportunity for women than one might expect. Indeed, some (e.g., Casas et al., 2001) contend that Latino culture might be more matriarchal, given the degree to which aspects of the culture are oriented toward respecting the mother figure and division of home labor. It may be the case that this approach, traditional values outside of the home and progressive values within the home, sets the stage for increased gender role difficulties. For example, the constant need to present one face to the world and another at home can be wearing. Furthermore, it increases the odds that the two roles might conflict, in that an older man might enjoy some of the benefits received from behaving one way in public and decide to bring those behaviors home. As problematic as these examples might be, however, it is more likely that the push and pull happening between the dominant culture and the culture of origin will result in a tendency to disengage as one ages in order to protect oneself.

American Indian Men

More so than any other ethnic group, American Indian populations are a highly heterogeneous people. Significant differences exist between tribes with regard to social structure, language, and cultural practices. This means that care should be taken to ensure familiarity with the specific tribal nation from where the client hails.

Duran and Duran (1995) perhaps best captured the challenge facing American Indian men and the dominant culture's definition of masculinity when they explored the role played by alcohol in the life of some 17th- and 18th-century American Indians. In a story about the power to assign meaning, these authors noted,

> The definition and significance of alcohol is centered around the struggle of related terms and their binary opposites: tradition/assimilation and savagery/civilization. Alcohol was used as a metonomy by both sides of a power struggle to define both the meaning and value of Indian versus white identity. (p. 119)

Alcohol therefore acted as a proxy through which an identity, as well as certain characteristics, could be cast upon American Indians.

A similar process likely operates when it comes to masculinity, as older American Indian men may be trapped between two worlds, both of which describe gender and gender role very differently. That is, gender role labels such as "masculine" or "feminine" do not easily translate to American Indian languages. As a result, it is quite likely that some traditionally oriented older American Indian men may be overwhelmed and have difficulty coping. Certainly, some may have developed an adaptive balance between their cultural heritage and the demands of their current life situation. For example, American Indians are well represented in law enforcement and the U.S. armed forces. Still others, however, may believe they face a choice between rejecting their culture of origin and endorsing dominant masculinity or rejecting the dominant culture and cutting off any chance of economic success.

Sexual Orientation

Unfortunately, "the vast majority of men participating in [masculinity] research so far [have] been nongay and heterosexual in nature" (Simonsen, Blazina, & Watkins, 2000, p. 85); in respect to older men, this is an understatement, as very limited information is available about older gay men. This is problematic, because from a gender role perspective, the development of a positive gay identity is a direct violation, and perhaps the most severe violation, of the traditional male gender role (e.g., Schwartzberg & Rosenberg, 1998). Interestingly, Kilianski (2003) recently proposed the idea of an exclusive male identity to explain this paradox. He described how some men develop both a masculinized ideal self and a feminized undesired self that result in their striving for society's definition of masculinity while at the same time rejecting anything associated with violating that gender role. Such violation might place them at risk for gender-role-related distress, as they face not only society's "strong heterosexist and homophobic bias" (Barber & Mobley, 1999, p. 168) but also condemnation for failing to "fulfill the male role and achieve a complete [i.e., heterosexual] male identity" (Harrison, 1995, p. 359). Negotiating these two perspectives as one grows older becomes even more complex, as it requires either a rejection of one's self-identity or a rejection of society and its gender role expectations.

Religion and Spirituality

The majority of older American men believe in God, with representation from a wide array of religious affiliations. Christian religions tend to be dominant, although a trend has emerged in recent years in the growth of non-Christian religions. Although religion may not be perceived as traditionally masculine, religious or spiritual beliefs will play a role in the lives of many older men. The therapist must recognize that a man's religious beliefs, some stemming from early childhood, will influence his values and shape gender roles and relations; beliefs about the afterlife are also strongly related to religion or spirituality. In psychotherapy, religious issues may arise in areas such as an older man's sexuality or relationships and may emerge in issues involving end of life.

DEALING WITH DIFFERENCE

Some therapists may feel that they have little in common, be it in terms of age, gender, ethnic or racial background, worldview, religion, sociopolitical orientation, or overt experience, with their older male clients. Therapists treating clients who are demographically different from themselves often experience additional strain in the therapeutic process (Spiegel, 1965). Similar to ethnocultural transference, which is based on a client–therapist dyad with each from differing ethnic backgrounds (Comas-Díaz & Jacobsen, 1991, 1995), a younger therapist and older adult client dyad comprises unique processes and dynamics with the potential to hinder core therapeutic issues (Vacha-Haase, in press). For example, there may be a therapist's "denial of ethnocultural differences," in this case the belief that everyone over 65 is the same. The "clinical anthropologist syndrome" may also occur, as the younger therapist is excessively interested in the older man's culture, with an overzealous curiosity of what it is like to be 90 years of age. Or the younger therapist may experience increased "guilt and pity" for the older male client, feeling sorry for the 80-year-old man with chronic back pain, limited finances, and loss of family members. Left unexplored, such views impact the complementarity of the working alliance such that it may make it difficult for some therapists to appropriately experience or communicate empathic feelings for the older man, highlighting the need to recognize countertransference and take steps to develop a healthy therapeutic relationship with the older male client.

Therapist Biases

Practicing self-reflection to monitor personal biases, assumptions, stereotypes, and potential discomfort in working with older men increases the likelihood of increased self-awareness and ability to recognize differences between one's own and the older male client's values, attitudes, and goals. On the basis of the psychodynamic concept of countertransference, therapists may have views, either negative or overly positive, of older adults stemming from their own relationships with their parents, grandparents, or older relatives. What did they learn from their fathers or grandfathers about how older men act and think? And how might this affect the psychotherapeutic process with an older male client? For example, having memories of one's stereotypical, gray-haired, loving, and accepting grandfather who played catch throughout one's childhood could potentially influence the therapist's approach to a similar male client. Or watching one's parents act in a parental or controlling way with their own aging parents could conceivably impact the therapeutic approach with a widowed older man who presented to therapy to explore decisions about future living arrangements and care. Or what if a therapist had a father or grandfather similar to Captain Montgomery? How could this impact the treatment or reaction to Captain Montgomery in comparison to another man presenting the same symptoms?

In addition to their personal experiences, therapists need to be mindful of the society in which they exist and the degree to which they have been socialized into the perceptions held by that society. In the youth-oriented culture of Euro-America, for example, aging may carry a negative connotation for many. Ageism, prejudice, or discrimination based on an individual's age can be subtle and is often manifested in negative views of aging held unintentionally, even by therapists interested in working with older men. One such stereotype is that all older adults are the same, with homogeneity occurring simultaneously with aging. Myths of the aging experience also include erroneous beliefs that older men are rigid, sickly and frail, and cognitively impaired. However, existing literature clearly refutes these stereotypes within an aging population, and therapists must strive to combat ageist misperceptions. When presented with the possibility of treating a male client differently because of his age, therapists should further explore personal biases, perhaps identifying that they worry about their own age (What do I know about what it's like being 80?) or societal influences (He looks like a kindly grandfather. He wouldn't abuse alcohol, would he?).

THE PSYCHOTHERAPEUTIC PROCESS

The psychotherapeutic process is complex, with many twists and turns, some expected and some not, but with no clear road map to navigate the uniqueness each client brings to the therapy session. Older men will present for therapy for multiple reasons and with various expectations for the outcome. Some men will desire a reduction in symptoms; others will crave increased self-awareness. Ultimate goals will range from adjustment or acceptance of current transitions and loss, to freedom from the torment of the past, to education in implementing a new way of doing things, to the opportunity to brainstorm and have a sounding board in making decisions.

Therapists themselves also add to the journey of psychotherapy, contributing their own individual characteristics, as well as experiences, years of practice as a therapist, and identified theoretical orientation. However, regardless of the numerous combinations possible, the general path of the psychotherapeutic process follows a set course broadly defined, including an initial stage of assessment and goal setting, followed by a working stage, finishing with an ending or termination aspect.

Focused Assessment and Specific Treatment Goals

The essential goal for the first session includes the establishment of initial steps toward the development of a working alliance, as well as a focused assessment and differential diagnoses clarifying the presenting problem. For example, during an intake with an older man presenting with symptoms of anxiety, medical causes and recent medication changes, in addition to recent cognitive and personality changes, should be explored.

Employing a cooperative approach, the therapist and older man combine efforts to establish clear objectives for psychotherapy, ultimately identifying the beginnings of an outline for a potentially effective, realistic, and acceptable intervention following a multifaceted treatment plan. Given the degree to which many men are socialized to be goal focused, setting specific goals may be a central part of the assessment process and identification of treatment. Assessment is framed as a method through which the client and the therapist collaboratively collect as much information as possible in order to design a treatment plan with the highest likelihood of achieving success. That is, despite the importance of therapist behaviors such as empathy and support, some older men may initially be more comforted by a direct approach to assessment and future actions, leaving out the "touchy-feely business" that Captain Montgomery found so alien and irrelevant.

One way of ensuring openness to a gender-aware context is to make an effort to overtly engage the older man in a manner in which he potentially feels most comfortable: the masculine voice, mentioned earlier. For example, Captain Montgomery seems to have adopted a more instrumental, action-oriented coping style than the typical client. The therapist should therefore consider adopting a similar stance in treatment, perhaps in the form of behavioral or cognitive behavioral assessment focused on content and outcomes rather than process and experience. Such a stance would potentially allow the therapist to harness the solution-focused aspects of this client's personal style and use it to further the goals of treatment. Conversely, if a client is more comfortable engaging in a more interpersonal, affective style, the therapist should be willing to adapt to allow the client time to explore the underlying cause to his psychological distress.

By utilizing an age-sensitive, masculine role view, that is, seeing the situation through the older man's eyes, the therapist can employ an adaption of the client's gender role socialized behavior to the changing demands of his current life situation. To help the older man cope with the physical changes associated with aging, for example, the therapist may consider playing on his socialized preference for overcoming obstacles through overt effort, themes prevalent in the winner and independent scripts. In the intake with Captain Montgomery, recognition of his goal-focused, achievement, and direct approach with him in a leadership position dictating the direction of his goals for psychotherapy would be critical. Focusing more on the achievement aspects or final outcomes, rather than emotions, underlying causes, or the process, allows the therapist to join Captain Montgomery's worldview. He can be reassured that there will be no "touchy-feely business" or need to "mull" over his feelings. Instead, focus will be given to specific goals for improving identified aspects of his current situation based on what he identifies as being of merit and chooses to improve utilizing his strengths in approaching problems. Through psychotherapy, Captain Montgomery can utilize his education, training, and experience to outline a plan to improve his life. In the spirit of complementarity, Captain Montgomery retains control, utilizing a set of well-known and practiced gender-role-specific behaviors to overcome those very behaviors that have become maladaptive. Consistent with his fierce independence, no one can change Captain Montgomery except the Captain himself.

It should be noted that appropriate interventions will not only vary given the clinical problem but also be influenced by the context and characteristics of the client. For example, even if the diagnosis and context are similar, the psychological intervention may be different if the older man is a naval officer such as Captain Montgomery or if he earned his living as a migrant farmworker. Even if they have both recently been diagnosed with terminal cancer, an 89-year-old Hispanic man living independently in the community will require a different approach than a 77-year-old man who is bedridden in a long-term care facility.

Socialized Gender Influences in the Therapy Room

Because of the privilege the gender role has afforded many older men, as well as the accomplishments associated with that privilege, extra effort needs to be expended in developing client insight into the negative consequences associated with their socialized gender role. Captain Montgomery's arrogance and his sense of entitlement are prime examples of learned traditional male roles. Sprenkel (1999) suggested embracing these characteristics, rather than combating or directly fighting against them. The process of change in therapy can be reframed as more congruent with men's socialized need for control and competence in order to shift the target of that arrogance to the behaviors targeted for needed change. For example, Captain Montgomery may be presented with a stark choice: change his behavioral style and take control of his actions and the current situation or continue with his maladaptive ways and surrender control to others. The final decision in the chain of command really is his.

Many therapists are aware of the degree to which socialized male gender roles lead to psychological distress. However, at the same time there remains the potential for what Brooks (2001) described as the "dark side of masculinity" (p. 213), which tends to cast traditional male characteristics in a negative light. Working with older men requires an overt effort to acknowledge the degree to which men themselves suffer from the expectations placed on them by the traditionally socialized male gender role. Older men often engage in the very disengagement likely to both continue and exacerbate their maladaptive functioning at the behest of society, which tends to expect older men to fade into the background by not disrupting the lives of those around them. As treatment begins, the therapist may offer an overt effort to acknowledge and understand the conundrum presented to some men by their gender role, being in effect rewarded for behaviors that cause them physical as well as psychological distress.

Further illustration is found in the writings of Richard Majors (1986, 1994; Majors & Mancini Billson, 1992) in his discussion of how some behaviors of African American males (e.g., "cool pose"; Lazur & Majors, 1995, p. 341), although interpersonally problematic, need to be seen and understood as adaptations to racism and sexism rather than automatically labeled by those in the dominant culture as pathological. In the case of Captain Montgomery, this would involve accepting his behaviors of being goal oriented, demanding, and arrogant as being useful throughout his life and chosen profession.

However, therapists should guard against overusing acceptance of any behavior, as it might contribute to the client's avoidant behaviors, stimulate other defenses, or inflate his sense of entitlement. A balance, usually dependent on specific client circumstances melded with clinical judgment regarding the older man's individual characteristics, is needed so as to both meet the client where he is comfortable and also push for change. Duffy (1999) foreshadowed this when he wrote about the need for those working with older clients to tolerate "ambiguity and uncertainty" (p. 11) rather than pressure the client to resolve decisions without having fully considered the situation. One example might be an older man's need to move beyond specific behaviors based on the physical changes associated with aging. Eventually, Captain Montgomery will need to be challenged on those behaviors that have become maladaptive, and his treatment of those around him confronted, so as to make him more malleable to the therapeutic process. Such a departure from his known behavior pattern will most likely cause ambiguity, triggering fears regarding what he might lose during this treatment (e.g., Addis & Mahalik, 2003), and lead to an initial increase in the problematic behaviors. During the psychotherapeutic process, Captain Montgomery may well become more demanding, pushy, and arrogant. Therapists, uncomfortable with the escalation, run the risk of giving into this pattern in the name of the working alliance without fully considering the need to also balance client comfort with client growth.

Engaging the Client: Empowering Change

Resistance may at times seem to disappear, only to resurface in a later session, as the therapeutic relationship moves into a deeper development of interpersonal reactions between the client and the therapist. Those reactions, in turn, should be considered a signal to the therapist that the work has moved into content that should be considered therapeutically important. The constructs discussed next often wax and wane depending on the progress of the treatment, and it is not uncommon for all of the them to be operating at one time one session and none of them operating in the very next session.

Honor Men's Developmental Heritage

The importance of recognizing the role of history in the socialization experiences of older men cannot be overstated. Brooks (1998), for example, offered the concept of "transgenerational focus" (pp. 93–96; see also Bowen, 1978), referring to the idea that greater comprehension of individual men can be gained through understanding their relationships with their father, grandfather, and other male figures in their family history. This degree of historical understanding allows therapists to place events, feelings, and behaviors in context rather than misinterpret them or blame the individual. Issues, attitudes, expectations, and demands specific to the Great Depression, world wars, space race, and cold war can be taken into account given the power of those events to shape individuals. How did Captain Montgomery develop into who he is today? What were the dominant experiences that shaped his orientation to the world? Working toward an understanding of such developmental processes allows therapists to gain a unique perspective on the older man, as well as allow the client to begin connecting with his own socialization and its impact.

Empathy

"One of the bedrock principals in psychology is that people are more willing to examine their issues when they feel as if they have been understood, appreciated, and valued" (Wester & Vogel, 2002, p. 373; see also Brooks, 1998; Rogers, 1966). As such, this could be considered as the first step toward cementing the working alliance developed earlier and, even more important, ensuring that the client perceives the therapist's empathy (Rogers, 1966). Unfortunately, this may be difficult to demonstrate to older men given their distrust and avoidance of therapy as an activity while at the same time the male socialization has led most men to conclude that seeking psychological help means admitting weakness and failure. Older male clients might be experiencing a high level of concern about how the therapist will react to their disclosures in therapy, especially when the therapist differs in gender or age. For all of the importance Captain Montgomery has attached to his accomplishments, and the degree to which his behavioral pattern has contributed to those achievements, asking for or accepting help carries significant risk, especially exposure of being vulnerable. Indeed, such jeopardy is compounded in that he might see the therapist as a threat, someone standing in the way of his ultimate goal of once again commanding his crew.

Being open, remaining nondefensive, providing comfort with being challenged and with a sense of complementarity, and being willing to self-disclose (e.g., Duffy, 1999) are all methods in working with older men. Nontraditional techniques, in nontraditional settings, may also offer options for working more effectively in psychotherapy with older male clients. For example, some men develop trusting relationships over a more gradual period of time (Kiselica, 2001). They also tend to do so in atypical settings, such as outside the office, or through shared activities, such as playing sports or working together on projects. In addition, psychologists need to recognize that therapy for older men involves not only feeling better but also doing better (e.g., Sprenkel, 1999). That is, progress can be defined not only as emotional and interpersonal growth but also as the development of new understandings, new behaviors, and new coping styles.

The Working Through Phase

The heart of progress at this stage of treatment is the understanding and addressing of those factors that are causing the older man the greatest amount of psychological distress. Effort made earlier to develop a working alliance and a sense of perceived empathy pays dividends here, as the trusting, nonjudgmental approach of the therapist can provide the older male client with the support needed to acknowledge his concerns and overcome entrenched defensive styles. However, "the psychotherapeutic process, if successful, is a poignant example of a truly intimate relationship and it is therefore not unusual that, if successful [*sic*], it will lead to a strain on the therapist–client relationship" (Duffy, 1999, p. 13). This might exhibit as an impasse within the progress of therapy, in which neither the client nor the therapist is sure how to proceed. Or perhaps it looks like a turning point in which the client expresses a sense that he has made adequate progress and no longer requires therapeutic services. Clients such as Captain Montgomery might be more vulnerable to this phenomena given their socialized reluctance to express tender emotions, weakness, and vulnerability, feelings that they are taught to deal with through avoidance.

As therapy moves forward, older "men must be challenged to initiate a major reevaluation of their gender role values and assumptions in an effort to bring themselves into harmony with a changing world" (Brooks, 2001, p. 219). In effect, the therapist will have to work with the client so as to first give himself permission to modify a set of behaviors that historically have served him well but have become maladaptive. One of the more common consequences is a combination of sadness and fear. Sadness stems from the loss of a behavioral pattern that was passed down across the generations, a version of the "it was good enough for my father, it is good enough for me" syndrome. Fear conversely stems from having to learn new ways of behaving later in life as well as from risking the loss of the edge granted by behaving in a traditionally masculine fashion. Indeed, given the degree to which society continues to expect certain behaviors if one is to be considered appropriately masculine, this stage of therapy may prove to be challenging for both client and therapist.

Once the nature and content of an individual client's way of being has been established, it is important to begin challenging those aspects that are maladaptive and problematic to interpersonal functioning while at the same time validating those aspects that may contribute to success. Again, the goal is not to condemn all socialized masculine behaviors but to encourage the development of a wider range of cognitive, affective, and behavioral options. There is a sense of keeping what works for them at this time in their life and changing what does not in regard to male role behaviors. For example, the male ideal of competition and success has been hypothesized to interfere with the development of interpersonal relationships (e.g., Brooks, 1998) and could be partly responsible for the isolation some older men experience in retirement. However, rather than eliminating this aspect of his behavior, the client might choose to redirect his interpersonally competitive nature toward community advocacy, social change, or family involvement. This process of reframing encourages the development of new, more adaptive behaviors built on the foundation, rather than the ashes, of previous learning. In essence, it is encouraging the client to capitalize on his strengths, only in a more adaptive format for his current life situation.

Exploration: What the Future Holds as a Part of the Termination Process

An eye toward the future can be shortchanged because of short-term treatment modalities, the importance of addressing current levels of psychological distress, or the existential nature of working with older clients. However, acknowledging potential situations or occurrences in the upcoming years increases an awareness of ongoing developmental change within the context of the important role played by socialized gender role behaviors. This may help to prevent the older male client from returning to previously identified maladaptive behavioral patterns, especially once members of the client's peer group begin reasserting their influence. Consider an example to illustrate this: During one of the final scenes in *Star Trek VI: The Undiscovered Country* (Meyer & Nimoy, 1991), Mr. Spock and the indomitable Captain James T. Kirk are discussing the plight in which they find themselves. Mr. Spock admits that he allowed his biases regarding a fellow Vulcan's accomplishments cloud his vision such that he missed her treacherous behavior until it was too late; disaster almost resulted. Captain Kirk counters with the admission that his own refusal to admit, and move beyond, his prejudice against Klingons also produced significant potential for disaster. Both are at fault, Kirk argues. This prompts Spock to ask, "Is it possible that we two, you and I, have grown so old and inflexible that we have outlived our usefulness?" This is a significant moment for Spock, in that as a Vulcan he subscribes to logic and ability above all else, and the admission of any potential failure on his part casts significant shame on his identity. As such, at that moment he recognizes that he faces a future in which at times he must be open to change, engaging in a learning process in how to better think, feel, and behave given the current situation, rather than those of the past.

This scene is analogous to what some male clients may experience toward the end of any therapeutic relationship, and incorporating a focus on the future during the termination phase significantly contributes to the older man maintaining an awareness of his long-term goals. As with any ending, the termination process can bring about a mixture of feelings ranging from uncertainty and excitement to recognition of the many possibilities the future might hold. Indeed, returning to the *Star Trek* example, much of this film is a metaphor for growing beyond one's socialized limitations and embracing what comes next. Both Kirk and Spock could have chosen to resist change; they have done so on countless examples throughout the universe of *Star Trek* (e.g., Okuda,

Okuda, & Mirek, 1994). With the support and encouragement of each other, however, they decide to take on this new challenge. Kirk tells his friend directly that he needs him, and with newfound insight and ability to capitalize on new behaviors, they move forward to save the upcoming peace conference between the Klingon Empire and the United Federation of Planets.

CONCLUSION

Older men can best be understood through the lens of their individual characteristics, as well as within the context of age and gender. An awareness of the complexities of an older man's life allows the therapist to better understand the client's plight and avoid passing judgment on behaviors he may have exhibited across the life span. A working alliance with older men based on a sense of complementarity increases the likelihood that progress gained in therapy builds on the strengths and skills of the client. In addition, the therapist's self-awareness is essential, with a focus on potential biases. These sources might range from one's own experience with older individuals in general to one's experiences with older men in one's own life such as a grandfather or father. Reactions might involve difficulty in dealing with certain behaviors, a sense of "he looks like my grandfather," or perhaps a more general dislike of a traditionally masculine way of being, or stereotypes about race and ethnicity. Additional reactions could include one's own concerns about the end-of-life experiences and anxieties about the consequences of aging. Whatever the content, recognizing the reaction as well as its potential for affecting the therapeutic process is important to successfully working with older men.

TABLE 3.1   Guidelines for Psychotherapeutic Approaches With Older Men

- Overall competence working with older individuals, as defined by various organizations (see Appendix), is both critical and presumed.
- Basic clinical skills need to be modified when working with older male clients.
    - Working alliance is characterized by complimentarity.
    - A multidisciplinary approach is important.
    - Pay attention to age and gender issues regarding language use and client presenting issues.
- The introductory phase should include focused assessment.
    - Honor both the context and heritage of the individual, including those aspects of the male gender role that allowed him to succeed.
    - Develop a sense of empathy, and become fluent in the masculine voice.
- The working through phase allows for a strengthening of the therapeutic relationship and exploration of difficulties.
    - Challenge him to build new learning upon the basis of what he already knows and does well.
    - Help him to reevaluate his gender role assumptions.
- The termination phase can be used as a context for continuing change.
    - Focus on what can be accomplished in the context of new learning.

4

Transitions and Life Adjustments

Tomas Hernandez was a 65-year-old Hispanic man who worked the majority of his professional life as an artisan cabinetmaker. He began making cabinets with his father while in grade school and later went on to study carpentry at a local technical college, being the first member of his family to pursue education beyond high school. While working for a home builder and developer, Mr. Hernandez built cabinets in his home garage in the evenings and weekends; he took great pride in his ability to create beauty with his hands. His extraordinary ability, hard work ethic, and tenacity to care for his wife and children developed into a thriving small business. Over the years Mr. Hernandez had carefully taught his son in the art of building and the critical elements of business. George had been apprenticing for 15 years in preparation to take over the family business. By the end of his career, Mr. Hernandez felt he knew "everything one needs to know" about making cabinets and surviving as a small-business owner. Mr. Hernandez and his wife, Elsa, who was a stay-at-home mother, earnestly saved and prepared for their retirement, a time when they would be able to enjoy more leisure time, with contentment of providing for the financial security of their only son, the youngest child in a family of seven. However, as Mr. Hernandez's retirement date approached and he planned to turn over the business to his son, he realized that he enjoyed his activities so much that he "had not worked a day in his life." He began to fear losing the social interaction with customers and other small-business owners and the feeling of being an active and essential member of the community. He was also concerned that boredom and laziness would set in without the structure and physical challenge of his work. But, most important, he wondered what would happen to the special feeling he felt when he created something beautiful for someone else to use.

Change happens to everyone, regardless of age, gender, or ethnicity. However, there are situational difficulties that are often associated with the developmental process of aging, and there are certainly unavoidable changes or needed adjustments that are relevant to older men. These can include areas such as work and retirement in later life, as well as leisure and financial resources. Societal changes in the constitution of family, shifting relationships (e.g., interacting with adult children), and changing roles (e.g., caregiver of spouse; widower) can also be prominent for older men. With the increase of medical technology, end-of-life issues have increasingly become a matter of importance with age.

RETIREMENT: CHANGES IN IDENTITY, FINANCES, LEISURE, AND RELATIONSHIPS

Retirement from the world of work is one of the most significant transitions for older men as it influences a range of emotional, cognitive, and financial domains. Adjustment difficulties related to retirement for the older man most often stem directly from the context in which he constructed his masculinity. If his sense of identity as a man includes work as a significant component, then adjustment to retirement is likely to be of great concern for him. Work is so central to the Euro-American sense of masculinity that it is difficult to imagine a masculine script that does not include aspects of career and its meaning (e.g., Heppner & Heppner, 2001). However, it is possible that for some men the role of work is not as salient, in which case adjustments associated with retirement may be of less significance. Mr. Hernandez certainly placed a tremendous value on his work and the achievements, even suggesting that it was not actual work. As such, for all the positive aspects of his situation, his adjustment to retirement was still difficult.

Theoretical Frameworks of Retirement

Retirement has been examined through several theoretical frameworks. Sociological Role Theory (Ashforth, 2001) predicts older men will experience distress with retirement, as work is a central aspect of personal identity. With the loss of this role comes change in identity, leading to distress (Pinquart & Schindler, 2007). Continuity Theory (Atchley, 1989), however, suggests that stress associated with retirement is related to discontinuity with earlier roles in life. Therefore, if men are able to transfer central roles in their life they experienced through their employment, they will be less likely to experience psychological distress. If people do not transform their previous roles to new activities outside of the world of work, they can experience hopelessness, which can prompt significant stress (Pinquart & Schindler, 2007). Consider the example of Mr. Hernandez at the beginning of the chapter. He spent his entire life working for his community and family, which in return provided him with a sense of satisfaction for creating beauty for others and of contributing to those he cared about. Without transferring his love of building cabinets to another activity, Mr. Hernandez loses a core piece of his identity as an artisan and active contributor to his community. Thus, when an older man is unable to transfer the tasks, responsibilities, and positive elements of work to retirement, difficulty with adjustment will likely result.

Atchley (1976) conceptualized retirement as a process ranging from preretirement to postretirement. In this seminal work, Atchley explained that most men experience a relatively short "honeymoon phase" soon after retirement. This time is often spent engaging in what is described as typical retirement activities, such as travel or hobbies, and is experienced as a relief from work-related obligations; it is idealized in popular culture, such as "we will finally be able to travel" or "I'm going to take up golf" in retirement. However, Atchley (1976) noted that after the initial glow, individuals experience a decrease in their well-being when the reality of retirement sets in; the novelty of retirement fades and is replaced by the realization of a lack of proscribed structure or limited financial resources. In a final stage, men experience a reorientation phase when they develop realistic views of their new social and economic realities and are able to fully appreciate both the advantages and the disadvantages of retirement.

Trajectories of Adjustment

Current empirical research has found several distinct trajectories of adjustment to retirement (Pinquart & Schindler, 2007), establishing support that people who generally transfer the needs fulfilled by work to tasks, roles, and activities outside of work thereby leading to a relatively small transition into retirement. Pinquart and Schindler (2007) identified that approximately 10% of the older adults in their study experienced role loss when they retired; almost 15% reported experiencing a slight increase in life satisfaction, followed by despair, and then a subsequent leveling of satisfaction. Overall, this empirical study demonstrated that a bulk of the retirees used continuity to adapt to retirement and therefore had a relatively small change in life satisfaction. For Mr. Hernandez, then, the key might be to transition to alternative ways of meeting those needs mentioned—the creation of something beautiful for others to use—to his retirement activities.

Although adjustment to retirement has expected trajectories through normative means, variation exists, especially with regard to the individual differences and personality attributes. Research has identified that people who tend to adapt well to retirement are often from a higher socioeconomic status, married, and in relatively good health and actively replace work with other meaningful activities (Pinquart & Schindler, 2007). In the psychotherapy process with Mr. Hernandez, the therapist must consider his Hispanic culture, recognizing that although there is often tremendous individual variation, it is not uncommon for this to include activities that the dominant culture might associate with femininity given the degree to which the culture may indeed be more matriarchal, especially in regard to family and home circumstances. Bye and Pushkar (2009) found that the intrinsic desire for cognitive inquiry and challenge prompted greater cognitive activity and, thus, better coping in older adults transitioning to retirement. Inquisitive individuals were more likely to continue to challenge themselves cognitively, allowing for positive coping in the transition.

The context surrounding the decision to retire also has a large influence on how an older man interprets and accepts the transition. Certainly this refers to how someone constructed his masculinity, but it also refers to the situations surrounding the change itself. For example, a major factor influencing adjustment to retirement is whether the retirement was forced or voluntary (Calvo, Haverstick, & Sass, 2009). The research consistently indicates that when workers are forced to retire, adjustment to the process is significantly more challenging because of appraisal of the situation (Calvo et al., 2009; Isaksson & Gunn, 2000). In addition, when retirement is forced, emotional satisfaction and self-image are negatively impacted (Peretti & Wilson, 1975). Conversely, when people perceive control in their decision to retire, they are more likely to interpret the event with pleasure and enjoyment rather than as a drastic, forced, psychological, and economic change in lifestyle (Calvo et al., 2009). This seems to be the case with Mr. Hernandez; he is choosing to retire and has made significant preparations for his son to transition into managing the business he built. His seemingly positive relationship with his wife, and the degree to which they may have negotiated the changes in their division of labor, bode well for the long-term adjustment.

Researchers have also speculated that those who experience a decrease in life satisfaction related to work prior to retirement (e.g., loss of a job prior to retirement) tended to experience a relatively large increase in quality of life after retirement with a later decrease to more moderate levels (Pinquart & Schindler, 2007). This could be accounted for by having relatively few role options as well as the financial losses as a result of retirement. Again, the nature of an individual man's scripts and the context in which these scripts developed is informative. Mr. Hernandez attaches significant meaning to his career, both in terms of working hard and providing for his family and in the sense of creating things and providing items that can be used and admired by others. Thus, the context of the older man's life, the circumstances around the transition into retirement, and the meaning given to transitioning out of the world of work greatly affects his adjustment trajectory.

As with any event, individual understanding and interpretation of the event is the underlying mechanism that influences the resultant psychological outcome. When one is forced into retirement, the event has a higher probability of being interpreted as a loss, rejection, or a sign of personal inadequacy. Under conditions of little control, an older man may feel obsolete and unproductive, further questioning his self-worth and contribution to society. However, under similar financial and social circumstances, if an older worker chooses to leave, the psychological consequences related to rejection need not be activated. Instead, the transition can be interpreted as a "deserved time" to relax and focus on hobbies and other personal pursuits. Through psychotherapy the actual context of the older man's retirement as well as how he interprets the context or transition can be explored, with consideration given to challenging and reframing his individualized interpretation of retirement to facilitate adaptive adjustment.

Relationship Changes

In addition to facing changes in role and role definition, many older men face significant changes in their social support network as a result of retirement. In contrast to women, men tend to derive the majority of their social support network from relationships at work (Brooks, 1998). Hispanic men such as Mr. Hernandez, however, have the added dimension of presenting traditional values outside of the home and progressive values such as a sharing of duties within the home, which may set the stage for increased adjustment difficulties if they are not prepared for the loss of that public presentation of traditional values. In addition, public relationships may tend to be more task or activity oriented (Brooks, 1998; Wester, 2008), rather than emotionally intimate in nature. Research has noted that other than work relationships, the primary source of social support for many older men is their significant other (Sternbach, 2001), and some men who are widowed in late life tend to be considerably more socially isolated (Moore & Stratton, 2002; Tamir, 1982). Thus, retirement can be a time of increased social isolation for men in general, and a loss of that aforementioned public face of traditionalism for Hispanic men specifically, which is a hallmark of disengagement (e.g., Cummings, Henry, & Damianopoulos, 1961). If the older man is able to transfer his skills to have his social needs met outside of the world of work, similar to other challenges related to retirement, he is likely to fare better with regard to psychological functioning. Should Mr. Hernandez continue to visit his friends and help them with their businesses and remain active as a volunteer in his civic organizations, the social needs fulfilled previously through his relationships at work can be adequately and appropriately met during retirement.

In addition to the loss of primary social support found through work, some men may find difficulties with their significant others given the greater amount of time spent at home and the subsequent redistribution of household responsibilities. Consider the example of Mr. Hernandez; given that his wife did not work outside the home while he gave significant time developing the business, it is possible that gender roles were more strictly defined. This is more likely to be the case if Mr. Hernandez defined himself using the dominant culture as his reference group. If a man has spent most of his adult life exerting control and personal efficacy over his work life outside of the home, while his wife has been doing the same thing over the household, significant interpersonal conflict could result should the husband in retirement begin exerting control over household affairs. However, if Mr. Hernandez defined himself in relation to his Hispanic culture, it may be the case that although his situation—he worked while wife remained at home—might appear traditional to the external observer, in fact it is likely that the two of them shared duties within the household. Consistent with continuity theory, if an older man maintains continuity by meeting similar role needs in new environments, he would be expected to experience less distress. However, if the older man exerts more control in an area that has been managed primarily by his significant other, this could lead to significant interpersonal conflict. Both Mr. and Mrs. Hernandez must reestablish their relationship to accommodate the amount of time spent together and renegotiate household roles and responsibilities and the parameters of their relationships.

On the other hand, some men may have complex relationships in which they worked much of their life as a form of avoidance or escape from household or relationship conflicts. In this example, the newly retired man might find spending time with his family as stressful and without access to the coping strategy used throughout his life. This is a hallmark of both gender role conflict (e.g., O'Neil, 2008) and gender role strain (e.g., Pleck, 1995) theories, in that the skills he has relied on to be successful in his job conflict with those required to spend time with his family. Someone of Hispanic heritage might also face the challenge of having to reconcile both the dominant culture's expectations for men and what Hispanic culture expects of men. In this scenario several transitions must be made, including redeveloping comfortable interpersonal boundaries with his family and reestablishing new methods to cope with interpersonal conflict. In psychotherapy, most men respond well to framing the key to success for these transitions as the learning of new skills.

As a man transitions to the later years of his life, the relationship with his children will inevitably change and can become a source of discomfort and inefficacy. Men endorsing traditional gender role socialization may be most comfortable in being the head of the family, having others dependent on him, and having the final word on many household and interpersonal decisions. However, as the older man transitions out of the world of work, while his children move into the labor force and begin having children of their own, a reversal of parent–child roles can occur, leading to possible discomfort on the part of the aging male. An example of this might develop for Mr. Hernandez, as he would need to become comfortable with his son making decisions within the family business, an enterprise that Mr. Hernandez had devoted his life to developing. Relationships must be constantly renegotiated as the older man's life roles change with advancing age. Exploring the meaning older men attach to their roles in the family, as well as what it means for them to have those roles transform as their relationships change, is critical to increased understanding of these issues in psychotherapy.

In contrast to the potentially problematic relationship transitions older men may face as they transition into retirement, retirement and disentanglement from traditional gender role socialization opens the possibility of forging new relationships without such circumscribed gender-based parameters. As men leave the world of work and transition away from the expectation of being powerful, successful, and competent; putting their work before their family; and showing little emotion or affection, they may feel freed to have more genuine, emotionally connected relationships with family members. For example, as a grandfather, an older man does not have the obligation to be powerful and successful, allowing him to be attentive, playful, and affectionate with his grandchildren. Therefore, a positive relational side effect of retirement is that older men, no longer closely adhering to strict gender role expectations, may be able to take the liberty to engage in relationships in a manner they felt they could not at a younger age.

Financial Strains of Retirement

As a man leaves the world of work, he must confront the financial reality of retirement, which has changed significantly over the past 50 years, leaving many older adults financially vulnerable. Male socialization, which is especially prevalent for men of the current older adult cohort, centered on work as a means of financial independence, which in turn allowed for financial support of others and control over one's choices and lifestyle. A prototypical image of the male head of a household picking up the check for the family's meal at a restaurant is ubiquitous in American culture. Underlying this prototypical image is the broader social belief that the patriarch of a family should financially support the family and to a certain degree continue to control how money is spent. Within Hispanic culture, for example, there is also the fact that the definition of family is often more expansive than the parents and their children. Older parents, as well as grandparents and children of brothers and sisters, may make up the family unit. These individuals may fall under Mr. Hernandez's financial umbrella, thereby placing additional strain on monetary resources of retirement.

However, the reality of a fixed income comes with retirement. Many older men depend on Social Security or company-sponsored pensions as the primary means for financial security in older age. However, Social Security, when created in 1935, was created as a social insurance program to ensure that older workers would leave the workforce to make room for younger workers with families. If a worker lived to the age of 65, the mean life expectancy at that time, he was able to receive money from the government as a form of insurance. However, in the past 75 years, the life expectancy has increased to 78 years because of great advances in technology and medical care. However, the system originally created to provide only a few years of financial support to the oldest members of society in the 1930s is now being used as a primary means for retirement, thus financially straining the public system. Social Security currently provides only minimal financial assistance to older Americans and in the future will likely be an unsustainable program, thus providing older men with only minimal financial compensation and uncertainty about the future.

In addition to the problems associated with a reliance on Social Security as the primary funding source of retirement, many older men worked hard throughout their lives, with the expectation that their company-sponsored pension would provide for them in retirement. In 1978, America's retirement system was revolutionized with the inception of 401(k) employee-managed options through passage of the Revenue Act of 1978. In addition, because of financial strain and difficulty, many large companies have cut or eliminated their company pensions. In general, older men who are currently approaching retirement have less financial security than they anticipated.

Although many older adults function well on fixed incomes, the financial security and comfort they may have felt during the working years of their life are likely limited. For men who strongly endorse the success, power, and competition expectations of being a man, being unable to financially "flip the bill" when out with family, maintain the household, or support others represents a significant loss of power, autonomy, and personal efficacy. Being unable to pay the heating bill in the family home or purchase needed medications may cause the older man to label himself as a failure or embarrassment, as if he has let himself and others down and failed as a provider. Being a sole financial supporter allows a man the control to decide family activities, permitting a man to feel needed, essential, and protective. As such, adjusting to a fixed income has the potential for adjustment difficulties related to quality of life and lifestyle as well as the role and emotional loss of no longer being the needed provider.

OPTIONS FOR LIVING ARRANGEMENTS

Today, older men have more options than ever regarding housing options for the later years of life. The desire of older adults to remain independent has brought about an increase in active adult and independent living communities, spurring community-based care services designed to help older adults remain in the community through social support programs, adult day care, home-based care, and other care services. Housing alternatives now include choices such as retirement resorts, independent living communities, active adult communities, and senior apartments. Should older adults require more care, options range from assisted living, where older adults often have private units similar to apartments and receive nursing, meal, and cleaning services to assist in maintaining a degree of independent living, to long-term care facilities units that offer a place of residence to older adults who can no longer perform activities of daily living and who do not have at-home caregivers to assist them. Memory care facilities help older adults with decreased functioning due to dementia live meaningful lives without endangering themselves.

Older men may use therapy as an opportunity to explore their options of living arrangements, as well as their reactions to such a transition. Listing positives and negatives of such a move or of two different places may be helpful. Perhaps unlike the older man's family members, the therapist is an objective partner in helping him to truly consider all options so that he can make the best decision for himself. In some cases, the older man may indicate that family members are "pressuring" him to move to a different level of housing, as they would feel more reassured of his safety and well-being. In another situation, an older man's family may be emotionally invested in their childhood home and their own needs for their father to remain as the head of the household and, thus, oppose his interest in moving to a senior living community. Regardless of the reasons for the positional move or the level of care the older man is relocating to, these decisions can be emotionally charged and bring out a number of socialized male role conflicts, such as the need to be independent and remain in control of one's own life.

In addition to the various living options and level of care offered, hospice care, an approach to providing comfort and care at life's end rather than heroic lifesaving measures, has become increasingly available via in-home services, specialized units, or hospitals. Decisions to enter hospice or opt for palliative care initiate a number of additional emotional issues as the end-of-life approaches.

One aspect of working on these issues with older men is the degree to which many of them resist seeking help, in whatever form, despite the evidence that they need such assistance. An older man admitting, for example, that he might no longer be able to afford or be physically able to maintain a home directly challenges the traditional masculine identity; to admit that he must leave his home because of medical, cognitive, or psychological issues would surely suggest unacceptable weakness. In the case of Mr. Hernandez, enlisting the culturally appropriate community-based systems of care, such as extended family, may be useful.

END-OF-LIFE ISSUES

With medical and technological advances, Americans are living longer but also bearing the burden of chronic illness and increased disability, bringing about decisions of whether to continue life-sustaining treatment at the cost of quality of life. In previous generations, death was an uncontrolled, inevitable element of life. Acquiring a disease or infection without ventilators, organ transplants, or hemodialysis likely meant death, and individuals or family members were not required to weigh the decision of length of life versus quality of life.

Advance Care Planning

Advance care planning involves meeting with the individual and his support network to discuss treatment alternatives and his values and preferences and to create a plan suited to the individual (Lorenz, Rosenfeld, & Wenger, 2007). Creation of an advanced directive can provide an older man security and concrete assistance when making decisions for family members as well as the autonomy to make decisions about the end of life that are congruent with his value system. With the passage of the Patient Self-Determination Act in December 1991, individuals are afforded the right to make independent decisions at end of life even should they become unable to do so verbally in the moment. Through this document, an older man can clearly indicate preferences about care to friends and family members as well as health care providers. Making decisions about life-sustaining treatment in the absence of a clearly stated advanced directive can be not only difficult for family members but emotionally painful, although having an advanced directive does not guarantee ease with this conversation (Wilson, 2000).

Having these conversations both with an older man in psychotherapy and with him and his family members requires weighing the individual's personal and cultural values as well as family dynamics and problem-solving skills. With regard to salient issues at end of life, people typically express the desire for pain control, awareness, existential and spiritual acknowledgment, and the ability to gain a sense of completion (Steinhauser et al., 2000).

Good medical and physical care is considered important to most, but it is only one part of the larger experience of the end-of-life process. In facing death, an older man can be encouraged to examine his values and desires while concurrently considering how his family dynamics may influence his decisions. As the caretaker and head of the family, older men may feel reluctant to acknowledge their vulnerability as they approach death, instead "staying strong" for their family members. They may also struggle with balancing their own preferences with those of their family members. For example, an older man who has been living with chronic pain for the past 10 years and has a number of critical medical complications may prefer to refuse any future aggressive life-saving measures. However, his family members, who are not ready to be without him in their life and fearful that he is "giving up," may strongly encourage him to "fight" these diseases and do everything medically possible to prolong his life. Through psychotherapy the older man can further explore his own thoughts and feelings about his decisions in context to those of his children, coming to some clarity about how to best approach his family and how to further talk about this together. The therapist can help him to better understand his family's point of view but also support his own needs, with an overall goal of coming to a resolution with which he is content.

Men with strong gender role socialization, who are often unable to show vulnerability or emotionality, may be at a disadvantage while having this conversation. Again, because the gender role mandates avoiding the presentation of weakness or failure, many men operate under a number of coping mechanisms learned as a boy, not all of them adaptive, to avoid this discussion. However, at the same time, gender role socialization may also have imparted adaptive traits for older men as they face end-of-life issues. A man may be more willing to approach end-of-life conversations with decisive planning to take the burden away from his family and end life with a similar level of efficacy and control. The key for those working with older men at this stage in life is to tap their preference for a solution-focused orientation and point it in the direction of end-of-life concerns. Assessment of whether gender role beliefs and how those beliefs interact with family dynamics must be completed as an older man approaches end-of-life conversations.

Being in the Decision-Maker Role

In addition to dealing with end-of-life decisions for themselves, older men may also be charged with the responsibility of acting as a surrogate to their significant other or spouse, which includes executing an advanced medical directive or supporting the wishes of another person. This can be a stressful decision to make, as the older man may have personal beliefs about his significant other's care, feel confused about what the other individual would have wanted, or find that the loved one's wishes differ from the written instructions created when the individual was well. Having an up-to-date advanced directive on file can be helpful for an older man having to make decisions about the medical care of his wife, as it provides concrete guidance of her wishes. Gender role socialization may affect positively or negatively in this situation. For example, older men may find themselves more adept at coping with this situation because of their tendency to use problem-focused coping strategies. In this pursuit, a man may be able to focus on the specific, and perhaps written, decisions of his spouse with relative adaptiveness and ease. The key to this seems to be flexibility on the part of the man and his own willingness to adapt his gender role behaviors to the demands of this situation.

However, at the same time, for those men who have developed a more dependent relationship (e.g., Huyck & Gutmann, 1999) with their wife, agreeing to no further treatment per her wishes, although this is in direct conflict to his, can be an extremely difficult position. If Mr. Hernandez faced this decision, the more matriarchal nature of Hispanic culture, while subject to within-group variation, might make this an even more complex decision. Certainly, those men who have developed a systonic dependence, characterized by a more passive behavioral style and the overreliance on others for their caregiving and support, might find themselves paralyzed in the face of having to make such significant decisions. On the other side of the coin, dystonic dependence would be one in which the goal would be to avoid the public suggestion of vulnerability. Hence, when feeling overwhelmed by the need to care for their significant other, these men would be most at risk to not ask for help, while feeling ashamed of their seeming inability to cope in the situation (Levant, 2001a).

Shifting Perspectives

Another critical aspect in the end-of-life realm and the making of decisions about continuing life-sustaining treatment is recognition of the perspective from which people are viewing the decision; where one is in the process may influence the point of view. Research has demonstrated a trend for those who are more physically disabled and frail to request more invasive physical treatment than those who are well (Winter & Parker, 2007). This phenomenon has been termed a "response shift" and occurs when people reestablish different standards about what is a good quality of life after living with chronic illness and/or disability (Gibbons, 1999). Thus, depending on the physical state of the older man leading up to a decision on whether to have or to continue life-sustaining treatment, the likelihood of opting for that treatment and subsequently feeling content with that quality of life will differ. This becomes particularly important with regard to frail elders, as older adults with a more compromised health state are less likely to refuse further health intervention (Winter & Parker, 2007). The decision about whether to continue or discontinue treatment is multifaceted and dependent on the person's idiosyncratic values, cultural values, family support, and the perspective from which the person is making a decision.

Therapist Reactions

Therapists working with older men must also be aware of the existential nature of their work in regard to the impact of these issues on one's self. The aging process and death become relevant at some point for everyone. Care must be taken to be self-aware of one's own perceptions about end-of-life issues. What are the therapist's experiences surrounding death and beliefs about death and what happens after?

Providing psychotherapy to older men obviously increases the potential for client deaths, as working with a late-life population increases the likelihood that clients, or loved ones in their life, will die. Monitoring internal thoughts and feelings that may influence professional behavior is recommended to allow for adjustment of behavior accordingly in focusing on needs of the client, family, and treatment team. There should be an introspective awareness that regardless of countless experiences or even familiarity, the exposure to ongoing suffering and ending of life can also provide its own distress. Basing the title of his book *Staring at the Sun* on this concept, Yalom (2008) wrote, "It's not easy to live every moment wholly aware of death. It's like trying to stare the sun in the face: you can stand only so much of it" (p. 5). Therapists will be more effective in psychotherapy with older male clients if they remain sensitive to their own reactions to end-of-life experiences and be willing to remain aware and process their unique reactions to client death. Just as therapists must be cognizant of the differences between normal grief reactions and complicated grief in older male clients, they too must be introspective regarding their own reactions to death and their overall emotional well-being.

Bereavement Over Loss of a Spouse or Partner

Some older men will experience the loss of family members and friends, in addition to a significant other or spouse. Many individuals who experience a significant loss have symptoms associated with depression, which has been coined the "loss effect" (Stroebe & Stroebe, 1987). Symptoms associated with a loss effect, rather than a clinically diagnosable psychological disorder, often dissipate within two years of loss but mimic symptoms of depression (Stroebe & Stroebe, 1987), thus a certain level of psychological distress after the loss of a significant other or spouse is expected. Thompson, Gallagher-Thompson, Futterman, Gilewski, and Peterson (1991) found psychological distress to be greater among widowed compared to nonwidowed older adults for up to a year after the loss, with reestablishment of psychological well-being after that year. However, self-reported grief and the expression of grief (e.g., missing a spouse, wishing to be with a spouse, crying over loss of a spouse, and fondly remembering a spouse) can last for several years after a loss and is often independent of psychological distress and symptomatology (Thompson et al., 1991).

Common immediate reactions to bereavement include emotional symptoms (e.g., distress, depression, anxiety, guilt, anger, yearning, and shock), cognitive symptoms (e.g., rumination, preoccupation with the deceased, denial, suppression, helplessness, and self-reproach), behavioral problems (e.g., fatigue, agitation, restlessness, weeping or sobbing, and social withdrawal), and physiological symptoms (e.g., loss of appetite, energy loss, sleep disturbance, and somatic complaints) (Stroebe, Schut, & Stroebe, 2007). However, these symptoms are not experienced by all individuals and are thought to dissipate with time as a normative part of the human experience (Stroebe, Schut, et al., 2007). Further complicating this process is the tendency of some men to mask their depressive reactions through active coping styles but also substance use. At the same time, many are able to adapt through a series of "tasks" including accepting the loss, experiencing the emotional pain of grief, adjusting to life without the deceased, and moving on (Worden & Monahan, 2001). Approximately 9% to 20% of all bereaved individuals experience chronic or complicated grief, with individuals losing children experiencing a higher rate of complicated grief.

Davis and Nolen-Hoeksema (2001) argued that meaning making is an essential process that occurs in the adjustment to loss, echoing Addis & Mahalik (2003) regarding the social construction of masculinity. For someone like Mr. Hernandez, this is likely to be a multidimensional experience, as he negotiates between the gender role demands of both the Hispanic culture and the dominant Euro-American culture (e.g., Wester, 2008) as well as what those demands meant for the relationship with his spouse. Thus, Davis and Nolen-Hoeksema suggested that older men might search for more than a causal explanation for a death, seeking a comprehensive, philosophical explanation for the loss. Unlike individuals who may die at a younger age, older adults often have the logical existential explanation that this was the natural course of life and inevitable outcome for an older adult; however logical, the death of the loved one remains emotionally grueling. Imagine waking up every morning for the past 60 years with the same person by your side; together there have been good times and bad times, children have been raised, jobs have come and gone, as have financial concerns and other major life events. After the many years and momentous experiences shared, the loss of his wife—a lifelong partner—can be devastating for an older man. Some men will indicate that 60 years "was not enough time together" and deeply grieve her loss. Religious or spiritual beliefs are also meaningful constructs that can help comfort some bereaved (Davis & Nolen-Hoeksema, 2001), which may in turn make the emotional coping process of bereavement more bearable. It should be noted that although many would expect these rationales to comfort older adults after the loss of a spouse, if people interpret the death as random or unfair, the meaning-making process and thus adjustment and coping can be thwarted. Davis and Nolen-Hoeksema claimed these beliefs stemmed from individual worldviews and have a great impact on the individual adjustment to a loss. An essential aspect of psychotherapy is the exploration of the client's interpretation of the event based on his worldview beliefs rather than his socially held beliefs.

In addition to normative styles of bereavement, several behaviors are associated with complicated grief and disturbed adjustment. Ruminative coping is when an individual passively engages in negative thoughts and focuses on negative emotion without attempting to engage in problem-solving behavior (Nolen-Hoeksema, 2001). Negative rumination has been conceptualized as an avoidant coping strategy or way to avoid forgetting the deceased that leads to complicated grief and psychological symptoms by not allowing for complete integration of the loss (Stroebe, Boelen, et al., 2007). Torges, Stewart, and Nolen-Hoeksema (2008) suggested that how people coped with perceived regrets influenced adjustment to loss, as those who resolved their regrets had lower psychological symptoms, less rumination, and greater psychological well-being over a year after loss. However, Torges et al. also suggested that coping with loss in a ruminative manner might serve to reciprocally impact adjustment to loss by fostering more regrets and negative thinking. Findings imply that reacting to loss with depression, negative rumination, and unaddressed regrets may serve to hinder adjustment and negatively impact quality of life.

Of note, it has been found that older men fare better than women with regard to depressive symptoms and psychopathology following a loss (Thompson et al., 1991). This may be due to an overall finding that women experience a greater level of depressive symptomatology than men (Nolen-Hoeksema, 1987) because they engage in relatively higher rates of ruminative thinking. Again, however, it is important to fully assess for the presence of depressive symptoms in an older man using a typology that accounts for the masking of depression as well as the presentation of problems not typically associated with depression and the employment of more maladaptive coping styles (e.g., Cochran & Rabinowitz, 2000).

Another way of coping with the death of a loved one that has questionably deleterious outcomes includes continuing emotional bonds to the deceased. Although evidence cannot definitively support whether maintaining or severing close emotional ties to the deceased facilitates or hinders adjustment to loss, as it depends on the individual, researchers have suggested that individuals having difficulty adjusting may need to "relocate" the deceased individual emotionally to provide emotional flexibility in future relationships (Stroebe & Schut, 2005).

On the aggregate, the impact of bereavement on men is thought to be greater than the impact for women with older men faring worse than women across health-related outcomes. Men tend to have more health-related consequences as a result of losing a spouse, including a greater number of self-reported health problems, a greater number of chronic conditions, and greater disability (Stroebe, Schut, et al., 2007; Stroebe, Stroebe, & Schut, 2001). When comparing widowers to men who have a living spouse, widowers tend to have higher psychological distress, use more medication, and have a higher rate of mortality than otherwise comparable older adults (Stroebe, Schut, et al., 2007; Stroebe et al., 2001). They also tend to have a higher incidence of mental illness in widowhood than women. A comprehensive review of the literature (e.g., Stroebe et al., 2001) suggested widowed men have an increased risk of mortality compared to men who have not been widowed, which is a much stronger impact for men than for women (Stroebe et al., 2001).

The impact of spousal bereavement on older men is influenced by individual response, gender role socialization, social support, and individual coping. Bereavement researchers have suggested that men experience more consequences than women in response to bereavement because men have limited social support in comparison to women (Stroebe et al., 2001). In addition, the negative impact of bereavement on men has also been explained using stress theory (Lazarus & Folkman, 1986), which suggests that when an older man interprets an event as overly taxing to his coping resources, failure to cope and health and psychological consequences result. According to this theory, overstressing one's coping resources can be buffered by social support or other psychological resources, and men and women likely have differential access to such resources as a result of gender role socialization and role in the relationship (Stroebe et al., 2001). In psychotherapy, there can be exploration of the older man's primary appraisal of the situation (e.g., how upsetting, traumatic, or unexpected he individually saw the death) and the secondary appraisal (e.g., what the loss of a spouse means) in order to fully address the older man's level of distress and subsequent coping.

Adherence to gender role socialization also has the potential to impact adjustment to bereavement and coping with the subsequent health and psychological consequences of widowhood. Gender role socialization suggests that men should be strong, emotionally restricted, and in control (e.g., O'Neil, 2008). However, loss of a significant other is a situation warranting emotional expression and cannot by definition be coped with through increasing control. Thus, problems may occur if men apply gendered belief systems to a situation in which they are ill fit. In addition, with regard to coping with the physical and psychological consequences related to bereavement, findings from the help-seeking literature (Addis & Mahalik, 2003) suggested men tend to seek informal or formal help less often for physical and psychological problems; therefore, those who experience physical consequences secondary to bereavement may be hesitant to seek appropriate medical care, in turn contributing to worse health outcomes, disability, and mortality. Jin and Christakis (2009) demonstrated that after the death of a spouse, men tended to have poor informal care, lower coordination of care, and a decreased ability to advocate for their self in a health care situation, further illustrating that widowed men may experience health-related problems due to past dependence on their wife for health maintenance behavior.

In addition to the psychological adjustment to the loss of their wife, many older men experience increased social isolation and difficulty with instrumental household tasks. Although conceptualized as slightly less for men than for women, men losing a wife whom he depended on for instrumental and emotional support tended to have a more difficult time adjusting to her death than those who depended less on their spouse (Carr et al., 2000). Researchers have suggested that this occurs because people with closer, less conflicted marriages tend to interpret the loss of their significant other as more disturbing (Carr et al., 2000).

CONCLUSION

Many older men experience major life events and transitions, including retirement, living arrangements, and eventually end-of-life issues. With retirement comes a number of changes, often revolving around relationships, such as those with his wife, adult children, and support networks. An additional obstacle may be the transferring of work-related roles and activities to those accessible in retirement.

During the later years, where to live and end-of-life issues may become prominent for older men. Grief and bereavement due to the loss of a spouse becomes a reality for many men, bringing additional emotional turmoil and adjustment challenges.

TABLE 4.1   Guidelines for Working With Men Experiencing Transitions and Life Adjustments

- Retirement is a significant transition, including adjustment to a change in self-identity, role, and activity.
  - Encourage successful transfer of what he gained through work to areas outside of work, allowing transition to retirement to be more positive.
  - Relationships with his wife and adult children evolve, with possible conflict and need to renegotiate the relationship but also with increased freedom from socialized masculine roles.
  - Financial limitations may impact the retirement experience.
- A number of living options for older men are available, from retirement resorts to high-need medical care offered through long-term care facilities.
- End-of-life issues may become prominent for older men in their later years.
  - Advanced care planning allows the older man to maintain control over decisions made at the end of his life and also provide family guidance in this responsibility.

5

Depression

Harold Arnold looked around the waiting room as he sat calmly waiting for his appointment with the therapist. He wasn't sure why he was actually here, but his wife had said he "needed help." She believed that he was different since the car accident a year ago, when his longtime friend didn't see the red light and ran into oncoming traffic. After having driven a bus route for over 40 years before retiring at the age of 70, Mr. Arnold saw the collision coming but could do nothing to stop it. Mr. Arnold had been in the passenger side at the time and received only a few cuts and bruises, but his friend who had been driving sustained massive injuries and died a few hours later at the hospital. Yes, it was hard to have a friend die, but at the age of 84, Mr. Arnold had lost a number of family members and friends, and he expected to lose many more in the upcoming years. Maybe he had lost some weight over the past few months and was having difficulty sleeping at night, with a few more headaches during the day. What did his wife expect at his age? After his stroke several years ago, he never returned to the outdoor activities of hunting and fishing that he once enjoyed. He was feeling a bit tense; these types of hassles would be hard on any guy. But he was used to change—growing up as a "military brat" and having been the son of an army colonel who had served in the First World War, he learned as a young boy how to "keep a stiff upper lip" and "never show weakness" as well as adapt to change. And at times he missed his son who had moved to Florida several months ago after his own retirement to be closer to the grandchildren—Mr. Arnold's great-grandchildren. It was hard for Mr. Arnold and his wife to no longer have their only child living nearby, and they rarely heard from him. Had he been a terrible father and an even worse grandfather? Maybe it was hopeless.

Counter to popular belief, most older men are not cranky, depressed, or overwhelmed with grief. In fact, based on a recent review of detailed interviews of over 50,000 people spanning more than three decades, results consistently identified that older adults were happier than younger adults (Yang, 2008). Current research has reported that although older adults note a larger number of health problems, they tend to report fewer difficulties overall, including less financial, interpersonal, and crime problems. In general, older adults tend to identify experiencing more loneliness, but they also indicate feeling more serenity.

Although the latest research challenges previous negative findings and stereotypes suggesting depression as a normal part of aging, there is no denying that some older men will eventually experience emotional distress. Projections suggest that by the year 2050, the number of adults age 18 and older diagnosed with a depressive disorder will grow to 46 million. The increase is anticipated to be most pronounced in men over the age of 65, with 2.7 million men being diagnosed with a depressive disorder, a 125% increase (Heo, Murphy, Fontaine, Bruce, & Alexopoulos, 2008).

Depression is one of the most common psychological disorders in older adults, with the consensus being that depression continues to be underdiagnosed in older men, most likely because of traditional views of masculinity. Older men have been described as being less likely to express emotion through feelings of sadness or hopelessness, as there may be embarrassment in stereotypical female behaviors such as crying or tearfulness. In their seminal book *Men and Depression: Clinical and Empirical Perspectives* (2000), Cochran and Rabinowitz labeled this phenomenon "masked depression" (p. 51), in that many men do not exhibit the classic symptoms of depression, instead presenting behaviors seemingly incompatible with depression yet more compatible with their socialized male gender role, alcohol abuse, anger, and reckless behavior. Thus, throughout the psychotherapeutic process, older men experiencing depression may be more comfortable expressing frustration, irritability, or anger, and they tend to be resistant to talk about or label feelings, using words other than "depression" or "sadness" to describe the negative emotion that is present. In addition, men may focus more on physical symptoms, or express themselves in cognitive terms, rather than communicate on an affective level.

O'Brien, Hunt, and Hart (2005) found that men in their study often emphasized the importance of remaining "strong and silent" about emotional difficulties. During the 14 focus groups the authors conducted with a diverse sample of men, participants tended to label their symptoms as "stress" rather than "depression." As in the case at the beginning of this chapter, Mr. Arnold described his emotions as "tense" and minimized his feelings by referring to the "hassles" he was experiencing and noting their difficulty for "any guy." Courtenay (2000) suggested that emotional control and the denial of vulnerability are important parts of masculinity and argued that the "denial of depression is one of the means men use to demonstrate masculinities and to avoid assignment to a lower-status position relative to women and other men" (p. 1397). That is, depression may be feminized in society, as women are twice as likely to have been diagnosed with depression when compared to men.

Although depression may occur earlier in life and recur periodically, it can also present for the first time in men in their 70s, 80s, 90s, and beyond. Older men over the age 85 are more vulnerable to stress and depression than any other age group, as they lose relationships with family and friends. Feelings of loneliness, rather than perceived social support, may best explain the relationship between social isolation and depression in older men (Alpass & Neville, 2003). In addition, age-related losses, such as the loss of professional identity and physical mobility and the death of family and friends, tend to negatively impact a man's ability to maintain relationships and independence, which in turn may lead to a higher incidence of depressive symptoms (Alpass & Neville, 2003). Thus, Mr. Arnold's loss of friends and family, as well as the death of his lifelong friend in a car accident, may be contributing to his feelings of depression.

In addition to increased stressors, many older men may also lose access to the coping skills that they implemented as younger men to successfully ward off depression. In a man's earlier years of life, distraction through keeping physically active or focusing on work may have helped to reduce a man's attention on negative events or feelings. With age, however, often comes retirement, and exercising, playing sports, or participating in activities such as playing pool or bowling may no longer be an option. Older men often relate their feelings of depression to their retirement or to an inability to perform physical or manual labor tasks as they had when younger (Miller & Iris, 2002). In Mr. Arnold's case, hunting and fishing may have been opportunities to increase his mental well-being, serving as his coping mechanisms. But now that these activities are no longer available to him given his physical limitations after his stroke, Mr. Arnold is without aspects of the coping skills he relied on as a younger man. Given his retirement from driving a bus for over 40 years, Mr. Arnold may also find he has "too much time on his hands." With retirement comes the additional aspect of no longer having work to "escape to," and many men often find they have open time that may be difficult to fill, allowing for increased rumination about distressing events.

In another example of the potential for loss of previous coping resources, focus is given to the marital relationship. For many older men with a traditional marriage, their wife provided emotional support over their adult years. However, after his wife's death, not only does the older man suffer from the emotions associated with the loss of his spouse, but he also finds himself without her support that he leaned on during difficult times over their many years together. This may be the first time he has had to cope with a devastating event on his own since he was in his youth. Note that in the example at the beginning of the chapter, it is Mr. Arnold's wife who identified his distress, encouraging him to seek help. He clearly trusts her judgment enough that he is willing to seek help through psychotherapy.

Late-life depression is particularly concerning given the possibility of devastating outcomes. Depression not only causes distress and suffering for the older man and his family but also leads to impairments in physical, mental, and social functioning (U.S. Department of Health and Human Services, 2006); worsens age-associated medical comorbidity; and increases mortality (Alexopoulos, 2005). In a national sample of community dwelling adults, depressive symptoms reduced active life expectancy (remaining years free of disability, and mortality) by 6.5 years for men age 70 and 3.2 years for those men over the age of 85 (Reynolds, Hayley, & Kozlenko, 2008).

In addition, older age appears to exacerbate suicide risk in older men, as they are disproportionately likely to die by their own hand. The suicide rate for non-Hispanic White men 65 years of age and over is higher than in all other groups. In 2005, the suicide rate for older non-Hispanic White men was two to three times the rate for older men in other race or ethnicity groups (Centers for Disease Control and Prevention [CDC], 2007). Suicide rates for men aged 75 to 84 was twice as high as those of women in that age group, with a rate of 36 per 100,000; men over 85 had the highest rate of 45 per 100,000 (CDC, 2007). Firearms tend to be the most commonly used method of suicide among men, with men opting to use guns to end their own life in 56.0% of all suicides (CDC, 2007).

OLDER MEN AND DEPRESSION

Health care professionals may miss depressive symptoms in older men, as socialization influences tend to result in concealment of men's symptoms. In a gendered analysis of his own experience as a man with severe clinical depression, Smith (1999) emphasized the importance of maintaining control, ignoring pain, and suppressing emotion. In a broader study analyzing 16 in-depth interviews with a wide range of men diagnosed with depression, a clear association between depression and men's gender identities emerged (Emslie, Ridge, Ziebland, & Hunt, 2006). A number of men referred to the importance of being "one of the boys" and tended to deal with their depression through construction of their own masculinity, often by reestablishing control and responsibility to others (Emslie et al., 2006). These authors found that one way men created their own masculinity was by associating themselves with real or fictional characters with varying claims to hegemonic masculinity. For example, a 75-year-old man compared himself to two strong men who suffered from depression: Churchill (Britain's prime minister during World War II) and Hemingway (an American author renowned for his drinking and womanizing who eventually committed suicide). In the example with Mr. Arnold, he did not compare himself to anyone of notoriety, but he did note the difficulty "any guy" would have with similar experiences.

In a culture where "big boys don't cry," many older men may be reluctant to discuss feelings of sadness, loss of interest in normally pleasurable activities, or extremely prolonged grief after a loss. Thus, older men suffering from depression may find it more socially acceptable to complain primarily of physical symptoms, causing difficulty in discerning a co-occurring depressive disorder in older men who present with other illnesses such as heart disease, stroke, or cancer, which in themselves may cause depressive symptoms or may be treated with medications that have side effects resembling depression.

It should also be noted that although the focus is often on older men and their tendency to downplay depressive symptoms due to socialization, depreciation of negative emotion can also occur between the therapist and the older man in an unspoken mutual agreement, of which neither may be aware. That is, in addition to the traditional role the older man may be playing, the therapist may also be influenced by societal expectations of masculinity, as well as older age. For example, how open and receptive is the therapist to the potential depth of an older man's level of depression? If while talking about the death of his friend, Mr. Arnold began to sob uncontrollably, how would this affect the therapist, in comparison to if Mr. Arnold were an older woman or a 10-year-old boy? Thus, therapists are encouraged to be cognizant of issues that may contribute to countertransference or potential blind spots when working with men in later stages of life.

DESCRIPTION OF THE DISORDER

Depression in older men can be conceptualized on a spectrum, from a reactive sadness (stemming from minor occurrences), to grief (a normal response to painful loss), to complicated grief, to clinical depression with symptoms causing impairment in daily functioning. Masculine-specific modes of experiencing and expressing depression may not match criteria detailed in the *Diagnostic and Statistical Manual of Mental Disorders* (*DSM-IV-TR*; American Psychiatric Association, 2000). Again, the construct of masked depression (Cochran & Rabinowitz, 2000; see also Rabinowitz & Cochran, 2008) is relevant, as many older men suffering depression symptoms may present as externalization through irritability and anger, rumination, interpersonal withdrawal, and preoccupations or obsessions with work, hobbies, and other distracting routines, possibly turning to alcohol and drug abuse. There may be guilt-related feelings of worthlessness or of not being able to measure up to society's or family's expectations, such as in Mr. Arnold's case in wondering what kind of father or grandfather he had been.

Pollack (1998) proposed a change in the diagnostic criteria used to assess depression in men that would allow those working with men to recognize masked depression and treat it accordingly. In describing his category of Major Depressive Disorder, Male Type, he stressed the importance of linking potentially unrelated symptoms that are not traditionally seen in people suffering from depression but often seen in men coping with stress in their lives. Symptoms such as increased withdrawal from relationships, overinvolvement in work or hobbies, increases in angry outbursts, extreme levels of self-criticism, and an inability to cry when such a reaction would be appropriate represent a syndrome more congruent with the masculine way of being. The challenge involved for those seeking to apply this to older men is separating age-related changes from symptoms representative of depression. Disengagement may occur, for example, because of the loss of friends and family due to death or moving away rather than because of depression in and of itself. Increased involvement in hobbies may be a legitimate reaction to retirement rather than an automatic indicator of depression.

Grief

Although there are many misconceptions about grief, empirical findings reveal that grief is a natural process of emotional expression, with no set time frame to be completed. Grief can best be conceptualized as a permanent state with varying levels of intensity that can be reactivated indefinitely and requires accepting the loss rather than forgetting about the deceased. Delayed grief is rare and generally occurs in a very small percentage of people who do not grieve at the time of the death. An estimated 15% of those who are bereaved may experience prolonged grief, often referred to as complicated grief. Although there is no single or formal definition of complicated grief, it is often acute, persisting more than six months, and characterized by painful emotions that occur in pangs triggered by reminders of loss and guilt specific to bereavement and related to having let the loved one down. Older men suffering from complicated grief may also demonstrate a strong interest in things related to the loved one and prominent intrusive images of the deceased and note a yearning for contact with the deceased. At times, the older man suffering from complicated grief may experience uncontrollable bouts of sadness, with intrusive thoughts about death and feelings of life being meaningless. Complicated grief has been linked to higher incidences of drinking and suicide attempts.

In working with Mr. Arnold in psychotherapy, the therapist should be cognizant that complicated grief might be present given the death of his friend over a year ago, as well as other family members and friends who have passed away. Consider Mr. Arnold and his possible guilt at being able to see the likelihood of the accident but unable to do anything to stop it; additional guilt may be from surviving the crash when his friend did not. Anticipatory grief may also be a factor, as Mr. Arnold indicated the belief that he will lose additional friends and family members in the future.

Suicide

Risk for suicidal ideation increases with depressive symptoms and, as noted previously, is a serious issue in the older male population. Researchers have thought that suicide by older men is often related to physical illness and, more specifically, pain. In a study exploring the rates of depressive symptoms and suicidal ideation among homebound older adults, men with chronic pain reported the highest levels of suicidal ideation (17.8%) whereas men without chronic pain had the lowest rate (5.9%) (Sirey et al., 2008). In addition, a lack of social relationships is thought to contribute to the increase of suicide by older men. Ethnic and cultural differences may explain the fact that older men in other ethnic groups are less isolated and affected by such processes when compared to White men.

EFFECTIVE SCREENING AND ASSESSMENT

There are significant clinical implications based on the assessment and differentiation among (a) older men who are suffering from depression, (b) those with "understandable" sadness (representing a "normal" response to an adverse life event), and (c) those tormented by complicated grief. Caution must be taken to minimize the risk of misdiagnosing a mental disorder when present are only normal reactions to a difficult experience or environment, a physical illness, or a reaction in a different manner than the expected masculine tradition. For example, in the case of Mr. Arnold, caution is required to not overpathologize Mr. Arnold's reaction to his only child moving across the country. A decrease in mood is an expected and understandable response to this type of change and, as such, does not represent a mental disorder.

As noted previously, a complicating issue may be the predominant complaint of somatic symptoms by older men, with less mention of mood-related symptoms, such as sadness, diminished concentration, anhedonia, and anxiety. Older men may experience depression without sadness, as depressive symptoms are expressed or experienced in a physical, behavioral, or cognitive, rather than emotionally based, aspect. Older men, with and without depression, may also present with concomitant cognitive dysfunction and medical illness, as well as frequent use of multiple medications. A tendency to resist psychological assessment can add to the diagnostic complexity.

A thorough screening for depression should include a comprehensive evaluation of symptoms and severity, medical illness, previous suicide attempts, use of alcohol and other substances, and current stressors. In a masculine-sensitive assessment of depression, Cochran (2005) focused on the need to use both traditional methods of assessment and more gender-specific methods. He delineated three tasks in accurately identifying depression in men: (a) review of symptoms based on *DSM* criteria, (b) recognition of comorbid disorders such as personality features or alcohol and substance abuse, and (c) consideration of cultural influences that may shape the experience of depression. Masculine-related symptoms include somatic or physical complaints, interpersonal conflict, and wounds to self-esteem. Of particular value for assessment of older men are the culturally influenced manifestations of depression, such as class and race, level of awareness and adherence to masculinity, and norms for expressing emotion in family of origin. With an older male, attention to cohort group and military experience should also be included. Cochran (2005) encouraged assessment of suicide and homicide risk, including focus on alcohol or drug intoxication, psychotic or delusional features, and capacity for cooperation with professionals.

When depression is identified, a key question to consider in regard to treatment is "To what extent is this depression due to psychological factors, and to what extent is this depression due to biochemical disturbance?" With an older male population, the answer often includes a combination of both, rather than one or the other. As stated previously, more than any other population, older adults will experience the highest coexistence of physical and emotional ailments.

Little is known about the issues most relevant for culturally sensitive assessment when working with ethnic minority older men. As Chiriboga, Yee, and Jang (2005) summarized, "Even when a minority elder overcomes multiple barriers and comes to the attention of a mental health care provider, little is known about the effectiveness of psychosocial assessment tools when applied to minority populations and subpopulations" (p. 360).

Assessment Instruments

In addition to doing a thorough clinical interview, therapists have several assessment instruments available for screening depression in older men. The Geriatric Depression Scale (Yesavage, 1988) is widely used for detecting depression in late-life adults, as are the Hamilton Depression Rating Scale (Williams, 1988), Patient Health Questionnaire (Kroenke, Spitzer, & Williams, 2001), and Zung Self Rating Depression Scale (Zung, 1965). The Cornell Scale for Depression in Dementia (Alexopoulos, Abrams, Young, & Shamoian, 1988a, 1988b) incorporates information from both the client and a collateral source and is best used when attempting to make a diagnosis when cognitive impairment is present.

Suicide

Given the prevalence of suicide in older men, a thorough risk assessment must be completed, with a heightened awareness of potential threats. As noted previously, research suggests that men who report chronic pain and loneliness are at a higher danger for suicide. Thus, assessing chronic pain (discussed in detail in Chapter 7) is essential in a man presenting with depressive symptoms. Exploring an older man's social support system, but, more important, his perception of relationships and his level of interaction, may help identify older men who are in high-risk groups known to have elevated rates of completed suicide.

Although there are objective tests to assess lethality, there is no replacement for a thorough clinical interview with direct questions posed to assess the degree of concern warranted. Asking "Are you thinking about hurting yourself" or "Do you have thoughts of ending your life?" is a direct approach to determine risk level. If the answer is "no," following up with questions such as "Have you ever tried to hurt yourself" or "Have you ever thought about hurting yourself" is appropriate. If an older man responds in the affirmative to having thoughts of ending his life, the therapist should assess lethality by asking about his plans with questions such as "What are you thinking about doing?" or "How would you go about killing yourself?" The focus should be on assessment of the overall plan, including means to which the suicide would be accomplished, access to possible means, and the intent to complete. The level of detail or specificity is critical, as is the access to means. For example, an older man who answers, "Head up to the mountains like the Native Americans did" most likely is at a lower risk for a suicide attempt compared to the older man who shares, "When my wife goes shopping with our daughter, I would shoot myself with my hunting rifle that I keep in the closet."

It is essential to distinguish between men expressing suicidal ideation with a true desire to die and those men who, because of an inability to express themselves in other ways and a need to express the degree of their emotional or physical pain, state wishes for death. For example, an older man who is not adept at recognizing or verbalizing descriptions of his feelings may summarize emotional pain as "I can't live like this any longer; I need to kill myself to end it" or "I should just shoot myself." In these situations, there is no active plan to bring about death; instead, the sentiment of the emotional pain and desperation he is suffering is being shared and must be further explored by the therapist.

In addition, these types of statements should be differentiated from those indicating the older man is "ready to die." Many older men who are not suffering from depression will openly state, "I wish it was my time" or more directly indicate that they would like to die. On further exploration, these older men are expressing they have enjoyed a full and productive life and view their death in somewhat objective and realistic terms. As one 83-year-old man summarized, "I've had a good life. I am ready to go when it's my time."

PSYCHOTHERAPY AND TREATMENT APPROACHES

Although there has been long-standing concern regarding the lack of treatment for older men experiencing depression, there are indicators to suggest a positive trend. For example, in a review from 1992 to 1998 of 20,966 community-dwelling respondents aged 65 and older who were Medicare beneficiaries, 70% of men diagnosed with depression received treatment, generally taking the form of an antidepressant; to be more exact, almost 40% received an antidepressant, 12% participated in psychotherapy, and 18% reported both taking an antidepressant and participating in psychotherapy (Crystal, Sambamoorthi, Walkup, & Akincigil, 2003).

A study asking older adults about their views regarding treatment options for depression, exploring the attitudes of 100 individuals ranging in age from 66 to 98 years of age, suggested that of those with a depression diagnosis who were receiving psychiatric care, psychotherapy was considered both effective and acceptable but not widely available. Antidepressants were also considered to be effective and acceptable although likely to cause side effects (Kuruvilla, Fenwich, Haque, & Vassilas, 2006).

In general, psychotherapy with men experiencing symptoms of depression should (a) target clinical and biological predictors of adverse outcomes of depression; (b) address unmet needs through linkage to appropriate social services; (c) enhance the competencies of the older man so that he can make use of his resources; (d) attend to psychoeducation and preferences and increase treatment engagement; (e) coordinate care and mitigate the interacting medical, psychiatric, and social problems; and (f) provide continuity of care, prevent relapses or recurrences of depression, and preempt medical events and social stressors (Alexopoulos, 2005). Identification of predictors of treatment response and personalization of treatment (i.e., matching treatment with the client) has long been contemplated as a strategy to increase efficacy, to prevent relapses, and to preempt disability, worsening of medical morbidity, and cognitive decline. Kilmartin (2005) noted that therapists should teach men with depression about the importance of gender in order to help them "resist the cultural pressure to be masculine when it conflicts with life goals" (p. 97). He suggested building on positive masculine qualities such as courage (emphasizing that it is brave to take risks by expressing feelings and challenging culturally dominant definitions of masculinity) and leadership (through showing other men more effective ways of dealing with emotional lives).

In psychotherapy with Mr. Arnold, a thorough assessment of his symptoms should be completed, identifying what can be attributed to expected reactions to normal life changes, consequences from his previous stroke, depression, or complicated grief. Exploring how Mr. Arnold might have been affected by his experiences of being from a military family and the son of an army colonel seem relevant, as well as how he most likely internalized traditional male stereotypes and masculinity. Similarly, focusing on Mr. Arnold's history of ability to change and to adapt in difficult situations may help Mr. Arnold more clearly identify his strengths. Providing education about topics such as depression, complicated grief, and gender identity might be beneficial, as well as recommending Mr. Arnold visit a senior center to explore opportunities for increased activity and interaction. Finally, exploring Mr. Arnold's views about the term "depression," as well as thoughts about participating in psychotherapy and medication management, is recommended to help guide the overall treatment approach.

Psychotherapy Modalities

Since the early 1980s, several well-controlled clinical trials have demonstrated that psychotherapy can be an effective intervention for late-life depression (Cuijpers, Van Straten, Smit, & Andersson, 2009), either alone or in combination with antidepressant medication. In a review of evidence-based psychological treatments for geriatric depression, Scogin and his colleagues (Scogin, Welsh, Hanson, Stump, & Coates, 2005) identified six treatments shown to be beneficial: behavioral therapy, cognitive behavioral therapy, cognitive bibliotherapy, problem-solving therapy, brief psychodynamic therapy, and reminiscence therapy. According to the standards set by the APA for psychologists, two of the existing psychotherapies are currently considered evidence based for treatment of depression: cognitive behavioral therapy (CBT) and interpersonal therapy (IPT). Both can be adapted and modified to accommodate traditional masculine views, age-related cognitive changes, and contextual challenges so that older men may better accept and process new information.

CBT is based on the premise that depression is caused by a combination of coping skills deficits, problems with emotion regulation, and an overly negativistic view of the world and the ability to function adequately. Older men's ability to learn new skills and material is paramount, and when working with depression in older men, therapists should focus on what extent there may be compromise because of cognitive changes associated with normal aging or additional illness. A CBT manual for late-life depression was created by Thompson and his colleagues (Thompson, Gallagher-Thompson, & Dick, 1996), with a focus on teaching new skills to help regulate depression, increase activity levels, counter negativistic thinking, and apply these new skills in daily life.

In a situation of severe depression due to complicated grief, one strategy borrowed from the CBT treatment of post-traumatic stress disorder requires the individual to recall the death in detail while the therapist records the session. The tape is to then be played daily at home. The goal is to show that grief, like the tape, can be picked up or put away; it offers the older man an opportunity for additional control of his feelings or reactions. At the same time, this treatment allows the individual to learn to handle the grief, with encouragement to set new goals. In a clinical trial, this treatment was found to be twice as effective as the traditional IPT used to treat depression or bereavement (Shear, Frank, Houck, & Reynolds, 2005). Should the therapist determine that Mr. Arnold's symptoms are primarily stemming from the motor vehicle accident and death of his friend, this treatment option could be presented to Mr. Arnold during a therapy session. In setting new goals, Mr. Arnold might decide to return to attending his weekly game of cards with his male neighbors, something he and his friend use to do on a regular basis.

In his 2008 article on interpersonal psychotherapy (IPT) as a treatment for depression in later life, Hinrichsen identified that IPT was originally developed as a time-limited psychotherapy for major depression, emphasizing the importance of relationships and focusing on current issues, rather than historical or developmental issues tied to depression. The focus on interpersonal conflict including unresolved grief, role transitions, interpersonal role disputes, and interpersonal deficits reflects challenges experienced by many older men. Hinrichsen (2008) clarified, "In contrast to cognitive behavioral therapy, the focus of IPT is not on changing maladaptive cognitions coexistent with depression but on improving interpersonal behaviors associated with the current episode of depression" (p. 307).

In a review of 20 controlled outcome studies to assess the effectiveness of reminiscence and life review on late-life depression, results indicated that reminiscence and life review are potentially effective treatments for depressive symptoms in older adults and may thus offer a valuable alternative to psychotherapy or pharmacotherapy (Bohlmeijer, Smit, & Cuijpers, 2003). The authors concluded, "Reminiscence and life review can be delivered easily, do not stigmatize and appear to connect well with cognitive processes in elderly people, and they may very well increase treatment rates of depressed elderly and reach them in the early stages of depressive disorders" (p. 1093).

Chiriboga et al. (2005) reviewed the critical elements of cultural competence for clinical practice in treating late-life depression. The authors identified the significance of showing respect for the older man's cultural heritage, providing treatment in his preferred language, and understanding the possible effects of cultural background on symptoms and treatment. These authors also highlighted the importance of the interpersonal skills of the therapist.

Suicide

A number of options are available for addressing suicidal ideation with older men in psychotherapy. One option is for psychoeducation; that is, explaining the increased risk of suicide for older men. The loss of power and control, perhaps for the first time ever, can be quite overwhelming. Helping the man to understand that he is looking at the world through "depression glasses" may also help to provide a "big picture" perspective of what he is experiencing. These are examples of increasing the client's tolerance for depressive symptoms, in effect normalizing those symptoms and bringing about recognition that they can be dealt with appropriately.

Given that this generation of men grew up when "a handshake meant something," in addition to a verbal agreement that there will be no self-harm, asking for a handshake to confirm this intention can be effective. The therapist may also want to focus on reasons that the older man would refrain from an attempt at taking his own life. For many men, religious beliefs, feelings of not wanting to hurt their family, and even fear emerge as reasons for not attempting suicide. In addition to ensuring safety, both of these approaches can serve to strengthen the therapeutic alliance by indicating a level of trust within the relationship, while also reminding the older man of his interpersonal connections and responsibilities.

Pharmacological Treatment

Antidepressants can play an important role in the treatment of late-life depression. In a study by the National Ambulatory Medical Care Survey analyzing data from 2001 and 2002 to assess patterns of depression diagnosis and treatment provided during physician office visits made by patients aged 65 and older, results indicated that when there was a depression diagnosis, an antidepressant medication was prescribed over 50% of the time, with 90% of the time it being a selective serotonin reuptake inhibitor (SSRI) or an atypical antidepressant (Harman, Veazie, & Lyness, 2006). Although there are more than 20 medications to choose from when prescribing a treatment for depression, which one will be most effective for a particular person remains a mystery. Menza and Liberatore (1998) reported that 69% of older adult participants had a positive response to initial treatment with antidepressants, but therapists should be aware that many of their clients will need to try two or three drugs or drug combinations before experiencing relief. Response by the fourth week of chemical treatment is often a critical factor in determining the probability of a positive response by 12 weeks. However, older adults may have higher rates of recurrence of depression, suggesting a need for more rigorous maintenance in this population.

CONCLUSION

Although traditional masculinity tends to artificially decrease the number of men who are diagnosed and treated for late-life depression, progress has been noted in the understanding of, and sophistication of, assessment and comprehensive treatment for older men. Focus should be given to both traditional diagnostic criteria for depression and gender-specific characteristics such as anger, irritability, and increased use of alcohol and other substances. Because older men are at significant risk for suicide, the level of threat should be carefully assessed and monitored. Psychological treatment for late-life depression includes CBT and IPT, as well as pharmacological intervention.

TABLE 5.1   Guidelines for Assessment and Treatment With Men Experiencing Depressive Symptoms

---

- The traditional view of masculinity may impact the experience of depression, decreasing a willingness to show or admit to typical symptoms.
    - Emotional expression may be limited, without indications of sadness.
    - Depressive symptoms may be "masked" or present through externalization such as anger, irritability, or substance use.
- Differentiate among normal reaction to change, depression, and complicated bereavement.
- Older men are at a high risk for suicide.
    - There is an increased risk if chronic pain or loneliness is present.
    - Educate the client about risk factors.
    - Continue to carefully assess and monitor for threat of self harm.
- CBT and IPT are considered evidence-based treatment modalities.
- Antidepressants can increase effectiveness of psychotherapy in cases of severe depression.

CHAPTER

6

Anxiety

James LaCrane started his first therapy session with a summary: "I've had a really good life. But now I'm faced with losing my wife. I was at the doctor's office last week, and he told me the cancer in my brain is back. I've got to sell everything I own: my home, my car. ... In addition, my oldest son just told me he's getting a divorce. I haven't had to deal with any of these things before and now all at once at the age of 75. I don't know how I am going to get through this. I had a panic attack several days ago; the last time I had one was in my 30s when I lost my job. And I know what a panic attack is because I had them as a kid. In junior high I was teased a lot at school because my father was White and my mother was Asian. It comes on all of a sudden. Just like that I can't breathe, my heart starts beating hard and fast, I have chest pains—it feels like a heart attack, but I've been checked out by the cardiologist, and I'm fine. Overall, I just think I am losing control. If I'm honest, I'd say I've always been a worrier. Even my friends have noticed that I've been on edge; I'm just always tensed up. I'm even restless all night; seems like I can't ever shut my mind off.

There is an old saying that "worrying is like a rocking chair; it gives you something to do but takes you nowhere." Although trying not to worry is easier said than done, the consensus is that older adults tend to worry less than younger adults. And within older adult groups, the oldest old (age 75 and over) have been found to worry less than the young old (55 to 64 years old) or the middle old (65 to 74 years old). When older adults do worry, their reported concerns appear to be different from those of other age groups. A review of the literature concluded that in general, older adults tended to worry about health and death or injury to self or loved ones, compared to younger samples that focused on work, finances, and interpersonal matters (Mohlman, 2004).

MEN AND LATE-LIFE ANXIETY

Everyone worries to some extent, and older men may experience anxiety in a variety of ways and for a mixture of reasons. For example, anxiety is a common symptom of physical illness or a reaction to medication. Varying levels of worry, or a range of anxiety symptoms, can be caused by psychosocial issues such as death of loved ones, fear of declining strength or disability, or loss of finances. Mr. LaCrane, in the case example at the beginning of this chapter, shared with the therapist a number of stressors he is encountering. Although the majority of older men who present for psychotherapy most likely will not have a history of panic attacks or experience the number of significant life challenges as Mr. LaCrane, many will be facing significant life challenges and suffering from angst.

The past decade has marked an increase in research on late-life anxiety, providing an expanded knowledge base on anxiety in the older population; however, more questions than answers continue to exist. Random-sample epidemiological surveys have reported a wide range of diagnosable anxiety among older adults living in the community, ranging from 1% to 9% and possibly as high as 12% in primary care. Of the five principal anxiety disorders, 90% of presentations of late-life anxiety are accounted for by either generalized anxiety disorder (GAD) or a specific phobia, with GAD representing at least 50% of cases among older adults, of which the majority are exacerbations of disorders present at a younger age. The remaining 10% of anxiety disorders are accounted for by obsessive-compulsive disorder (OCD), post-traumatic stress disorder (PTSD), and panic disorders.

Research has indicated that when compared to women in their cohort, older men tend to report less anxiety. In a study of people 60 to 64 years of age, 2.50% of the women in comparison to 1.99% of the men reported anxiety. For both genders, poor physical health and less physical activity were consistent with increased anxiety (Leach, Christensen, Mackinnon, Windsor, & Butterworth, 2008). Results have indicated that in men over 65 years of age, 4.3% had experienced GAD in the past 12 months, and 6.9% reported at least one GAD episode in their lifetime (Vesga-Lopez et al., 2008).

However, there is a possibility that any reported gender difference may be due to men underreporting anxiety symptomatology rather than an actual lower occurrence in the male population. Many older men may not view "worrying" as an acceptable male characteristic given their gender role development. For example, when under stress, an older man may outwardly present traditional male behaviors such as acting aggressive, albeit tricky when feeling nervous or worried. The masculine scripts of the tough guy and give-'em-hell identify anxiety as a weakness and encourage older men to expend significant effort to denying symptoms of anxiety, possibly through using expression of anger or blaming the situation or the people around them.

Others, like Mr. LaCrane in the case example, may have internalized the belief that they should be in control. With increased physical disability, illness, or pain, many older men can be vulnerable to a loss of perceived control, whether it is over their health, environment, or life. Because perception of control protects people of all ages from vulnerability to anxiety (Batiuchok, 2009), the physical and psychosocial stressors associated with aging can cause older men to be increasingly susceptible to developing anxiety-related disorders. Schulz, Heckhausen, and O'Brien (1994) argued that late-life anxiety results from loss of ability to control life outcomes combined with a personal inability to deal with this threat using controlling strategies. Thus the loss of perceived control contributes to an anxiety response. In fact, it may not be until later life that a man first experiences events and situations that he truly has no control over and cannot fix or handle. In reality, Mr. LaCrane has no ability to control the presence of his or his wife's illness or their son's relationship change. This most likely is in contrast to the challenges Mr. LaCrane faced as a younger man, such as when he lost his job. Although Mr. LaCrane may have had no control in some particulars of that situation, he took charge and with great diligence found a higher paying position with better benefits through the government as a mail carrier. In his current situation, there is little Mr. LaCrane can do to have much power over the circumstances of his life, and thus he experiences increased symptoms of anxiety.

At times, older men may truly not recognize signs of anxiety, or they assume that anxiety symptoms are a natural part of the aging process, or they may misinterpret somatic anxiety symptoms as signs of organic disease. For example, disorders like Parkinson's disease and cardiovascular disease can cause physiologically based symptoms of anxiety but remain treatable with psychological intervention. Because of misconceptions, some older men will not recognize the need for diagnosis and treatment of anxiety; others may manage their anxiety through avoidance behaviors or by self-medication with alcohol or other substances, often because of their gender role socialization.

Anxiety might be considered a "geriatric giant" for late-life men because of the devastation it can cause for the older man and his family. Anxiety disorders frequently affect the cardiovascular system, central nervous system, and endocrine system and are linked with increased depression, decreased quality of life, memory difficulties, and greater physical disability. Associated cognitive aspects of underlying anxiety disorders include hypervigilance to threat, seeing oneself as vulnerable, and perceiving the demands of life as exceeding the available resources to cope. Older men with anxiety report increased comorbidity to the extent that late-life anxiety is considered "silent," missed, or difficult to diagnose as older men may present their symptoms as somatic difficulties, including stomach problems and feelings of a heart attack. In addition, by the time they seek treatment, many men often have multiple medical and medication issues.

DESCRIPTION OF THE DISORDER

There are five general categories of anxiety disorders: GAD, specific phobia, OCD, panic disorders, and PTSD. Each of these involves a cognitive component of worry and a physiological aspect of increased stimulation. Older men may have one or more of the five general disorders, as they can each occur within another anxiety disorder. GAD is characterized by excessive worry that interferes with general functioning or causes significant impairment. Older men with GAD often present to primary care practitioners with unexplained physical symptoms, including fatigue, aches and pains, gastrointestinal symptoms, or sleep disturbance. This is both consistent with the male gender role socialization regarding the denial of psychological distress and a likely outcome of the cohort effect; in comparison to what older men experienced as they stormed the beach at Iwo Jima, a "case of nerves" pales in comparison.

Specific phobias are characterized by a persistent irrational fear of a situation, object, or activity and the desire to avoid the phobic situation. OCD is identified by impairment due to obsessions (persistent thoughts) or compulsions (repetitive behaviors) that although the older man sees as unreasonable or excessive, he is not able to stop. OCD rarely, if ever, begins in later life, although it may reappear over the life span. Older men with a panic disorder present with feelings of anxiety and suffer unexpected panic attacks. This disorder has been associated with increased suicidal ideation and suicide attempts.

PTSD is the outcome of exposure to a traumatic event and can occur in those older men who, for example, experienced war or the Holocaust. Again, the cohort effect is relevant; after years of living without symptoms, older men might find traumatic memories reactivated by present-day events such as 9/11 or their recent personal losses, bereavement, diminished health, or retirement. Current occurrences might overwhelm long-established coping mechanisms that evolved to suppress traumatic memories while also allowing the man to be a contributing part of society. Indeed, many such men found solace in their ability to function, using long hours at work climbing the career ladder for distraction, leaving little time for contemplating history with the added benefit of being congruent with society's expectation of men. Despite the commonly held belief that PTSD symptoms ameliorate with age, retirement tends to worsen symptoms of PTSD. Factors involved in this are thought to be the loss of the ability to submerge the earlier trauma in the world of business or family life. Also, retirement-age men experience other stressors such as the loss of friends to illness and death and a general decline in economic resources. In a review of PTSD among older adults, Owens and her colleagues noted the presence of medical comorbidities, the development of potential cognitive deficits, and issues revolving around loss, all of which could be potential stressors for exacerbating PTSD (Owens, Baker, Kasckow, Ciesla, & Mohamed, 2005).

EFFECTIVE SCREENING AND ASSESSMENT

Screening for anxiety in older men who present with depression, especially those with a history of military service, should be standard practice (Markowitz, 2007). However, the clinical presentation of anxiety in older men may not follow established criteria, making symptom clusters less cohesive and potentially more difficult to detect. Anxiety disorders can be challenging to diagnose in older men because of the tendency to somatize psychiatric problems, comorbidity with depression (e.g., impaired sleep, concentration, attention, memory, and agitation), or medical illness (e.g., including chest and abdominal pain, headaches, and shortness of breath). Often, the experience of anxiety for older men is masked by the use of maladaptive coping mechanisms, alcohol being common. It is also important that the possibility of an anxiety disorder not be dismissed based on the "crotchety old man" stereotype; that is, an irritable older man may be presenting symptoms of anxiety in the only manner he perceives acceptable.

Clinical Interview

An in-depth clinical intake, with a thorough review of the older man's mental and physical history, is critical to the accurate diagnosis of late-life anxiety. Obtaining a history from the older man, as well as from family members, may be helpful. Focus is given to information that helps to clarify if there is a new-onset presentation, a medication- or substance-induced disorder, a new medical problem, or a recurrence of a previous disorder. Questions should be direct, focusing on past occurrences and current symptoms. Encourage the older man to further explain how he experiences the symptoms by asking, "What does it feel like for you? How do you experience anxiety?" The therapist may need to clarify that everyone experiences anxiety differently, and it is helpful in understanding his situation if he provides additional details about what it is like for him to be anxious. Given this cohort, the therapist should explore whether the man served in the armed forces and, if so, what branch he was affiliated with in the military and whether he served in combat. Additional questions should explore recent medication change and use of substances such as nicotine, caffeine, alcohol, or other drugs. Also consider lifestyle choices that may be contributing to symptoms of anxiety or coping abilities, such as exercise, diet, and sleep schedule. In some cases, a physical examination by a medical care provider or laboratory tests used to screen for physical factors that could be contributing to the anxiety may be required. A consultation with the older man's medical provider is often useful in the assessment of anxiety and should occur the majority of the time.

In addition, the therapist should be sensitive to nonverbal communication from older men, which for some may be a more accurate indicator of the level of their anxiety than the actual description they provide. Watch facial expressions, and listen to tone and rate of speech; behaviors such as tapping their cane, fidgeting in their chair, and any trembling of the hands should be noted. Awareness of these types of unspoken signs is an example of a "recognition of masculine ways of being" (Wester & Vogel, 2002) or acknowledgment of the masculine voice; that is, the therapist is knowledgeable about the contextually unique way in which men may present themselves or communicate. This includes recognizing and valuing gender or cohort differences of behaving but not overemphasizing gender-typical ways of being.

Given the high comorbidity of anxiety and depression, some older men with a significant level of depression may present with anxiety or nerves as their main complaint. They may state that they have not been themselves lately or "just don't feel right." As a general rule, if a man over the age of 60 presents with symptoms of generalized anxiety for the first time in his life, the diagnosis of depression may be most accurate until additional information is identified to prove otherwise.

In working with Mr. LaCrane, the therapist would follow up the client's summary with a thorough review of his mental and physical history, with attention on how existing symptoms stem from his current stressors and how medical diagnoses intertwine with information from his past; careful attention to any recent medication changes given his health status would be useful. Asking Mr. LaCrane about a possible history of serving in the military would also be important. The therapist should request that Mr. LaCrane sign a release of information so that a consultation with his medical provider could occur.

The therapist should further explore Mr. LaCrane's reactions to each of the recent changes in his life, his wife's health, his son's divorce, and his own diagnosis of a terminal illness. Requesting additional detail about the level of difficulty each of these has for Mr. LaCrane would be vital; that is, which of these concerns does he spend the most time worrying about or which recent occurrence causes him the most anxiety. Depending on the answer, the direction of psychotherapy would be greatly influenced. For example, Mr. LaCrane may give little thought to his own medical situation, but given his strong family values and own experiences of being raised in a home with parents from a different ethnic background from each other, he may be highly affected by the end of his son's marriage. He may have considerable concern about how his son will cope with the end of the marriage and constantly worry about his grandchildren's well-being and their reactions to the loss of an intact family unit. Or, on the other hand, Mr. LaCrane may be very understanding of his son's divorce, noting that he wonders where his son will live now that he is no longer with his wife, but he might deny any other concerns regarding his grown child's affairs, indicating that he and his wife raised an intelligent and insightful son whose decisions they never question. However, his true concern may be about his wife of 55 years, who is in the last stages of Alzheimer's disease and has been in a long-term care facility for the past several years. Although Mr. LaCrane believes his wife is well taken care of, he constantly worries about her well-being and is concerned that he is not able to spend enough time at the facility visiting her. Given all of the arrangements he must make for selling the house and moving to independent living, the majority of Mr. LaCrane's distress can be contributed to the decrease in the time available to visit his wife and his apprehension about the possibility that she may somehow react negatively to his increased absence.

Assessment Measures

There are a number of assessment instruments to measure anxiety; however, none are specific to an older adult population. In a review of assessment of anxiety in late life, Kogan, Edlstein, and McKee (2000) warned that the majority of available assessment instruments "lack sufficient evidence for their psychometric soundness for use with older adults. Moreover, most of the studies examining the psychometric properties of these instruments have methodologic shortcomings (i.e., homogeneity of samples, small sample sizes, restriction of age ranges, concerns regarding method variance) that limit the usefulness of their findings" (p. 127). Should therapists want to consider utilizing an assessment measure for anxiety in an older man, they must carefully consider advantages and disadvantages and use caution in the interpretation of the results.

One of the most popular questionnaires tapping worry content, the Worry Scale (WS; Wisocki, Handen, & Morse, 1986), contains several age-specific items relevant to an older person (e.g., "I will lose control of my bladder" and "My eyesight will get worse"). The Hamilton Anxiety Rating Scale (Ham-A; Hamilton, 1959) consists of 14 items that are answered using a graphic depiction of a scale ranging from 0 (*not present*) to 4 (*very severe*). The concreteness of the pictorial representation of the scale to rate anxiety symptoms may aid the older man in more accurately rating his level of anxiety. Additional instruments available to assess general anxiety symptoms include the Anxiety Disorders Interview Schedule (ADIS; Miller, Brown, DiNardo, & Barlow, 1994), Beck Anxiety Inventory (BAI; Beck & Steer, 1990), Generalized Anxiety Scale (GAS; Lindesay, Briggs, & Murphy, 1989), and Penn State Worry Scale (Meyer, Miller, Metzger, & Borkovec, 1990). The Fear Questionnaire (FQ; Marks & Mathews, 1979) is a 15-item inventory designed to assess the severity of avoidance behaviors related to agoraphobia, social interaction, and blood injury. To evaluate symptoms of

OCD, therapists can consider the Padua Inventory (PI; Sanavio, 1988), a 60-item questionnaire with four subscales assessing fear of losing control over mental activities, motor behaviors, severity, and contamination of checking rituals.

PSYCHOTHERAPY AND ADDITIONAL TREATMENT OPTIONS

In a review of clinical recommendations for treatment of anxiety in an older adult population, Krasucki, Howard, and Mann (1999) summarized, "In the literature on this field, the recommendations tend to outstrip evidence" (p. 38). In a similar vein, Mohlman (2004) more recently concluded, "We are still in the early phases of understanding the mechanisms of improvement of this enigmatic disorder as it appears in the elderly" (p. 164). However, there are emerging indications that some psychotherapeutic and pharmacological interventions utilized with younger individuals may be useful with older men.

Cognitive Behavioral Therapy

Cognitive behavioral therapy (CBT), both individually and in a group format, is the treatment of choice for anxiety disorders for children and young adults, and there is a growing body of evidence for its usefulness among older adults. In a review of evidence-based psychotherapy treatments for anxiety disorders in older adults, 17 studies for evidence-based treatments (EBTs) were identified (Ayers, Sorrell, Thorp, Wetherell, & Loebach, 2007). In samples of adults with GAD or mixed anxiety disorders or symptoms, evidence was found for efficacy of four types of EBTs, including relaxation training, CBT, and, to a lesser extent, supportive therapy and cognitive therapy. The authors noted that CBT for late-life anxiety has garnered the most consistent support, and relaxation training represents an efficacious, relatively low-cost intervention (Ayers, Sorrell, Thorp, Wetherell, & Loebach, 2007).

CBT treatment of anxiety disorders addresses the interaction between thoughts, feelings, and behaviors and is based on behavioral exposure to anxiety-provoking situations, reducing escape and avoidance behaviors, and cognitively restructuring appraisals and beliefs that increase fear. The therapist must first identify specific cognitive distortions that are contributing to the older man's anxiety. For example, "I am going to die, and my wife will be left alone, which she'll never be able to handle" or "Although I have a good retirement income, what if my money runs out, and I'm forced to move to a nursing home?" Focus is then given to promoting the older man's self-support during moments of fear or distress by challenging thoughts and assumptions that underline certain fears. In each of these examples, the older man would be encouraged to search for evidence that disconfirms these fears and to see the cognitive distortions for the illogical thinking they represent. He might also be encouraged to use reframing to help him put his concerns into perspective or possibly find a new viewpoint or different way of looking at the situation. In this example, the older man may actually realize that his wife is stronger emotionally than he originally gave her credit for and recall that prior to his retirement, she handled their finances, as she managed the home and raised their children.

Mahalik (2005) identified the complementary nature of CBT with masculine socialization. Many older men may be more comfortable with CBT given the focus on thoughts, behaviors, and actions rather than solely on emotions or need to describe feelings. He provided examples of how gender may contribute to cognitive distortion, such as the beliefs "Winning isn't everything, it's the only thing" and "Taking dangerous risks helps me to prove myself" (Mahalik, 2005, p. 224). When working with older men who clearly identify with these traditional views of masculinity, the therapist must be aware of the adaptive nature of these ideas and how they may have worked for the older man at other times in his life, with focus on how these might now be causing him distress. Also acknowledging the role of a man's cohort is critical, as many men may need assistance putting their anxiety into perspective and seeing it as something worthy of overcoming given the other challenges they faced in their lives. The therapist should also be on the lookout for cognitive distortions broad in nature, such as overgeneralizing (making a rule based on a few negative events), personalization (making an unrelated event personally meaningful or about one's self), mind reading (inferring what others are thinking or feeling and knowing for a "fact" their intentions), and all-or-none thinking (dichotomous thinking with the belief that things must be exactly one way or there is failure).

Mr. LaCrane, the older man in the case example, may be under the belief that asking for help is a sign of failure, thus accepting that he must cope with his and his wife's health alone, while also trying to sell his house and find appropriate alternative living arrangements. To challenge this, the therapist may encourage Mr. LaCrane to think of times that he helped others, which did not cause him to have a negative opinion of them. He may also want to identify times in the past as a younger man when he accepted help, which did not take away his manhood or make him appear incompetent. As an older man, Mr. LaCrane may be particularly sensitive to presenting as a competent adult rather than being unable to care for himself and his wife, believing that regardless of age, illness, or situation, he should "always be tough as nails" (Mahalik, 2005, p. 27). Again, challenging Mr. LaCrane to recognize the reality of the situation, and the lack of logic in doing everything himself and wanting to appear without weakness, increases his ability to identify the distortions in his thinking. In fact, Mr. LaCrane has five sons who live nearby, each who would appreciate the opportunity to give back to their father for all the times he has come to their aid, both as children and when they were young men. Mr. LaCrane's sons may be very active in not only helping with business matters but also taking turns visiting their mother each day, alleviating Mr. LaCrane's concerns of his wife being without him so much of the time.

Additional CBT techniques for older men may include cognitive rehearsal, where the man imagines dealing with an upcoming anxiety-producing event. In this case, the older man is encouraged to picture the upcoming event with destructive thoughts being replaced with more productive images. Another option is the thought-stopping technique; that is, anytime the older man becomes aware of having a negative thought, he says out loud or to himself "stop" and immediately thinks about an affirming event or person who brings positive memories or feelings. Activity scheduling (outlining a daily or weekly schedule on paper) and graded tasks (breaking down intimidating tasks into smaller steps) can be empowering for an older man, providing him the increased feeling of being in control and the active approach he craves.

For example, if Mr. LaCrane is particularly worried about asking his sons for help, the therapist may facilitate Mr. LaCrane visualizing himself feeling calm and confident, updating his sons about the current situation, and identifying what assistance he needs from each. Prior to meeting with his sons, Mr. LaCrane might also be encouraged to compose a list of specific tasks to be accomplished, identify a timeline for himself, and even break down larger projects such as selling the house into smaller steps, calling the realtor, making a list of home improvements to be completed, and contacting his mortgage company to obtain an updated payoff sum.

With the use of techniques during the therapy session, as well as options for additional activities, recognition of the older man's interest and ability to complete homework assignments outside of the therapy session should be assessed. Session length should be adjusted to meet the older man's tolerance level, and efforts to accommodate his schedule will be beneficial. For example, Mr. LaCrane has "difficulty getting going in the morning" and noted he certainly could understand if that was the only day available, but for the past several years, he has spent every Thursday afternoon at the facility with his wife, listening to the band that comes to play for residents and their families. Thus, the therapist can be sensitive to Mr. LaCrane's life circumstances by finding an optimal appointment time for him on any day other than Thursday, preferably sometime after lunch, such as 1 p.m., rather than earlier in the day.

Stress Reduction Interventions

An accompanying recommendation to CBT may be for the older man to consider decreasing his environmental stimulation during times of anxiety. For example, reducing the number of people he is around, playing soothing music, or watching something enjoyable such as a favorite movie or a sports program to provide distraction can be beneficial.

Older men can also be effectively taught relaxation methods, such as deep breathing, and the tensing and releasing of each muscle group, starting with the facial muscles and progressively moving down the body. Implementing imagery or visualization techniques to decrease symptoms of anxiety is also an option for older men. For example, the older man may want to visualize the anxiety as a bright color, such as red, covering his body. Using imagery, he can slowly start to see his body turn to a calmer color, such as a muted blue or green. Or at the first awareness of a symptom, he can visualize "bullets" of anxiety as he imagines a bulletproof shield around him, thus effectively stopping the penetration of the anxiety. An older man may also be encouraged to visualize himself in a relaxing or comfortable situation. For example, if golfing is a favorite pastime, he may want to visualize himself on the golf course, noticing the beautiful sunny day, seeing himself walk with ease and confidence on the greens, and so on.

These descriptions serve as examples and should be tailored for each older male client. The exact approach is much less important than the older man's willingness to implement the relaxation technique. It is imperative that by working together, the therapist and older man identify a visualization or image that is meaningful to the older man. For example, the therapist at the beginning of the chapter is aware that Mr. LaCrane was a postal carrier prior to retirement; through further discussion Mr. LaCrane indicates that those were some of the "happiest times" of his life, as he enjoyed the autonomy and physical exercise while being outdoors when delivering mail on his route. Given this has significant meaning to Mr. LaCrane, in times of increasing anxiety, imagery may be used to assist Mr. LaCrane visualizing himself walking outside on a beautiful day, seeing himself happy and relaxed, feeling more relaxed with each mailbox he fills with mail.

Pharmacological Treatment

CBT has been shown to reduce benzodiazepine use, which, in turn, reduces the risk of cognitive changes or falls and fall-related deaths in this age group. However, for many older men, a combination of CBT and antidepressant medications may be necessary for optimal management of symptoms. Thus, effective psychological intervention for symptoms of anxiety in older men should also include discussing the use of medication (Markowitz, 2007).

Unfortunately, research on pharmacological treatment of anxiety disorders in late life is sparse, and guidelines are generally based not on randomized controlled trials of older adults but on extrapolation from research with younger age groups (Krasucki et al., 1999). The three classes of medications that are most commonly used for late-life anxiety include antidepressants, benzodiazepines, and buspirone. Antidepressant medication is the pharmacological treatment of choice for older adults with generalized anxiety, providing long-acting, even benefit. Regrettably, benzodiazepines such as alprazolam (Xanax), clon-azepam (Klonopin), diazepam (Valium), and lorazepam (Ativan) are frequently overprescribed for older individuals with anxiety, tending to cause serious side effects in this age group, including cognitive impair-ment, rebound withdrawal symptoms, dependence, incontinence, and falls leading to hip fractures and fall-related deaths.

Because of concerns about the type of medication or side effects such as sedation, dizziness, and decreased balance, many older men may not be compliant with pharmacotherapy. Given that overall benefits can be diminished because of nonadherence to prescribed medication, psycho-education is necessary, as well as further exploring the older man's views about medication and identifying barriers to taking the medica-tion as prescribed.

CONCLUSION

Everyone worries at some time in his or her life; however, there will be a portion of older men who suffer increased symptoms of anxiety, some to the degree of experiencing significant impairment in their daily func-tioning. Although both the assessment and the treatment of late-life anxiety appear to be in their infancy, therapists can focus on informa-tion gathered from in-depth clinical interviews, identifying current and past symptoms and medical illness. CBT with medication management tends to be the most prevalent treatment approach.

TABLE 6.1   Guidelines for Working With Men Experiencing Anxiety

- Symptoms of anxiety may present as or be caused by physical illness.
- Assessment must include an in-depth history, including current and past symptoms of anxiety and medical issues.
  - Be aware of the limits of assessment instruments, and use caution in interpretation of any results.
- CBT can be an effective intervention.
  - Watch for gender-specific and general cognitive distortions.
- Pharmacological treatment is often used in combination with psychological intervention; however, side effects of medication must be closely monitored.

7

Health, Chronic Physical Illness, and Disability

His legs were swelling, and he felt tired all the time. What was going on? He was "sick and tired of being sick and tired," but of course he wasn't really sick. Fred Yao Ming just reminded himself that he needed to go to bed at a more reasonable time each night. And he needed to eat at least two regular meals a day; for some reason he had lost weight over the past few months. Since his wife of over 40 years recently died after a 10-year battle with cancer in which he had served as her primary caregiver, Mr. Yao had considered making an appointment with his primary care physician. But maybe his body just required rest given the strain of the past few years. And, at the age of 68, who didn't get run down and have blurred vision at times? The aches and pains were just a part of aging; everyone knew that pain went with old age. When his wife was alive, he joked with her about his pain, calling it "the grip," and on some days when the pain was severe, all Mr. Yao had to do was share that "the grip was winning," and she knew exactly what he meant. He had planned to mention the burning in his feet and poor balance when he and his wife last went to see their family physician, but he had been so focused on making sure they talked about everything he could do to make his wife comfortable that he had forgotten. While he was taking care of her, there was never really time for him to make an appointment to follow up on the pains and cramps. And now, he just didn't think there was much Dr. Bermingham could do.

Poor physical health is not an inevitable consequence of aging; in fact, many older adults live long and healthy lives. In his book on positive aging, Hill (2005) recognized aging as involving a "state of mind," supporting the concept that men's satisfaction with life appears to be influenced by their perception of health; if they feel healthy, their outlook on life is maintained or improved with age (Freysinger, Alessio, & Mehdizadeh, 1993). In a recent study involving in-depth interviews about aging, men often reported being positive about their health, identifying the disparity they experienced between their chronological age and how old they actually felt (Clarke & Griffin, 2008). The authors provided an example of an older man with multiple chronic conditions who shared, "I don't feel old even though I'm going on 77. I don't feel old. I still think I'm 50" (Clarke & Griffin, 2008, p. 1088).

DEFINING HEALTH AND ILLNESS

In regard to physical well-being in old age, health cannot meaningfully be defined as "the absence of disease" because of the prevalence of diagnosable disorders in an older population. Instead, health should be understood as being multifaceted, including diagnoses, mortality risks, functional capacity, and subjective health. Thus, an older man's health status may be better understood by identification of the diagnosis of the disease(s), complemented by assessment of discomfort associated with the symptoms (e.g., pain), the level of life threat, treatment consequences (e.g., side effects of medications), functional capacity, and, as noted previously, his own view of his health. Because health is a subjective appraisal, there is often much room for interpretation and misinformation; therapists should take care to understand the older man's perception of his own physical well-being, regardless of accuracy or observable functioning.

Living Longer and Healthier

Hill (2005) identified four characteristics to living a longer and higher quality of life, including the importance of coping with age-related decline; choosing a lifestyle to preserve well-being; maintaining cognitive, emotional, and behavioral flexibility; and focusing on the positives, rather than the negatives, of the aging process. The medical profession promotes the ideology that as one ages, avoiding disease and disability is the key, with focus on lifelong health promotion and disease prevention, also highlighting "it is never too late" to adopt this philosophy. This includes living a healthy lifestyle and obtaining medical care to promote early detection and treatment.

As simple as it sounds, many men fail to follow these steps. As noted previously, such avoidance most likely stems from the stigma associated with appearing weak or seeking help, coupled with the fact that doing so would admit that the older man is incapable of dealing with his problems without assistance. In essence, this is cognitive dissonance in action; despite the multitude of messages aimed at encouraging men to make healthy choices, including preventive care, many older men will continue to avoid such activities.

Perhaps the best advice for older men who wish to avoid disease and disability in later life is the general recommendations to focus on exercise, follow a healthy diet, limit the use of alcohol or other recreational substances, and be cognizant of family history. Additional suggestions include limiting sun exposure, or at least wearing sunscreen for those men who are outside, practicing safe sex, and not smoking and stopping exposure to secondhand smoke. From as early as age 15, men are encouraged to perform regular testicular self-exams, with regular medical prostate exams starting at the age of 45.

DISABILITY, CHRONIC ILLNESS, AND PAIN

Regardless of avoidance practices, with older age and longer life expectancy comes increasing possibility of chronic diseases and conditions associated with disability and limitation of activity. Unfortunately, many older men will experience chronic illness and pain as they age. Often, the sooner a disease is diagnosed and treated, the better the chances of survival and ability to live a relatively normal and happy life. If not treated or appropriately managed, chronic disease can limit daily life and lead to increased physical and emotional decline. In a recent study including over 500 older male participants from a normative aging longitudinal research project, 24% reported health problems as the most serious problem or concern they had experienced in the past month (Yancura, Adlwin, Levenson, & Spiro, 2006).

The reality is that the majority of these men will likely devote vast amounts of energy to keeping their illness contained and disability invisible or less obvious (cf. Charmaz, 1991) in hopes of promoting the continued presentation of masculinity. Mr. Yao, in the case example at the beginning of this chapter, may exhibit this behavior, perhaps even to a greater extent than would an older Caucasian man, because of the possibility that he has lived his life in search of the middle ground between the acceptance and rejection of the dominant culture's masculine norms (Liu, 2003). Although there were some slight changes because of age, Charmaz (1994) summarized that over the life span, "Men with chronic illnesses try to lead normal lives. In doing so, they implicitly, and often explicitly, devote much effort to preserving self-aspects of a self known and valued in the past" (p. 278). Thus, many older men will continue to abide by the strong and silent and tough guy scripts, regardless of actual ability or medical status.

Disability

Although older men may experience a variety of chronic physical illnesses, some diseases will cause greater disability than others. According to the National Center for Health Statistics (2009), disability is defined as "a complex concept and can include presence of physical or mental impairments that limit a person's ability to perform important activity and affect the use of or need for supports, accommodations or interventions required to improve functioning" (p. iii). Livneh (1991) identified five distinct stages that a man can experience when his life is affected by a disability. These include the initial impact, the defense mobilization where bargaining and denial occur, initial realization, retaliation when anger and frustration are turned outward at others, and reintegration, which includes acknowledgment, acceptance, and adjustment to the changes in one's life because of the disability.

Disability can occur instantly from a traumatic event, such as a spinal cord injury or major stroke. Or it can develop slowly over time, stemming from a common chronic illness, including those that cause extreme discomfort such as arthritis and osteoporosis, to those that can be debilitating and eventually life threatening, such as diabetes and high blood pressure. Much like in Mr. Yao's case, the symptoms can gradually appear, causing more discomfort some days than others, little by little decreasing ability and causing more restriction in daily activity over a period of time. The pressure to deny symptoms and focus on living up to the ideal of a model minority (Chua & Fujino, 1999) may have allowed Mr. Yao to succeed throughout his life, while also caring for his ailing wife. Now, however, the same behaviors have become maladaptive.

In 2005 to 2006, the percentage of older adults with limitation of activity ranged from 25% of 65- to 74-year-olds to up to 60% of adults age 85 years old and over (CDC/NCHS, National Health Interview Survey, unpublished analysis). Arthritis and other musculoskeletal conditions were the most frequently mentioned chronic conditions causing limitation of activity, followed by heart and circulatory conditions (National Center for Health Statistics, 2009). In 2006, heart disease was the leading cause of death for adults age 65 years and over (National Center for Health Statistics, 2009). Among noninstitutionalized adults age 85 years and over, senility or dementia, vision conditions, and hearing problems were often mentioned causes of activity limitation (Kramarow, Lubitz, Lentzner, & Gorina, 2007).

Common Illnesses Experienced by Men in Later Life

Arthritis, a painful, chronic stiffing of joints, is common in the United States, with over one half of adults over the age of 65 suffering from this disease. Osteoporosis, often considered a "woman's disease," may include symptoms that are not initially noticed, thus leaving an older man with weakened bones, increasing risks for a fracture or break. Although osteoporosis is more common in women, many men also encounter weakening bones and should be aware of this possibility. In addition, men over the age of 50 may be at risk for prostate problems. Not caused by aging in itself, urinary incontinence, or the loss of bladder control, can range from mild to uncontrollable in older men. Although cancer can develop at any age and in either gender, older adults are also more likely to experience this disease. In particular, men are at risk for prostate and testicular cancer and, although rare, penile and breast cancer. Unfortunately, African American men with a family history, the men most at risk for aggressive prostate cancer and likely death, are the least likely to be screened (American Cancer Society, 2008). Symptoms such as pain or difficulty with urination, a lump in the testicles, and pelvic pain are warning signs that men should not ignore.

Diabetes, caused by blood levels of glucose being too high, can lead to dangerous health problems in older adults including kidney failure, vision loss, and neuropathy. As Mr. Yao was experiencing, but unaware of the possible cause, symptoms of adult-onset diabetes Type 2 include frequent urination, increased appetite and thirst, blurred vision, fatigue, and slow-healing or frequent infections. The longer one goes without treatment, such as in Mr. Yao's case if he continues to ignore the symptoms and not seek medical help, the harder it is to manage diabetes-related complications. Approximately one in five adults over age 60 is affected by peripheral nerve dysfunction.

High blood pressure, or hypertension, is often referred to as the "silent killer" of older men because of the lack of identifiable symptoms. However, left unidentified or treated, high blood pressure can lead to stroke, heart disease, and kidney failure. According to national figures, 65% of men age 75 years and over either had high blood pressure or were taking antihypertensive medication in 2003 to 2006 (National Center for Health Statistics, 2009). Strokes, the third-leading cause of death in the general population, occur when blood is unable to flow to a part of the brain, causing cells to be damaged or die. In an aging individual, strokes are a leading cause of physical and mental disabilities.

Chronic Pain

Despite the belief that "real men don't feel pain," a study focusing primarily on older men with chronic health conditions found that out of the more than 500 older patients who were interviewed, over 60% reported having pain that was present most of the time for six months or more during the past year (Krein, Heisler, Piette, Butchart, & Kerr, 2007). Little is known about racial and ethnic differences in self-reported rates of treatment for chronic pain and ratings of pain-treatment effectiveness. However, regardless of demographics, more often than not, chronic pain in older men continues to be untreated or, at best, undertreated.

An extensive literature review by Bernardes, Keogh, and Lima (2008) indicated the gender differences relating to pain are socially and culturally constructed. Men receive very specific messages about pain as they grow up, most of them subsumed within the tough guy script. Boys are taught to rub dirt on an injury and to "shake it off" rather than pay attention to the problem. Those who do not do so, or cry, are deemed weak and unfit for being in the company of real men. Thus, even in later life, older men experiencing a high level of pain will adhere to the male role. Growing up in an era with comic books that idealized the powers of Superman and Batman as examples of the ultimate masculinity, older men today understandably have a fear of not appearing manly, mistakenly accepting that showing pain can rob them of their identity, with the ongoing belief that "pain is for sissies."

Some older men may believe that pain is associated with old age, perhaps something they were taught by their own parents or even grandparents from previous years when the medical advancements of today were not available. Similar to Mr. Yao, these men believe that little can be done for older adults who do not feel well or have pain. The construct of model minority also becomes relevant for Mr. Yao. He was born in 1942 and most likely developed his social construction of masculinity (Addis & Mahalik, 2003) in the context of post–World War II America with strong pressure to conform to the dominant culture's values of hard work, as well as a minimal demand on social services. Thus, developing a balance between the gendered messages of his culture of origin and the dominant culture was important. However, at this time in his life, it may be interfering with his ability to realistically evaluate his condition and seek needed help.

EFFECTIVE SCREENING AND ASSESSMENT

Therapists working with older men will encounter the presence of numerous physical illnesses, varying levels of disability, and chronic pain. As can be noted with Mr. Yao, presenting issues may be intertwined and difficult to uncover, as problems may include undiagnosed depression, social issues, cultural pressures, limited daily means, and coexisting health problems. Differential diagnosis becomes imperative, albeit complicated, as pain and emotions are often tightly partnered, even for older men who were taught to suppress emotion and deny pain.

Those who report multiple physical symptoms that cannot be explained in specific clinical groupings may be suffering from a depressive disorder requiring treatment. In the example of Mr. Yao, depression and diabetes may be contributing to his change in appetite, insomnia, fatigue, lack of energy, and psychomotor disturbances. Only through careful, culturally sensitive evaluation, as well as collaboration with other medical providers, will an accurate picture emerge of Mr. Yao's diagnosis and the appropriate treatment.

Chronic Pain

Pain is not a psychiatric condition, and there is no associated psychiatric diagnosis. However, here too it is important to gather comprehensive information, with particular attention to the assessment of the frequency, duration, and debilitating effect of the pain. Older adults in general, and even more so men, underreport pain when simply asked about its presence or absence. Even direct questions about the level of pain may not be adequate, as pain can have a different meaning to men depending on their socialization and life experiences. For example, if one asked Mr. Yao if he is in pain, he most likely would answer something such as, "No, not really." To admit such pain would be tantamount to admitting failure as a man and, thus, for Mr. Yao, bring shame to him and his family. Therapists who work with Asian clients recommend caution when considering the use of direct questions given the likelihood that the response will be what they think they must say in order to avoid shaming themselves (e.g., Kochman & Mavrelis, 2009).

In addition, pain may be relative for many older men. Thus, when they are asked if they are in pain, their answer may be "no," as they compare current symptoms to previous experiences. For example, compared to when an older man was in the military and survived a helicopter crash during training maneuvers, he genuinely is not in pain given his current situation. Nothing could compare to the injuries he sustained in the crash and witnessing the pilot sitting next to him being crushed to death by heavy metal.

To obtain a more accurate assessment of pain, provide the client with a scale on which he can describe his level of pain without overtly admitting weakness or bringing about shame. An example of this might be, "On a scale of 1 to 10, with 1 being virtually no pain, and 10 being almost unbearable at this moment, what level is your pain?" To this specific question, Mr. Yao most likely will answer, "6 to 7," allowing a more accurate assessment of his current level of pain. This has the added benefit of providing a shared point of comparison, as the therapist can focus on Mr. Yao's context for his pain and the degree to which it affects his life.

Assessment Tools

Although nothing can replace a thorough clinical interview, the use of a formal tool is known to increase the frequency of diagnosing pain with older adults (Kamel et al., 2001). For a graphic rating scale, the 0–10 Numeric Pain Intensity Scale (Agency for Healthcare Research & Quality, 1992) is available. The multidimensional Brief Pain Inventory–Short Inventory (BPI; Cleeland, 1989) is recommended for a more thorough assessment of pain. Using a 0 to 10 scale and focusing on the previous 24 hours, the BPI asks for location of pain on a body map and then solicits the level of severity and interference with areas such as general activity, mood, walking ability, normal work, relations with others, sleep, and enjoyment of life. Several items also focus on use of pain treatments and their effectiveness.

A number of pain and disability tools exist in addition to those previously mentioned. Many of these tools can be located and easily downloaded for clinical use at the Web site for Pain Treatment Topics, a noncommercial organization with the mission to provide access to news, information, research, and education relating to the causes and effective management of pain (http://pain-topics.org/clinical_concepts/assess.php).

PSYCHOTHERAPY AND ADDITIONAL TREATMENT OPTIONS

Traditional male gender role socialization interacting with culturally held beliefs about health and wellness and cumulative effects of illness leave older men vulnerable to the effects of chronic illness. Thus, a necessary component for evoking behavioral change in older men is understanding the unique cyclical interplay of older male clients. One of the more recent trends in the psychology of men literature has been the development and evaluation of methods designed to increase men's involvement in, and retention during, psychotherapy (e.g., Rochlen, Blazina, & Raghunathan, 2002; Rochlen & Hoyer, 2005; Rochlen, Mohr, & Hargrove, 1999; Rochlen & O'Brien, 2002a, 2002b). The key to those methods has been the presentation of therapy in a manner congruent with male gender role themes, in effect drawing on themes of strength and courage and reframing the act of meeting with a therapist about health or level of pain as a decision that requires significant bravery in the face of adversity (e.g., Kantamneni, Christianson, Smothers, & Wester, in press).

In psychotherapy with Mr. Yao, the therapist should recognize his adherence to the Asian culture, as well as his gender, age, and generational cohort. Although this client may not identify clearly with the defined masculinity roles of the dominant culture, care should be given to recognize the influence of each. Understanding the level of Mr. Yao's conformity to the majority cultural values in respect to maintaining traditional cultural orientation will be helpful in how to best approach him throughout the psychotherapeutic process. For example, his polite and acquiescent responses should not be assumed to be agreement with the therapist. When identifying his strengths, Mr. Yao may be modest, which would most likely not indicate depression or low self-esteem but be reflective of his Asian culture. In addition, he may continue to incorporate his deceased wife into responses about himself and his abilities, as "self-worth, masculinities or other characteristics cannot be defined outside of a relationship" (Sue, 2005, p. 358).

When using psychotherapy for health or pain management with older men, consider providing direct guidance or feedback, as some men respond to an "expert" approach. Rather than framing within a psychosocial or psychological context, focusing on action or behaviors in relation to adequate pain management may be useful. Helping an older man to understand how pain management could improve his "functioning" or identifying what adequate pain medication would allow him to do increases focus on the final outcome. That is, it is important to help an older man to strategize about the goal that he is focused on achieving through use of pain management, such as "Regularly taking the prescription for pain medication will allow you to walk to the park in the morning with your wife, just like you use to do" or "Biofeedback may help you get on top of your back pain so you can ride your Harley again." In Mr. Yao's case, the therapist could point out that adequate pain management might allow Mr. Yao to have the good night sleep that he so desperately wants or feel well enough to actually take the cooking lessons he has been thinking about.

In his chapter on counseling men in medical settings, Courtenay (2005) outlined several interventions in the clinical practice guidelines he developed for health professionals who work with men. With a clear emphasis on using effective communication skills, Courtenay (2005) identified that when working with men about their health, the first step is humanizing; that is, validating or normalizing their health problems and concerns, acknowledging that they might be feeling vulnerable and have difficulty accepting help, as neither are not stereotypically masculine, and guiding them if needed in redefining their lives or view of manhood. In another step, the importance of comprehensive education is highlighted, including early detection and treatment. In addition, Courtenay (2005) recommended focusing on the man's strengths, helping him to locate support systems, and customizing each plan, tailoring treatment so that realistic health maintenance behaviors are implemented.

Utilizing this approach with Mr. Yao, the therapist might first provide empathy and validation, focusing on how difficult the past few years must have been for him, seeing his wife fight cancer, being her caregiver (which is strenuous for anyone), and then losing her after so many years of marriage. Feelings of helplessness of not being able to stop the disease, constant worry about her well-being, and the need to protect her must have been overwhelming for Mr. Yao. Not to mention the physical exhaustion of taking care of not only her needs but also the household chores that they once shared. And now, with her having passed away, the sadness, as well as loneliness, that he must be feeling would be challenging for any man. Culturally sensitive education about the grief process, as well as caregiver stress and the tendency for caregivers to not only experience burnout but ignore their own health concerns, may be enlightening for Mr. Yao, as might the involvement of culturally specific community-based systems. The therapist can encourage him to recognize his physical symptoms as being significant and that just as he would have identified the importance of his wife seeking assistance from their family physician, he too needs to access good medical care by seeking treatment from a medical provider. As he learned with his wife's disease process, early detection and treatment is key to the best possible outcome given the reality of the situation. The therapist may also support Mr. Yao in exploring fears about "not being strong" or believing that he just needs to "pull himself up by his bootstraps" to get through this time of his life. Asking Mr. Yao how he managed other challenging times in his life might help to stimulate conversation about his strengths and positive coping strategies employed throughout earlier years; no one completes 68 years of living without learning a few ideas about living and surviving difficult times. Or gently question Mr. Yao about what his wife might say to him if she could talk to him right now: What would she tell him to do? How would she want him to live his life? What directions would she give him on how to best take care of himself? In addition, focus might be given to whom Mr. Yao has in his life who might be able to provide him with additional support, whether it is adult children, siblings, friends, or members of his community. Based on Courtenay's (2005) model, all of these activities would be most effective if the therapist was specific to Mr. Yao and his situation, with future plans or goals tailored to what fits for or is acceptable to him and concordant with his views and wishes.

Pain Management

When an older man with chronic pain is advised by his physician to see a therapist, he may balk at the idea, assuming the message is that his pain is imaginary and only in his head. However, more and more research is demonstrating that the services mental health providers can offer, for example, cognitive behavioral therapy (CBT) and biofeedback, can ease pain by teaching coping mechanisms. In a review of 22 pain management studies, Hoffman, Papas, Chatkoff, and Kerns (2007) found that CBT and self-regulated treatments (such as biofeedback and hypnosis) eased pain intensity, improved quality of life, and reduced symptoms of depression. More recently, a meta-analytic review of 12 treatment studies on cognitive and behavioral interventions for chronic pain in older adults indicated that cognitive and behavioral interventions were effective on self-reported pain experience (Lunde, Nordhus, & Pallesen, 2009). Even relatively short and simple mindfulness meditation training can have a significant positive effect on pain management, as a single hour of training spread out over a three-day period can produce the same kind of analgesic effect (Zeidan, Gordon, Merchant, & Goolkasian, 2009).

Guided imagery, meditation, relaxation therapy, biofeedback, and hypnosis or hypnotherapy are useful adjuncts to pain treatment, either individually or as a part of a comprehensive treatment plan. These techniques can help to reduce stress, take the older man's mind off the pain, and/or empower the older man to have increased control over the pain experience.

CBT has the most empirical support for pain management within an interdisciplinary framework, based on the premise that thoughts impact feelings and behaviors. Given the crucial role of psychological and environmental factors in the experience of pain, CBT typically enhances the older man's feelings of self-control by combining stress management, problem solving, goal setting, and pacing of activities. Action-oriented, CBT techniques such as labeling cognitive distortions, reframing, and even giving homework assignments are utilized in the process of instilling hope and encouraging resourcefulness. The goal is to change thoughts and behaviors in reference to the pain, allowing for implementation of positive coping mechanisms and mastery over the pain.

Utilizing a Transdisciplinary Team Approach

Disease management with older men may be most effective when care is coordinated across a group of diverse professionals, including physicians (primary care and specialist), pharmacists, dieticians, and occupational and physical therapists. The therapist should help to focus on comprehensive care that is consistent and nonredundant by using a transdisciplinary team approach. An integration of treatment of targeted psychological variables associated with the illness or chronic disease can provide an effective disease management program that might include medical information about the disease, clear discussion about treatment options, training in use of medical skills (e.g., use of inhaler), focus on treatment compliance, and exploration of lifestyle changes.

A number of alternative treatment options are available for older men experiencing illness and chronic pain. For example, many older men may be able to benefit from physical therapy to strengthen weak supporting muscles and relax tight joints. Occupational therapy may be able to reduce irritation of or dependence on painful body parts by teaching new ways of moving, standing up from a chair, sitting, or lying down; adaptable equipment may also be available to better manage pain so the older man can continue to complete daily activities. Acupuncture has proved to be an increasingly popular treatment for persistent and intermittent pain and is thought to work by increasing the release of endorphins, chemicals that block pain signals from reaching the brain. Other options include massage and hydrotherapy, which is the use of hot or cold water to reduce inflammation and promote healing.

In a psychotherapy session with Mr. Yao, the therapist may encourage Mr. Yao to make an appointment with his primary physician if he has not already done so, requesting a release of information so that consultation could occur. This allows the therapist and physician to share information about a specific physical illness, emotional aspects, and identification of pain issues, leading to a comprehensive outline of the most effective treatment plan tailored to meet Mr. Yao's specific needs. Included is an added benefit of allowing the therapist to advocate for Mr. Yao, rather than leaving the direct disclosure of the level of pain to him, which might run the risk of him downplaying his symptoms in an attempt to avoid shame. On the basis of mutual agreement, perhaps an occupational and physical therapist could be brought in to help Mr. Yao increase his balance and decrease the risk of a future fall, as well as strengthen muscles or identify changes in movement to decrease pain. Given the death of Mr. Yao's wife, whom he presumably shared meal preparation with, and his lack of desire to cook and his tendency to skip meals, a referral for a dietician may also be of benefit for a nutritional assessment and educational purposes.

Pharmacological Intervention

When nonpharmacological treatments do not work or do not provide the level of relief required, turning to medication for appropriate pain management may allow for a higher quality of life. Pain management guidelines issued by the American Geriatrics Society (2009) indicate that over-the-counter pain medicines, such as Tylenol and aspirin, are not recommended for older adults with persistent pain, as the risks outweigh the benefits according to most recent clinical trials. Because the older adult population does not appear to be at a high risk for addiction (especially without any prior history), current thinking believes that opioids may be an option. For moderate to severe chronic pain, recommendations include opioids such as morphine and morphine-like drugs or a slowly released opioid such as oxycodone (OxyContin), or fentanyl (administered through a skin patch or lozenge on a stick), which help to minimize or eliminate the hills and valleys of pain. Of course, older adults are more sensitive to medications and may experience a higher degree of the usual side effects such as sedation, nausea, and confusion.

Because these medications are classified as narcotics, therapists should be aware that older adults and physicians often have negative emotional reactions to these medications and even possibly have misinformation about them. Attitudes preventing older men from taking medication for pain may include the idea that chronic pain does not change, thus the fear of addiction or dependence. Many men believe that words such as "opioid" or "narcotic" in reference to pain management equates with addiction and other adverse consequences as a long-term outcome. Thus, they worry about addiction to these type of pain medications and ultimately refuse to take them, even when in severe pain and in their last years of life.

There are various categories of drugs for treating chronic pain. Although in the past over-the-counter and prescription nonsteroidal anti-inflammatory drugs have been used for pain, recent studies suggest they should be used only short term, if at all, because of effects on blood flow to the kidney and worsening of other diseases including hypertension, congestive heart failure, and ulcer disease.

At times, some medications that were originally marketed for other uses are now part of pain control, including antidepressants such as venlafaxine (Effexor) and duloxetine (Cymbalta). Antiepileptics such as gabapentin (Neurontin) and pregabalin (Lyrica) are also used for pain control depending on the need.

Finally, there should be an awareness of the difference between pain medication that is scheduled to be taken at certain times of the day or intervals and medication that is prescribed as "prn," which is Latin for *pro re nata* and is commonly used to mean "as needed" or "as the situation arises." Each approach has different benefits. Prn allows medication to be taken only when it is needed, thus allowing time without the added drug in the older man's system. However, prn requires that the pain first be experienced, causing increased distress and often a higher dosage to alleviate the symptoms for treatment of chronic severe pain. In this situation scheduled intervals are thought to be more useful, as scheduled intervals of medication for chronic pain tend to require lower doses and minimize the degree of pain experienced. For many older men, asking for pain medication may be a sign of weakness, thus prn may not be the best approach. As noted previously, many older men have lived a lifetime of believing "real men don't feel pain," thus there is valor in not asking for pain medication; however, when the same medication is prescribed and to be taken on an indicated schedule, there is no loss of masculinity, and a more optimal level of pain management is reached.

CONCLUSION

The ultimate approach to health for older men is prevention through living a healthy lifestyle while keeping a positive attitude, in addition to early detection of any illness. However, with advancing age a number of men will experience declining health, disability, and chronic illness. With the stereotype of masculine traits of appearing healthy and strong, many men may not want to admit or accept physical symptoms as illness, as this not only challenges their manhood but possibly represents aging or their own vulnerability and even mortality.

Therapists can be effective in supporting healthy life changes, as well as treatment for men suffering from decreased ability. Adequate assessment and differential diagnosis is key, as well as a willingness to provide comprehensive care by working across disciplines. Men experiencing chronic pain can experience relief through a number of psychological interventions, as well as medication management.

TABLE 7.1 Guidelines for Health and Working With Men Experiencing Chronic Physical Illness and Disability

- Focus on prevention and early detection of physical symptoms, as older men tend to avoid seeking medical help.
- Disability and chronic illness must be addressed directly.
  - Recognize the older man's need to deny, remain independent, and focus on normalcy.
  - Utilize a transdisciplinary approach, working closely with those from other disciplines who are involved in the client's care.
- Chronic pain in older men continues to be undetected or often under treated.
  - Utilize a concrete assessment (1 to 10 scale).
  - Focus on function or behavior that the effective pain management will allow.
- CBT provides direct guidance for improving health related behaviors and pain management.
  - Assess the client's willingness to complete homework assignments.
- Medication is often required for appropriate pain management.

8

Management of Substance Use and Abuse

Samuel T. Benito Jr., or "Samson" to his friends, stopped the trac-
tor just a few inches in front of the barn door; he wasn't sure how
he came so close. Guess he hadn't been paying attention as much
as he should have been. Sure, he had a few beers with his lunch
and then another couple when Jack his neighbor stopped by mid-
afternoon to return the saw he had borrowed. It was a hot summer
day in July; who wouldn't need a little cooling off? Mr. Benito
knew it was dangerous to drink and then drive farm equipment, but
he could handle it—he had been doing it since he was a teenager.
If he couldn't drink a few beers and still do the afternoon chores,
who could? But he had to admit that at the age of 78, he seemed to
be starting to feel the effects of the alcohol more than when he was
younger. Actually, the more he thought about it, maybe it wasn't his
age. It might be the medication that Doc Hegge gave him last week,
something about his blood pressure being too high. Oh well, maybe
he should give up the beer for a while. But the last time he tried, he
was hot, sweaty, and even a bit shaky—which really was dangerous
when working around farm machinery. Maybe he would just try to
cut down a little; yes, that was the answer.

Although alcohol and substance abuse is the third-leading health problem among Americans 55 years of age and older, it has been only in the
past decade that the recognition of the pervasiveness of substance abuse
problems among older adults has come to light (Fingerhood, 2000). It
has been estimated that alcohol and prescription drug abuse affect up
to 17% of older adults, and the number of those who abuse alcohol and

other drugs later in life is expected to increase over the next several decades given the high birth rate of Americans during the post–World War II era.

Isenhart (2005) identified the extensive link between masculinity and the use of alcohol, explaining, "Men use alcohol to better fit into the traditional masculine role and to better manage the stress" caused by this pressure to conform (p. 135). With idolized characters such as James Bond 007 and the infamous vodka martini "shaken not stirred," older men grew up with a direct association between alcohol and "manliness." However, even with the many years of socialized romanticization between masculinity and alcohol, an older man's responsibility for his decision is not lessened and neither is his ability to be held accountable for his behaviors (Isenhart, 2005).

ALCOHOL USE

Alcohol use may be particularly problematic for baby boomers because of changing views, as generational cohorts who were raised prior to the 1960s tend to hold more conservative values about alcohol use when compared to cohorts raised since the 1960s who consider drinking more common and acceptable. Current estimates of alcohol abuse or dependence among older adults range from 1% to 10% in community settings and is thought to be considerably higher in clinical samples. According to the annual national survey on drug use and health sponsored by the Substance Abuse and Mental Health Services Administration (SAMHSA, 2009), 50.3% of individuals between the ages of 60 and 64 years used alcohol in the past month, and 39.7% of individuals aged 65 and older used alcohol in the past month. Six percent of adults aged 65 and older reported binge drinking, and 2.2% reported heavy drinking. In a separate study of Medicare recipients, Merrick and her colleagues (Merrick et al., 2008) found that 9% of community-dwelling older adults reported "unhealthy drinking."

Prevalence of alcohol use tends to be higher in older men than women. In a cross-sectional survey, 9.3% of men over the age of 65 were identified as "heavy drinkers," meaning they reported at least five or more alcoholic drinks on one occasion on a monthly basis or more (Lukassen & Beaudet, 2005). More recently, a national survey found that 22% of men aged 50 to 64 reported consuming five or more alcoholic beverages at a time during the past month. In that same cohort, 19% of the men drank two or more drinks daily, putting them in the "at-risk" group (Blazer & Wu, 2009).

In those over 65 years of age, men were almost twice as likely as women to be admitted for hospitalization through the emergency room with an alcohol-related cause and on average six years younger (71.8 versus 78.4 years) than those admitted to the hospital for other reasons (Saleh & Szebenyi, 2005). The latest statistics indicate that substance abuse treatment admissions for those aged 50 or older accounted for about 10% of all substance abuse treatment admissions, with the majority (76%) of adults aged 65 and older identifying alcohol as their primary substance (Office of Applied Studies, 2004).

PRESCRIPTION, OVER-THE-COUNTER, AND ILLICIT DRUGS

When it comes to illicit drugs, older adults are less likely than younger adults to report use. However, baby boomers, again unlike the cohort before them, were more likely to have experimented with drugs during their youth, and thus an increase of illegal drug use in later life may occur in the upcoming decade. But concerns do not exist only for the potential use of unlawful drugs in an older population; in fact, the misuse of prescription and over-the-counter (OTC) drugs may be even more of an issue. On average, older adults between ages 60 to 65 fill 13.6 prescriptions per year, and those 80 to 84 years old fill an average of 18.2 prescriptions per year (American Society of Consultant Pharmacists, 2003). Thus, although older adults represent only 13% of the population, they account for 30% of prescription drug use and 40% of OTC drugs sold in the United States (Menninger, 2002).

However, there appears to be two differing views of addiction to pain medication or OTC drugs. Proponents for the theory of "accidental" addiction to medication believe that dependence occurs as an outcome of the misuses of a medication that was originally suggested or prescribed by a medical provider. In contrast there are those who deny "accidental" addiction. For example, in a study exploring OxyContin use with both genders (64% men), ranging in age from 18 to 84 years, results indicated that the majority of individuals seeking addiction treatment reported their drug dependence as originating not from OTC or physician prescriptions but rather from illicit sources, such as family, friends, or other illegitimate sources (Carise et al., 2007). The authors contended that based on their study, indicators support that drug problems were clearly not "accidentally" secondary to OTC drugs or drugs prescribed for pain and other medical problems.

Although alcohol use and drug use in older men are each of concern, using alcohol and medication or illicit drugs concurrently create dire outcomes, as older individuals are more susceptible to the adverse reactions of drinking alcohol while taking OTC or prescription drugs. The physiological changes of aging can alter how a body processes and reacts to a medication, and the liver and kidneys may not as easily metabolize medications. Thus, moderate alcohol consumption is associated with a 24% increase in the risk for adverse interactions, given that "as many as half of the 100 most common drugs prescribed to older adults react adversely with alcohol" (Nemes et al., 2004).

DESCRIPTION OF THE DISORDER

"Heavy drinking" for men is often defined as drinking more than two drinks per day on average; drinking more than four drinks during a single occasion is the common definition for "binge drinking" (Centers for Disease Control and Prevention, 2007). However, when working with older men, flexibility is required, as consideration must be given to physiological changes with age. Alcoholism, also known as alcohol dependence, is a chronic disease that typically includes tolerance (need to drink greater amounts of alcohol to get "high") as one of four criteria; however, changes in the physiology of older adults makes this an invalid indicator. The other three predictors of alcoholism, however, can be applied to older men, including craving (a strong need or urge to drink), loss of control (not being able to stop drinking once drinking has begun), and physical dependence (withdrawal symptoms such as nausea, sweating, shakiness, and anxiety after stopping use of alcohol).

Early-Onset Versus Late-Onset Alcohol Use

Older men who abuse alcohol tend to fall into two categories: those who begin abusing alcohol in early or middle adulthood (early onset) and those who do not begin to abuse alcohol until after the age of 60 (late onset). Older adults who fall into the early-onset group outnumber the late-onset group by two to one (Fingerhood, 2000), with men more likely being a part of the early-onset group. These men tend to have a long history of difficulties, including behavioral problems and poor physical health. Mr. Benito, in the case example at the beginning of the chapter, most likely belongs in the early-onset group, as he indicated he had been drinking since he was a teen. Although few details were offered about his physical health, Mr. Benito most likely experienced significant physical symptoms that caused him to visit his physician, as men, especially those with traditional male views like Mr. Benito, tend to underutilize health care services (e.g., Addis & Mahalik, 2003). The winner and independent scripts may best describe Mr. Benito's socialization as a male in relationship to his health, as he associates masculinity with victory over adversity and obstacles in his life, such as physical problems due to long-term use of alcohol or even normal changes due to aging.

In an assessment of 61 male veterans aged 60 to 90 years who met criteria for likely history of alcohol abuse or dependence, participants identified their 20s and 30s as the ages in which the greatest frequency of problematic drinking symptoms occurred; they reported a decline in alcohol consumption in their 50s and 60s (Karel, Lynch, & Moye, 2000). Overall, the majority of these men reported variability in levels of drinking over the years (i.e., periods of heavy versus lighter drinking); few participants reported consistent levels of drinking over their life span. Men who begin drinking earlier in life most likely have attempted to stop their drinking numerous times and often have a number of failed attempts at treatment, as there tends to be limited compliance. In many cases, relationships with family members are strained, with those close to them tending to report experiencing burnout.

In contrast to those with a pattern of drinking over their life span, those who experience late-onset alcohol abuse is often associated with age-related stressors and losses. These might include retirement, death of a spouse, or physical decline. Although there is a general recognition that treatment would be successful for these men, they may suffer from their addiction in shame and remain silent, believing they should be strong and not depend on alcohol to cope. This most likely is due to the socialized male expectation to adhere to the strong and silent script, stressing the importance of men being stoic and unemotional lest they be labeled as less of a man. The tough guy script may also prevent many men who experience late-onset alcoholism from seeking treatment, as it stresses men's suppression of emotions so they can be called tough in the face of pain, both emotional and physical. Men who "turn to alcohol" when in pain and are honest about their use most likely do not achieve tough guy status. Because of men's tendency to conceal their drinking, late-onset alcohol abuse is more likely to be undetected by health care providers (Barrick & Conners, 2002).

Risk Factors

Regardless of when the misuse began, alcohol use has increasingly negative effects on an older man's body, as normal physical changes over the life span modify the body's responses to alcohol, including the manner and rate of absorption, distribution, and excretion. Older men obtain a higher blood alcohol concentration for a given quantity of alcohol compared to younger men, often placing the late-life man at increased risk for intoxication and other adverse effects, even at relatively low levels of use. Minor alcohol use can not only cause disease but also worsen current medical symptoms and increase resistance to treatment. For example, two to three drinks per day have been associated with hypertension and diabetes; as few as one to two drinks per day can increase the threat of hip fracture.

A number of risk factors have been identified with drinking problems in older men, including social isolation, loneliness, sleep disturbance, chronic pain, and other persistent medical disorders. That is, the misuse of alcohol by older men can lead to cirrhosis of the liver, peripheral neuropathy, depression, late-onset seizure disorder, confusion, dementia, poor nutrition, incontinence, peptic ulcer disease, and inadequate self-care. A higher rate of mortality is also reported in older men who abuse alcohol. In a study of White men aged 50 to 79 who received treatment for alcohol-related problems through community mental health centers, results suggested that a five-year mortality rate was 17.7% compared to 12.2% in the general population (Banks, Pandiani, Schacht, & Gauvin, 2000).

As identified in the case at the beginning of this chapter, Mr. Benito's alcohol tolerance is no longer the same as it once was. In addition, given that his primary care physician recently prescribed medication for his "blood pressure being too high," Mr. Benito most likely has hypertension, possibly from years of drinking alcohol. This may contribute to an internalization of loss of masculinity due to his decreasing physical function, strength, stamina, and activity (Gerschick & Miller, 1995). It is difficult to identify the extent of physical problems Mr. Benito experiences, but there seems to be an increased possibility of his life being shorted, either by medical disorders due to drinking or by an accidental death because of alcohol use while working on the farm. As many have suggested within masculinity theory, risk taking is a part of being perceived as manly, perhaps even to the extent of loss of life.

Much less is known about symptoms in prescription medication misuse or illicit drug use in older men. Concerning factors may include social isolation, loss of motivation, memory problems, family or marital discord, or recent decline in ability to manage activities of daily living. A history of substance abuse, medical exposure to prescription drugs with abuse potential, poor health status, and polypharmacy may be additional areas of risk for older men. Drug-seeking behaviors or doctor shopping should be viewed as significant concerns associated with substance use (Simoni-Wastila & Yang, 2006).

EFFECTIVE SCREENING AND ASSESSMENT TECHNIQUES

The overall goal for screening older men for alcohol use is to identify at-risk drinkers, problem drinkers, and/or older men with alcoholism. Early identification of and early intervention for substance abuse in older men is crucial. However, even though there is a significant need for screening older men and identifying those who may be at risk for substance abuse problems, alcohol use disorders among older adults remain underdiagnosed, misdiagnosed, undertreated, or untreated (Han, Gfroerer, Colliver, & Penne, 2009). There are a number of factors that contribute to why therapists may be at risk to miss an older man's substance abuse, including both the information provided and the presentation by the older man and the therapist's approach.

Therapist Contributions

Health professionals tend to overlook alcohol and drug misuse among older men, often attributing the symptoms to other common problems among older adults, such as dementia, depression, and other physical illnesses (Sattar, Petty, & Burke, 2003). Thus, poor self-care (e.g., lack of hygiene or self-neglect), frequent falls and unexplained bruising, malnutrition, and physical illness may be explained away by the therapist as age-related occurrences that are to be expected as men experience a gradual decline in later years. Even traditional signs of intoxication, such as slurred speech, lack of judgment, inhibition, and staggering gate, may be contributed to aging. Given Mr. Benito is a farmer, little notice may be given to lack of hygiene, as the assumption would be made that he was "in his work clothes, having been out in the field all day." In addition, he could easily explain away bruising from falls as "I just bumped into something in the shed" and his weight loss as "no women around to cook for me." In this example, Mr. Benito's use of the masculine stereotype of the achievement-oriented, hardworking male relying on the female to provide meals may on one level be protective, at least in Mr. Benito's view, as it helps to hide his drinking behaviors, but on the other hand be very dangerous, as the therapist is relatively hindered from identifying the alcohol use early and thus the possibility of providing treatment.

In addition, therapists may avoid the topic of alcohol or drug use because it can be a difficult topic to discuss, with the potential of it being awkward to ask an older man about his alcohol and substance use. Age alone may be a deterrent, as the societal belief of "respect your elders" can cause discomfort in confronting an older man about his substance use. In addition, it may not occur to the therapist to ask a friendly older man who presents as the stereotypical grandfatherly type about his alcohol use. An advanced education level or a higher socioeconomic status may also hinder direct assessment of alcohol or substance use.

Unfortunately, there may also be misconceptions that it is not necessary to screen for alcohol- or drug-related problems in older men as they cannot be treated successfully, or the time and energy required to treat substance abuse is too great for those who are close to the end of their life. The attitude of "just let him enjoy his last few years" or "that's just what men do" rather than the appropriate attention to assessment may be potentially very dangerous. Power, dominance, and control, characteristics thought to be necessary features in proving one's masculinity (e.g., O'Neil, 1981a, 1981b), are part of this process, and therapists should guard against inadvertently subscribing to an older man's sense of entitlement when it comes to substance abuse.

Therapists should also be aware of the influence of their own gender and cultural background on their response to older men with suspected substance abuse problems. Exploring one's internalized stereotypes of age, gender, or labels such as "addict" and "alcoholic" is crucial. Although an understanding of typical patterns is useful in anticipating problem areas or the possible course of treatment, experienced therapists resist the temptation to stereotype based on language, ethnicity, age, education, and appearance. Assumptions such as "This well-dressed 80-year-old retired banker is not the type to misuse his terminally ill wife's OxyContin" or "Of course this 72-year-old man likes to drink and have a little fun with his friends at the VFW on Monday nights" can be damaging to the accurate assessment of substance use. A therapist's personal history with substances is also a part of this equation; an individual who does not drink alcohol may have a different perspective of what constitutes alcohol consumption compared to a therapist who comes from an environment where alcohol is socialized as an appropriate aspect of life.

The Older Man's Contribution

On the other hand, older men may not be willing to be open or honest about their use of substances; given traditional masculine reluctance to accept help, many will not self-refer or seek treatment. Numerous older men will rely on being self-sufficient and avoid presenting any weakness and vulnerability. Although the majority of older adults (87%) see physicians regularly, an estimated 40% of those who are at risk do not self-identify or seek services for substance abuse (Raschko, 1990). In addition, memory difficulties may interfere with the ability of the older man to self-monitor intake or provide accurate information to his health care provider. Culture and gender may influence men's recognition of their problems (e.g., local cultural norms may condone or accept male drunkenness) and their reaction to the assessment process and recommended treatment interventions (e.g., substantial stigma may be associated with substance abuse treatment for older men).

For example, when Mr. Benito visited his family physician the previous week, he undoubtedly did not mention his change in tolerance when consuming alcohol, and he was not asked about his drinking habits by the nurse or his family physician, as less than half of family practice physicians screen alcohol use in their current older patients (Sharp & Vacha-Haase, 2010). In addition to the possibility of colluding to help Mr. Benito present as "strong" rather than vulnerable, Mr. Benito, as well as the professionals in the medical office, may view his alcohol use, especially with friends, as a part of the normal culture in the area.

Clinical Interview

Assessment of substance use or abuse can be completed by conducting a thorough clinical interview, with direct questions about past and, most important, current consumption of alcohol or other substances, including quantity, frequency, and any bingelike behaviors. The therapist may need to target questions to gain clarity or obtain specific information, such as what "a few" beers actually represent, or when an older man indicates he has "one glass of alcohol a day," does he really mean one shot of hard liquor or one cup, or is he continuing to keep the same glass filled with alcohol throughout the day? Exploring any consequences of alcohol or substances is also recommended; additional questions based on the CAGE Questionnaire (Ewing, 1984) to assess the use of alcohol or other substances include the following: Have you ever felt you should cut down on your drink/substance use? Have people annoyed you by criticizing your drinking/substance use? Have you ever felt bad or guilty about your drinking/substance use? Have you ever had a drink first thing in the morning to steady your nerves or to get rid of a hangover? Mr. Benito, if he were being honest, most likely would answer "yes" to many, if not all, of these questions.

The usual ways of detecting problems with substances (e.g., time lost from work, legal problems, or decreased participation in important social activities) when assessing older men are not helpful in identifying substance use, as older men generally have fewer activities and obligations. Older men often have an open schedule and autonomy, as they no longer are expected at work five days a week, or have frequent family responsibilities. Or, like Mr. Benito, they may live alone and have an occupation such as a farmer that allows independence and significant flexibility in a daily schedule. There is most likely no one who would notice if Mr. Benito did not show up for work or recognize if his work was subpar or remained unfinished because of his increased substance use. At the same time, an older man of a higher socioeconomic status may also be in a position to cover his behavior, given that access to financial resources allows one a great degree of flexibility in today's society.

Assessment Instruments

With the many entwined factors in diagnosing substance misuse in older men, the assessment should be sequential and multidimensional. "Sequential" suggests the assessment process be composed of a series of stages, each of which may or may not lead to the next stage depending on the information obtained previously. In this model, a broad-based assessment is conducted first. If the information obtained suggests that there may be a substance abuse problem, then a series of progressively more specific questions would be initiated to confirm and characterize the substance use. Utilizing a multidimensional approach to assessment includes the use of multiple sources of information (e.g., collateral interviews with family members, medical records), combined with cohort and gender issues that impact an older man's substance use.

Few studies have examined the process whereby older men in need of substance abuse services are identified or screened. The U.S. Preventive Services Task Force (2004) recommended routine screening for unhealthy alcohol use with the use of the Alcohol Use Disorders Identification Test (AUDIT) or CAGE questionnaires in primary care settings. The AUDIT is a 10-item self-report screening instrument that specifically identifies current use disorders, developed to identify people with hazardous levels of drinking. A shorter version of the test, the AUDIT-5, is often used with older adults (Oslin, 2005). The CAGE Questionnaire is considered to be the most widely accepted and researched instrument for alcohol screening. As indicated, the test has only four questions, can be quickly administered, and assesses lifetime prevalence of alcohol problems; however, because results do not differentiate between past or current problems, there may be some disadvantages to using this with older men. The Alcohol-Related Problems Survey (ARPS) is an 18-item self-administered screening measure that focuses on the relationship between alcohol use and medical problems, medication use, and functional status; results classify one as a "nonhazardous," "hazardous," or "harmful" drinker.

The Michigan Alcohol Screening Test–Geriatric Version (MAST-G; Blow et al., 1992) is an elder-specific 24-item self-report inventory. Although it is a screening tool with age-directed questions, the length may prevent routine use with older men; it also does not distinguish recent drinking from past drinking.

Another option for screening substance abuse in older men is the Drug Abuse Problem Assessment for Primary Care (DAPA-PC), a computerized instrument developed for primary care settings. Results of a study of those over age 55 indicated that the DAPA-PC was a useful instrument for screening older adults for alcohol and drug abuse in primary care settings (Nemes et al., 2004).

There are few, if any, validated screening instruments for detecting problems related to prescription medication abuse. Assessment for older men who may be abusing prescription medication should include a detailed history and exploration of signs of prescription misuse (e.g., excessive worry about whether the medication is working, attachment to a particular psychoactive medication, or excessive anxiety about the supply and timing of medications). Therapists can also explore excessive daytime sleeping, declines in personal grooming and hygiene, and withdrawal from family, friends, and normal social activities.

PSYCHOTHERAPY AND ADDITIONAL TREATMENT APPROACHES

There have been few studies examining the treatment of older male substance abusers, and little is known about why they stop using. In a study of 61 male veterans, aged 60 to 90 years of age, who met criteria for likely history of alcohol abuse or dependence, 46 (75%) appeared to have given up problematic drinking. Of those 46, the majority (89%) reported they had stopped the use of alcohol on their own. Written comments from these men included, "I just quit" and "Just stopped cold turkey." The authors (Karel et al., 2000) noted that they were unable to offer further clarification of why these men refrained from alcohol use, as over half (52.2%) indicated the option "other" when given the choice to explain why they were no longer drinking.

Treatment approaches to substance abuse can be thought of as being across a spectrum, ranging from preventive education, to clinical advice, to brief intervention, to formalized specialized treatment, to inpatient or residential specialized programs. At each level treatment may include an individual or group approach. Therapists may want to refer to the treatment manual titled *Substance Abuse Relapse Prevention for Older Adults: A Group Treatment Approach* (Dupree & Schonfeld, 1999), which is based on cognitive behavioral and self-management treatment techniques specifically adapted for use with older adults. Although the program was originally developed for outpatient group settings, it is designed to be adaptable for other settings including inpatient or individual psychotherapy.

Many have identified the need for effective treatment to consist of psychological intervention integrated with primary health care, as older primary care patients, particularly men, are more likely to accept collaborative mental health treatment within primary care than in mental health or substance abuse clinics. Research has identified that patients engaged in an integrated treatment model were much more likely to participate (71%) compared to those in a referral model (49%). Overall, integrated care was associated with more mental health and substance abuse visits per patient for both at-risk alcohol users and those with severe drinking problems (Bartels et al., 2004; Gallo et al., 2004). Similarly, the U.S. Preventive Services Task Force (2004) recommended brief therapy interventions in primary care settings to reduce alcohol misuse and referral to specialty treatment for those with alcohol dependence.

Mr. Benito serves as an excellent example for the increased likelihood of increased intervention through a primary care approach. Should Mr. Benito decide to participate in treatment for his drinking, he would likely be most comfortable working through an integrated approach, with his primary care physician Doc Hegge at the head of the transdisciplinary team.

Individual Treatment

In providing psychotherapy, therapists should be sensitive to issues such as loss, isolation, and serious physical health problems that older men in substance abuse treatment might be experiencing (Blow, Walton, Chermack, Mudd, & Brower, 2000). In addition to their substance abuse, older men may be suffering from grief, depression, anxiety, or developmental issues (e.g., integrity vs. despair). These issues should be considered in relation to the impact of alcohol and other substance use. At the same time, the therapist should not fall into the trap of excusing substance abuse either because of these reasons or because of a sense that the man in question has earned his beer given his age and accomplishments. A balance must be struck that allows older male clients to make their own choices while also opening the door for more adaptive ways of coping.

Older men may react most positively if questions are prefaced with a link to medical conditions or health concerns. Until rapport is well established, the therapist may want to refrain from labeling or using

stigmatizing terms such as "alcoholic." Older men may not respond well
to confrontation, as it may be viewed as disrespectful and interfere with
the treatment process (Blow et al., 2000). An older man might experience confrontation as the therapist challenging his masculinity, causing
him to react in a verbally aggressive or guarded manner rather than
with the increased honesty the therapist had intended. The special challenge in dealing with the issue of substances is that such behavior is so
strongly reinforced by society at large and the gender role socialization
in particular. Images of men enjoying liquid rewards at the end of a long
day are common, and many older men believe substance use is not only
accepted but an encouraged aspect of their gender role.

Cognitive behavioral therapy can be effective with older male substance abusers. Focus should be given to techniques that increase
emotional coping, self-control, and social skills. During the course of
therapy, time should be given to explore reasons for substance use. For
example, what pattern does the older man recognize in his drinking
behaviors if he considers the past 50 years? What was going on in his
life when he drank the most? The least? And how does he make sense
of that pattern for himself? With further insight, the older man may
eventually be at the point that he is ready to make a plan for treatment
or at least identify how he can start to change his behaviors and move
toward healthier choices.

Some older men will exhibit reluctance or ambivalence regarding
change of their substance use, as for many it may have served a functional
male purpose over the years. This should not be interpreted as denial; as
Isenhart (2005) explained, "Ambivalent behavior is consistent with the
traditional masculine role of maintaining power and control and questions convention and authority" (p. 139). Thus, he may not be ready to
completely accept that he is an alcoholic or stop drinking, but he may
be open to committing to a reduction in consumption (e.g., drinking
every other day instead of daily) or significantly limiting the amount of
alcohol. Or another older man may identify an initial step as honestly
recording the amount of pain medication above the prescribed amount
that he is using on a daily basis. Accepting where the older man is in his
processing of his use and need for change and the willingness to take
one step at a time will prove the most effective in the end.

An additional component of psychotherapy may be the brainstorm-
ing of how the older man will cope when in a high-risk situation. For
example, the therapist may encourage Mr. Benito to generate ideas of
how he might decline a beer should his neighbor stop by in the morning
to share a six-pack of beer. With another older man, the therapist may
help him to identify coping strategies other than taking additional pain
medication when he begins to experience symptoms of anxiety, which
causes his pain to increase.

In psychotherapy with Mr. Benito, the therapist should be sensitive
to the isolation and loneliness that he most likely is experiencing. As a
lifelong bachelor, he has little contact with family, and thus when a

friend does stop by to visit, he is likely to engage in social behaviors (such as drinking a beer) that prolong the visit and potentially encourage the visitor to return in the future. Mr. Benito may be hesitant to identify his behavior as problematic or be willing to change in any way, given he does not know different from having "a few beers" with friends during the day, as this has been a custom since he was a teenager, he was socialized the majority of his life to associate beer with masculinity, and he most likely has been rewarded by others for this behavior. One way to better understand Mr. Benito's perspective may be through the "gender role strain" (Pleck, 1995) that men experience when they become aware of the divergence between the male gender role they believe they must adhere to and the changes they should make to decrease personal consequences. To work most effectively with Mr. Benito, the therapist may help him to explore the societal messages that he received through the years regarding alcohol use, acknowledging the previous value of such behaviors but also the need to consider how this once beneficial behavior may no longer be advantageous given his health status. With increased awareness of the differing pulls, Mr. Benito may be ready to explore what, if anything, he might want to change at this time, particularly within the context of medical concerns.

Adaptations to psychotherapy with an older man struggling with substance abuse should be made to personalize treatment to accommodate variability in the physical and cognitive functioning of clients. This might include a reduced pace, slower transitions, repetition if there is decreasing cognitive functioning, and possible referrals for outside case management activities, such as arranging guardianship and alternative living arrangements (e.g., assisted living or long-term care) and identifying community resources to address the social, recreational, medical, and spiritual needs of the older man.

Treatment Programs

The underrepresentation of older adults in traditional mixed-age programs and the scarcity of specialized, age-specific treatment programs have contributed to the paucity of research on alcoholism treatment outcome for older men. Older adults tend to be underrepresented in drug and alcohol treatment programs, possibly because of the tendency for older adults to deny their drug use as problematic (Nemes et al., 2004) or encounter treatment initiation and access barriers. However, when older adults do participate, studies indicate that they benefit from formal substance abuse treatment; older adults tend to stay in treatment longer and have outcomes at least as favorable as those of younger adults in mixed-age programs (Atkinson, Tolson, & Turner, 1993; Satre, Mertens, Areán, & Weisner, 2003).

Older men may gain additional treatment benefits from elder-specific programs (Blow et al., 2000); however, few studies have examined client factors associated with treatment initiation in substance abuse programs specifically designed for older adults. In a study that sought to examine how individual characteristics predicted substance abuse treatment initiation among older adults, 124 male veterans over the age of 55 years who began substance abuse treatment where compared to 126 of their peers who did not participate in any treatment options. Results suggested that the negative effect of greater age on the process of treatment seeking occurred earlier and that by the time of the pre-treatment evaluation, those older clients who were going to drop out had already done so. Clients who initiated treatment following evaluation, compared with clients who did not initiate treatment, had more years of education, better cognitive status, more alcohol problems, and higher depression scores. Greater number of alcohol problems and better cognitive functioning independently predicted treatment initiation (Satre, Knight, Dickson-Fuhrmann, & Jarvik, 2004).

Blow and his colleagues examined multidimensional six-month outcomes of elder-specific inpatient alcoholism treatment for 90 participants with an average age of 71 years (range 55 to 91 years old); a little over half (58.9%) were men. On the basis of six-month outcomes, participants were classified into the following groups: Abstainers, Non-Binge Drinkers, and Binge Drinkers. The groups did not differ on any baseline measures (e.g., demographics, drinking history, alcohol symptoms and age of onset, comorbidity, or length of treatment). General health improved between baseline and follow-up for all groups. Psychological distress decreased for Abstainers and Non-Binge Drinkers but did not change for Binge Drinkers. Results suggested that a large percentage of older adults who receive elder-specific treatment attained positive outcomes across a range of outcome measures (Blow et al., 2000).

Hanley Center, a leading substance abuse treatment facility, is nationally known for being a trendsetter in older adult recovery; the center was the first to develop a program specifically designed to meet the unique needs of baby boomers. The Life Stages Track for Boomers program deals with unique characteristics of those just turning 65 years old but still has its roots in a 12-step, holistic, medically based treatment model (www.HanleyCenter.org).

Although a review of treatment for ethnic minorities indicated there are no consistent ethnic differences in overall prognosis or in response to the particular treatments being compared (Miller, Villanueva, Tonigan, & Cuzmar, 2007), a long history of debate exists regarding how addiction treatment should differ for or be adapted with special populations. Currently, relatively few, if any, efficacy studies are available thus far for each particular special population.

Pharmacological Intervention

There are currently three oral medications available to treat alcoholism. These include disulfiram (Antabuse), which makes the person sick after drinking alcohol; naltrexone (Depade or ReVia), which reduces cravings; and acamprosate (Campral), which reduces symptoms that follow lengthy abstinence. Naltrexone (Vivitrol), a long-acting injection, is also available. There are also medications to help manage symptoms of withdrawal, such as shakiness, nausea, and sweating. Like the majority of medications, there are risks and side effects for each of these prescription medications, with the likelihood of their being increased in an older adult population. Few clinical studies have been conducted regarding the effectiveness of these medications with older men, and little evidence exists supporting pharmacological intervention with older substance abusers (Fingerhood, 2000).

Although the study included adults aged 18 and older, several years ago the National Institute on Alcohol Abuse and Alcoholism (NIAAA) implemented the first national study to evaluate the effectiveness of behavioral treatments alone and in combination with medications targeting persons with the diagnosis of alcohol dependence. Results of the Combining Medications and Behavioral Interventions (COMBINE) found that the medication naltrexone and up to 20 sessions of alcohol counseling by a behavioral specialist were equally effective treatments for alcohol dependence when delivered with structured medical management. Overall, those who received naltrexone, specialized alcohol counseling, or both demonstrated the best drinking outcomes after 16 weeks of outpatient treatment. All patients also received medical management, an intervention consisting of nine brief, structured outpatient sessions provided by a health care professional. Contrary to expectations, the researchers found no effect on drinking with use of the medication acamprosate and no additive benefit from adding acamprosate to naltrexone (Anton et al., 2006).

CONCLUSION

A long history exists for the connection between substance use and the traditional masculine role. The use of substances is an increasing phenomenon among older men, even though abuse or dependence is often overlooked. Assessment and identification of substance misuse within an older male population may be difficult given an older man's tendency to not report or even downplay his use. Traditional indicators may not be present because of reduced social and occupational requirements of later life, as signs may more often present as poor self-care, unexplained falls, malnutrition, and medical illnesses. Treatment options range from preventative education to inpatient hospitalization.

TABLE 8.1   Guidelines for Working With Older Men With Substance
Abuse Problems

- Older men are at increased risk for substance abuse.
  - Consumption of alcohol has long been associated with the traditional
    male role.
- Effective screening should be sequential and multidimensional.
- Effective treatment can occur individually or in groups, and range from
  prevention education to inpatient formalized treatment programs.
- Psychotherapy with older men experiencing substance abuse problems
  must be adapted to recognize additional areas of concern and the
  potential for male identity conflict in regard to substances.
  - Confrontation may bring about increased defensiveness and be
    harmful to the therapeutic process.
- Pharmacological intervention to treat older men for substance abuse is not
  generally recommended.

9

Cognitive Impairment

Following a significant stroke, Denzel Smith, a 72-year-old African American man, obtained extensive physical and cognitive rehabilitation, relearning basic skills including coordinated movement and speech. Seven months later he appeared to have made significant gains in his cognitive and verbal functioning, reestablishing his ability to eloquently discuss and argue intellectual points. As a younger man, Mr. Smith had earned degrees in both economics and law and worked in the financial arena throughout his life as a hedge fund manager and financial consultant. For 30 years, Mr. Smith had focused on an entrepreneurial enterprise, building a lucrative financial business. He overcame racism and oppression to succeed in areas of business in a society where strangers, other professionals, and even family members consistently questioned him; his friends often described him as fearless, tenacious, headstrong, authoritarian, and demanding. Mr. Smith's career and providing for his family defined him, as he had achieved much success in these domains. He and his wife had two sons, and over the years Mr. Smith had encouraged them to join the family business, holding them to high but supportive standards. Both sons eventually followed in their father's footsteps and worked side by side at Mr. Smith's company. However, Mr. Smith's sons began to notice slight changes in his behavior following rehabilitation from his stroke. Mr. Smith, a widower for the past two years, now lived alone, and his sons became aware that he wore the same shirt and pants throughout the week, even if they became soiled. They noted that he appeared to be losing weight, although his refrigerator was stocked with now-expired food. Although Mr. Smith could still verbally spar with his sons and speak eloquently in casual conversation, they discovered that he devised business plans that were not logical or linear in thought or as thorough or detailed as they once

were. At one business meeting, Mr. Smith appeared mildly confused and left the room unexpectedly. Given the changes, his sons
became concerned about his ability to act as CEO of his company.
However, when Mr. Smith's sons addressed these issues with him,
he responded with anger, denial, and argumentation. He claimed
his sons were attempting to take over leadership of the company
without his consent. He refused in-home services such as cooking,
cleaning, and yard work, asserting he had single-handedly cared for
himself and his entire family for years.

Cognitive impairment is a reality many older adults experience, be
it personally or as a caregiver to someone with a diminished thought
process. For many older men, their own cognitive decline often involves
challenges associated with the loss of control over their daily functions
and the threat the loss poses for their identity as a man. In the caregiver role, older men are often required to learn new skills, as their
socialization generally has not taught them the various aspects essential in caregiving.

COGNITIVE FUNCTIONING

Cognitive changes associated with aging have been conceptualized as
two separate processes, one consisting of normal changes in cognition
associated with increased age and the other consisting of impairment.
Smith and Rush (2006) delineated the differences between the two,
labeling them as "benign" and "malignant." Benign changes are considered secondary to the process of aging, with nonspecific changes in the
brain; malignant processes are marked by atypical brain histopathology
and are not equivalent to aging.

Normative Cognitive Changes Associated With Aging

Most researchers agree that with age comes normal declines in cognition (Schaie, 1994), typically manifesting as slower processing speed
(Salthouse, 1996) across language, memory, attention, and executive
functioning. Because the speed with which older adults process information slows as a natural trajectory, older male clients, when compared
to younger men, may demonstrate a reduced speed encoding information, recalling information, and solving problems.

Two terms are commonly used to describe normative, nonpathologi-
cal cognitive decline in older adults: "age-associated memory impairment" and "age-related cognitive decline" (Smith & Rush, 2006).
Age-associated memory impairment is defined as cognitive decline
found in older adults relative to performance found in younger individuals as established through neuropsychological testing (Smith &
Rush, 2006). An older man might be considered to have age-associated

memory impairment if he performed less optimally than a younger person, yet with no indication that the change met the level of impairment or organic pathology.

Age-related cognitive decline, as defined by the American Psychiatric Association (1994), is a term used to categorize perceived memory impairment that has not been fully verified through memory testing. As such, older individuals complaining of problems with their memory (e.g., "I just can't remember things as well as I used to") but who are still performing at a level expected by someone in their age group are defined as having age-related cognitive decline. Accurate assessment at this stage of decline is often difficult, as symptoms tend to be dismissed, either because the older man considers it a normal part of the aging process or because he is reluctant to discuss any decline he might have noticed because what the loss of abilities might suggest about him and his ability to be a man. Although changes in cognition with advancing years can be a normative part of the aging process, some older men may experience a sense of inadequacy related to their inability to perform tasks as quickly or efficiently as they could when they were younger. They may also find these changes distressing, as they believe others may begin to view them in a negative light and treat them as senile or forgetful.

Given the life roles played by many men of the current older generation cohort, such as decision makers, providers, and leaders, experiencing the normal changes in cognition associated with aging may prompt frustration, defensiveness, and self-doubt. Even well-meaning suggestions that the older man might benefit from additional assistance with a task he once performed himself can bring about intense feelings of anxiety, defensiveness, sadness, or anger, prompting an offended or obstinate response. In addition, an older man might perceive that other people treat him as if he is getting old or acting senile based on subtle changes associated with aging, prompting thoughts of self-doubt and the need to defend or protect himself from others. Thus, when working with older men who are experiencing age-related cognitive decline, therapists can reassure clients by informing them about normal cognitive changes occurring in advancing years.

For Mr. Smith, the older African American man in the case example, Franklin's (1999) concept of invisibility, also discussed in Chapter 3, may be relevant. Mr. Smith spent his life defining himself as a successful, competent individual able to thrive despite the realities of race-based oppression in this country. Thus, Franklin would suggest that Mr. Smith made himself visible to those around him, defining himself on his terms rather than on those set by the dominant culture. As adaptive as this was, however, it might also cause increased difficulty for him in coping with cognitive decline. To lose the skills that he based his self-identity on, those abilities on which he built his balance between the demands of the dominant culture and those levered by his culture of origin, may multiply the threat beyond that of merely losing cognitive functioning. Mr. Smith may evidence significant fear that he is losing his sense of visibility and that as a result he may have little power to control his own destiny. This outcome is also likely to be evidenced in older African American men who may not have been able, either by circumstance or as a result of race-based oppression, to define their visibility so successfully. These individuals, who Wade (1996) would suggest are forced to base their racial self-perceptions more on external, dominant-culture-imposed ideals, may find it much more difficult to cope with cognitive decline, whether due to normal aging or pathology.

Some older male clients may also present for therapy with symptoms of depression or anxiety related to a perception that they are losing control and efficacy across life, yet at the same time they are determined to hide those symptoms for fear of further violating the gender role. Major's (1986) construct of cool pose is also relevant, as this may be one way in which African American men might deal with their perception of losing control. Therapists should be attuned to identifying whether the client has been experiencing personal and interpersonal conflict associated with normative changes in cognition but maintain vigilance in treating the client as a competent, self-determined adult. Culturally, implicit social standards suggest that when an older person shows cognitive weakness and slowing, others often take on roles of caregiving and protection, which is often disempowering to the older person. The therapeutic relationship between a therapist and an older man in psychotherapy can be an opportunity to reinforce personal autonomy and efficacy, which may be being undermined in the older man's broader social context. Older male clients should never be treated as less psychologically minded, less insightful, or unintelligent or senile. Instead, therapists should actively attempt to tailor therapeutic approaches to the slightly slowed processing speed an older man might experience, while concurrently reinforcing and encouraging autonomy and personal agency.

Nonnormative Cognitive Changes

In addition to addressing the normal cognitive changes associated with aging, therapists working with older men should be versed in the identification of signs of abnormal or malignant cognitive changes so that a client can appropriately be referred for further assessment and effective treatment. Cognitive impairment is generally defined as notable and measurable changes from previous functioning in domains of memory, language, reasoning, executive function, and visuospatial abilities, most likely secondary to a neurological disease process. As a result, cognitive impairment manifests behaviorally through difficulties with activities of daily living, behavioral and personality changes, and conflict in interpersonal relationships. Cognitive impairment as it relates to older adults can best be conceptualized on a continuum, ranging from mild cognitive impairment (MCI) to various forms of dementia, which often require additional evaluation and treatment.

Mild Cognitive Impairment

MCI, a relatively new syndrome, is defined to label presentation of memory decline that does not meet the full criteria for dementia due to lack of functional impairment but that includes a significant and measurable cognitive decline (Peterson et al., 2001). Although older men with this level of dysfunction can be amenable to psychotherapeutic treatment, therapists must continue to monitor cognition and functioning, as this form of cognitive impairment requires ongoing assessment and neurological treatment.

MCI is considered not a normal or benign cognitive change but instead a likely prodromal to dementia, most frequently Alzheimer's disease (AD). A proportion of individuals with MCI will continue at their current level of functioning, with no further development of impairment; approximately 6% to 25% will develop AD or a different form of dementia (Peterson et al., 2001). In a review of the MCI literature, Smith and Rush (2006) reported that approximately 12% of MCI patients progress to meet full criteria for dementia per year, with 7% to 10% of people diagnosed with MCI not meeting criteria for dementia on autopsy. Thus, MCI has been conceptualized as both a subclinical, prodromal form of AD and a categorization for subthreshold cognitive impairment that will not advance. Although it is difficult at this early time to differentiate MCI cases that remain static from those that progress into dementia, research on MCI (predementia and subclinical cognitive impairment) has suggested that these individuals have many biological markers similar to those with AD, although at a more moderate level. Specifically, researchers have found that people diagnosed with MCI had notable hippocampal atrophy (Jack et al., 1999) and changes in metabolic patterns in their brain (Kantarci et al., 2000) similar to those in people with AD.

Dementia

Malignant cognitive processes beyond MCI include a range of clinical dementias including the two most common forms of dementia: AD and vascular dementia. Although Alzheimer-type and vascular dementias can be distinct processes, studies (Welsh-Bohmer & Warren, 2006) have suggested that the two types of dementia co-occur in 75% of cases; vascular infarcts can prompt faster decline in individuals with AD as well (Sheng et al., 2007).

Alzheimer's Disease

AD is the most popularized diagnosis of dementia, likely because of the prevalence of this disease. AD accounts for approximately 50% of all cases of dementia (Breitner et al., 1999), and, unlike other forms of dementia, 98% of AD cases develop in people over the age of 50 (Smith & Rush, 2006).

AD is characterized by significant impairment in memory for new, rather than old, information and progressive deterioration of other cognitive abilities prompting increasing functional impairment and death. Individuals demonstrating Alzheimer-type memory concerns, primarily at the early and moderate stages of the disease, will demonstrate recollection of memories created long ago (as those memories were consolidated years earlier) but difficulty remembering recently occurring events because of the marked impairment in consolidation of new information into their memory. Resultant impairment found in these older adults includes difficulty remembering new information with little increase in recall even in the presence of recognition cues. Thus, an older male client suffering from AD may easily be able to recall details about his first car or his daughter's wedding several decades ago but may not be able to list what he ate for dinner the previous evening or identify when his daughter and her husband last came to visit.

AD presents as a gradual progression of increasing symptoms over time, with clinical signs including functional impairment and impairment in language including difficulties thinking of the appropriate word for an object, person, or situation (word-finding difficulties) or using similar but incorrect words (paraphasia). Initial indications of declining memory ability often include the older man repeating himself and easily becoming confused about the chronology of recent events.

Vascular Dementia

Vascular dementia is a form of cognitive impairment associated with vascular insults to the brain, ranging from a major stroke to a series of microvascular infarcts, leading to impairment in at least two cognitive domains with associated functional impairment. Vascular dementia is the second-most common form of dementia, accounting for approximately one third of dementia cases in older adults, with an incidence ranging from 6 to 12 cases per 1,000 people over 70 years old (Rojas-Fernandez & Moorhouse, 2009). Given that "vascular dementia" is a term used to describe cognitive impairment associated with vascular-infarct-related impairment in the brain, the pattern of deficits differs by person and area of the brain affected by the vascular event(s). Characteristic early-disease presentations of vascular dementia include sudden onset, uneven decline, difficulty with retrieval of new information, and variable executive dysfunction. Specifically, the nature of the cognitive and functional impairment tends to be stepwise in manner, as impairments arise concurrently with new vascular events and the culmination of TIAs, CVAs, and so on rather than a degenerating cognitive process. In the early stages of the disease, therapists may note that clients are able to remember information with the help of recognition cues, as the tracts associated with recall of memory, rather than consolidation of new memories, are damaged or impaired. Finally, given the multiple projections to the frontal cortex, which is essential in planning, initiating, and inhibiting behavior (i.e., executive function), deficits in executive functioning are often noted in older adults with vascular dementia.

Detecting Cognitive Impairment

When working with older men, the therapist must be astutely attuned to identifying the early stages of cognitive decline, as it will impact psychotherapeutic treatment outcomes. Assessing for change in cognitive ability includes awareness of the client's current functioning, level of carryover and retention between sessions, and change from baseline functioning. At the same time, it may be difficult to detect the early stages of cognitive impairment, especially with older male clients, as it is common for them to use preexisting coping strategies to compensate for impairment. Specifically, if an older man has a long pattern of being in control of most situations, he may activate this coping style when he is unable to recall information accurately or becomes confused. Reacting in a controlling manner, with anger or aggression, can often achieve the goal of hindering someone else's recognition of the older man's deficits or redirecting the other person's attention. Family members and friends may acquiesce to his statements and requests, attributing his behavior to him "just being Dad."

In addition, some older men may compensate for cognitive impairment through savvy interpersonal skills. Older men with pleasant, acquiescent styles (e.g., saying "yes" to everything) or those who are known to use humor are often not as easily identified as having problems with memory because they are interpersonally pleasing and accommodating to others. For Mr. Smith, culturally specific coping styles such as relying on family ties or being mindful of the needs of the community taking precedence over the needs of the individual may also be present. Other strategies used to cope with failing memory and cognitive functioning include the use of perceptive and observing behaviors, attending to cues from others.

Assessment Tools

Although an older male client with possible cognitive decline should be referred for a more thorough evaluation, several assessment instruments are available for initial screening or repeated measurement. The psychotherapist may want to administer either the Mini-Mental Status Exam (MMSE; Folstein, Folstein, & McHugh, 1975) or the St. Louis University Mental Status (SLUMS; Morley, 2003). The MMSE consists of 11 questions, testing five areas of cognitive functioning (orientation, registration, attention and calculation, recall, and language). This brief screening tool often takes less than 10 minutes to administer, and it differentiates from those experiencing cognitive impairment and those who are not. The SLUMS examination, which tends to take approximately 15 to 20 minutes to complete, consists of a 30-point screening questionnaire that tests for orientation, memory, attention, and executive functions.

Although both of these assessment instruments screen for cognitive impairment, neither are able to provide a diagnosis or should take the place of a more thorough evaluation. On a number of occasions, an older male client exhibiting cognitive change may be best served by a referral for a more complete medical or neuropsychological evaluation.

Working With the Diagnosis

Special attention must be given to objective measures of functioning, ways preexisting coping styles may be used to compensate for change in cognitive functioning, and how gender expression interacts with the older man's willingness to accept potential changes in cognitive ability. These issues are of particular importance for the older man to increase the probability of both receiving and accepting the appropriate treatment (e.g., medication for cognitive impairment if needed) and services in the home (e.g., in-home assistance or help from family members) to sustain the highest, most independent level of functioning possible. Referring to the case example, Mr. Smith is a successful African American man who had been accustomed to breaking through barriers by sheer will and determination, so acknowledging his potential weakness and need for help would be very threatening to him and his sense of self as a provider, authority figure, competent leader, and shrewd businessman. Recognition of his increasing limitations may challenge his socialized masculine role, possibly creating overreactive behaviors to prove his need to be viewed as someone who is intelligent, capable, and able to succeed in targeted endeavors. Thus, psychotherapy with Mr. Smith may be most successful if focus is placed on his strengths and previous accomplishments, such as verbal ability and being an effective businessman, to allow him to be agreeable to assistance in various domains of his life. Within the context of the therapeutic relationship, Mr. Smith may need to reexperience the process through which he first defined himself in relation to the dominant culture as well as his African American culture, in light of course of his changing ability levels.

Many older men may also resist recognizing or acknowledging cognitive and functional impairment because of male gender role socialization. Men who have defined themselves as leaders and authority figures throughout their lives may continue to interact in this manner even in the presence of cognitive and functional impairment. In addition, family members and significant others may fail to recognize the level of impairment given the older man's long-standing status and masculine stance. Again consider the case of Mr. Smith who was a prominent businessman, achieving despite overt and covert racism. Mr. Smith is well conditioned to push forward in the face of all obstacles, even dementia, based on his general mode of functioning. After having a stroke and completing an extensive course of rehabilitation with significant areas of improvement, Mr. Smith maintains many of his premorbid social skills, intelligence, and stamina; unfortunately, his memory and executive functioning are most likely impaired and not responsive to rehabilitation efforts. However, in social situations, he continues to be able to vigorously debate others, encourage his grandson to embark on creative new business ventures, and insist he remain at the head of his company. On initial presentation, Mr. Smith appears to be a wise, confident, healthy older African American man, without many, if any, residual effects from his stroke. However, on closer inspection of his functioning such as decision making, self-care, and complex planning, questions about his cognitive ability emerge.

Depression and Dementia

Cognitive impairment is frequently found in late-life depression, as cognitive decline can be intertwined or even present similarly to depression in some older men. Differentiating between the diagnosis of depression and dementia can be complicated, as can be the determination of their coexistence. Depression can be conceptualized as a prodromal presentation of dementia. Paterniti, Verdier-Taillefer, Dufouil, and Alpérovitch (2002) found that a combination of cognitive impairment with depression in older adults predicted further declining cognitive functioning four years later.

Alexopoulos and colleagues (1997) proposed that lesions in the brain due to vascular disease predispose, cause, or exacerbate depressive symptomatology. According to this theory, depression is conceptualized as depression with an onset in late life with concurrent medical evidence of vascular disease or risk factors and subsequent cognitive impairment with the following possible symptoms: executive dysfunction, psychomotor retardation, and limited insight or reason for depressive symptomatology (McDougall & Brayne, 2007). In a review of the vascular dementia literature, McDougall and Brayne (2007) found that vascular disease and depression were highly comorbid diseases and that vascular depression improved when an antidepressant was combined with a medication to treat cardiovascular disease.

Identification of the syndrome described as vascular dementia or coexisting cognitive impairment and depression is particularly important in older men given the incidence of cardiovascular disease in men, as well as the need for differential treatment of individuals who present with vascular-like symptoms or comorbid cognitive impairment. In addition, of those older men with cognitive problems associated with depression, some may resolve with treatment of depression whereas others will likely develop further cognitive impairment.

A further challenge, however, lies in separating symptoms from behaviors associated with male gender role socialization. Levant and his colleagues (e.g., Levant, Hall, Williams, & Hasan, 2009) described the construct of normative male alexithymia to explain the degree to which many adult men cannot access or describe their emotional experiences, in large part because of the long-term effects of being socialized to avoid such expressions. Differential diagnosis at this point is therefore essential for adequate treatment, as an older male client is more likely than not to demonstrate this symptom profile for several reasons, including potential vascular involvement, comorbid dementia, or a stoic experience of emotions secondary to male gender role socialization.

For example, a typical alexithymic vascular presentation often includes flat affect, avolition, and significant cognitive slowing. A male client with this behavior may also be unable to clearly identify why he feels depressed (e.g., depressive thoughts), instead seeming blunted, flat, and lacking any motivation or problem-solving skills. Or an additional challenge in working with Mr. Smith as an older African American male client may include that his culture traditionally allows, and even encourages, men to be more passionate in their emotional expression. Having a baseline becomes more important in this case so as to effectively differentiate between alexithymia, gender-role-based restriction of emotionality, and culturally based expression of emotionality.

DEMENTIA, CAREGIVING, AND GENDER

Older men can be impacted by the interaction between dementia and caregiving either as the caregiver or as the individual requiring care. Caregiving is often conceived of as emotional and instrumental support provided to an individual living with a chronic illness such as dementia. Caregiver burden (George & Gwyther, 1986) describes the aggregate impact of physical, psychological, social, and financial consequences related to caring for another individual (Pinquart & Sorensen, 2003). Ample literature exists regarding caregiving for an older adult with dementia given the pervasive and degenerative nature of the disease requiring long-standing supportive care, which is often provided at least in part by family members.

As dementia progresses from the mild range to the more advanced stages of the disease, problems worsen, thus increasing the burden on the caregiver. In addition, caring for individuals with cognitive impairment, even in the mild range, negatively impacts the emotional well-being of the caregiver such that depression, anxiety, and caregiver burnout intensify directly with the level of care provided (Garand, Dew, Eazor, DeKosky, & Reynolds, 2005). According to a comprehensive empirical review, caregiver burden and depression were significantly related to the level of physical and cognitive impairment of the care receiver, problematic behavior of the care receiver, hours of care provided per week, number of care tasks provided per week, and length of time filling the caregiver role (Pinquart & Sorensen, 2003).

Extensive research demonstrates a consistent pattern of results identifying that older women experience more negative consequences of caregiving when compared to men (Barusch & Spaid, 1989; Gallicchio, Siddiqi, Langenberg, & Baumgarten, 2002), including greater levels of depressive symptomatology (Bookwala & Schulz, 2000), less morale and greater strain (Collins & Jones, 1997), greater burden (Kao & McHugh, 2004), and greater cardiovascular reactivity related to caregiver-like stress (Atienza, Henderson, Wilcox, & King, 2001). However, Pinquart and Sorensen (2006) argued that the empirical literature does not fully support the assertion that men fare better than women in the caregiver role, noting any resulting gender differences were consistently small or limited.

For the studies that identified gender differences, there are several alternative explanations for the finding that women are more negatively affected by caregiving than men, one being men's hesitancy to report distress. Barusch and Spaid (1989) suggested that a degree of gender differences found in their data may represent men's unwillingness to acknowledge or report difficulties associated with caregiving, representing a gender role socialized behavior of not complaining, even if the extent of the challenge is great.

Men may experience less distress related to caregiving based on utilization of resources, social support, and coping mechanisms. Men have been found to utilize instrumental, problem-focused coping strategies in caregiving, which are related to less distress than emotion-focused coping strategies (Baker and Robertson, 2008). Therefore, an older man focusing on caregiving tasks such as going to appointments, cooking meals, or helping with showering may indeed do better psychologically than when implementing a coping strategy more specifically used by a woman to attempt to emotionally deal with the situation. Paradoxically, the task-oriented suppression of emotion can be an adaptive trait in older male caregivers, protecting them from the psychological distress associated with caregiving and allowing them to effectively perform the required duties. In this case, the socialized "just get it done" attitude serves as a positive buffer for the older man, whereas a more emotionally expressive individual may need additional assistance coping.

Older men in the caregiving role can also be conceptualized from the perspective of an adaptive activity congruent with gender role socialization for men. Of the limited research available, men have been thought to provide instrumental and problem-solving focused care rather than emotion-focused care (Baker & Robertson, 2008). In addition, several qualitative and quantitative research studies have suggested that men provide care as a duty to their spouse and sense of responsibility (Baker & Robertson, 2008; Mathew, Mattocks, & Slatt, 1990), engaging in caregiving through a manner that parallels dedication to their relationship in the past (Black, Schwartz, Caruso, & Hannum, 2008). Thus, through his role as a caregiver, an older man may derive a sense of honor and pride, congruent with his preexisting personal values, from performing challenging, demanding, and personal tasks for his significant other

(Black et al., 2008). This has also been conceptualized as men refocusing their dedication to work toward their new "work" as a caregiver (Harris, 1993). In these situations, men reported feeling appreciated and involved in meaningful activity as a caregiver (Matthews, Dunbar-Jacob, Sereika, Schulz, & McDowell, 2004), fulfilling personal needs previously met through their employment.

In addition, Black et al. (2008) suggested older men found a sense of pride and personal responsibility for providing care to their spouse, believing they were protecting their children from the burden. Within this framework, men may interpret caring for their significant others in later life as a transfer of their protective role from the workplace to personal care. Men holding strong gender role socialization may find caregiving to be a noble pursuit, caring for their spouse in a self-sufficient and goal-directed manner in order to fulfill promises made earlier in life. Caregiving can also allow older men a sense of purpose and control. Qualitative accounts have suggested that older men may at times approach caregiving from a perspective of personal power and autonomy; through creating a structured care schedule, the caregiver is able to reestablish a sense of control in an uncontrollable situation (Black et al., 2008). Although the *progression* of the dementia cannot be controlled, *how* the male caregiver deals with this progression can be controlled through the caregiving process.

It should be noted that the bulk of research on differences between men and women with regard to coping with caregiving has examined gender as a unitary construct rather than as adherence to gender role expectations and/or behaviors, which can lead to clinicians making generalizations rather than multifaceted assessments. As has been highlighted, masculinity and adherence to male gender role socialization is a heterogeneous phenomenon (e.g., Addis & Mahalik, 2003), and thus, a great deal of heterogeneity in reactions to caregiving exists depending on individual men and their expression of masculine gender. Exploration of the burden level, therefore, should include assessment of the potential protective and deleterious aspects of gender role expression impacting the relationship between caregiving and quality of life.

ADDRESSING MASCULINITY AND POTENTIAL LOSS OF ROLE FUNCTIONING DUE TO COGNITIVE IMPAIRMENT

There are numerous psychological and interpersonal implications of providing care to an older man with dementia, often being related to role definition, gender role expression, and help-seeking behavior. Men in general, and certainly in the case of Mr. Smith as an older African American man, who assume a more traditional gender role identity valuing strength, self-sufficiency, and autonomy, may find increased dependency on their caregiver uncomfortable and personally incongruent. As highlighted with continuity theory (Atchley, 1989), older adults operate in a manner consistent with previous roles and functions, applying past methods of functioning to current situations. With cognitive impairment and the associated functional decline, this can manifest in an older man refusing to acknowledge his cognitive and functional impairments (analogous to acknowledging weakness) and continuing to engage in tasks with an increased risk of injury or negative outcomes.

Mr. Smith, as an example, may continue to shovel snow from his walkway although he lacks the adequate judgment (due to his executive dysfunction) to determine appropriate boundaries of safety. When performing this task, he would be at risk for dressing inappropriately (not wearing gloves), walking haphazardly over areas of ice and snow, and having a delayed response time (physically catching himself when slipping on ice). His lack of insight and refusal to accept help, most likely due to the stroke as well as personality characteristics and socialized masculine traits, cause him to continue this dangerous behavior despite the physical risks and requests from his sons. Mr. Smith most likely would respond similarly to tasks associated with his personal finances and business. As a financial consultant, Mr. Smith prided himself on managing the family's day-to-day and investment finances. However, in light of his poor judgment, poor problem-solving ability, and impulsivity, Mr. Smith frequently forgot to pay bills, overdrew his checking account, and made poor decisions about his investments, thus leading to severe consequences. Addressing this in psychotherapy may require Mr. Smith to reconnect with his culturally acceptable reliance on those around him.

Mr. Smith may continue to refuse assistance, whether it falls within the domestic or business realm, in instrumental activities of daily living from either his sons or professional caregivers, as he may believe any acceptance of help is a sign of weakness. His long-term pattern of "never giving up" may also come into play. Working with Mr. Smith in psychotherapy, the therapist may embrace Mr. Smith's values by reframing household assistance such as cooking and cleaning as being similar to contracting with a specialty service as he would in his business. This allows the client to capitalize on his strengths in a manner nonthreatening to his gender role identity, which is essential to maintaining his personal worth, while permitting caregivers to provide assistance, creating a safer and more positive environment and overall increased functioning for Mr. Smith. In this case, a win–win situation would be achieved. Mr. Smith is allowed to continue to be "Mr. Smith," and his sons achieve some sense of reassurance of his safety and well-being as negative consequences within the home environment are minimized.

Each older male client will require a unique, creative approach in addressing challenges that present because of his declining cognitive functioning or his stepping into the caregiver role. For example, some older men will be relieved to be free of certain activities or responsibilities; others will opt or even demand to continue to engage in activities although they may not have the background or skill set or, in Mr. Smith's situation, cognitive or physical abilities to do so (e.g., paying household bills even though he has difficulty writing checks or shoveling snow even though he has difficulty with balance and gait). Exploring the functional nature of this behavior, as well as how the older man may be able to continue to feel efficacy in his life in a way that is most appropriate given his current level of functioning, is at the core of the psychotherapeutic process. The key is to carefully and fully clarify the older man's individual preferences, with attention to detail and specific issues, and then place this within the overall context of his individual personality traits, values, and socialized masculine identity. Focusing on what can be arranged rather than on possible difficulties or barriers, keeping an open mind and a willingness to be flexible, and using creativity will often result in discovering a viable solution that at a minimum limits loss or distress, with the potential to increase the quality of life for the older male client and his family. As another illustration, again keeping in mind Mr. Smith's worldview, the therapist may work with the client and his family to negotiate agreement that the management of the finances be shared with his sons under the condition that Mr. Smith continue to teach them about finances and investments. This would once more allow Mr. Smith to keep his self-identify, worth, and dignity, while sanctioning consequential decisions to be monitored by his sons and providing opportunity for the family to continue to work together and ensure well-thought-out, logical investment business plans.

CAPACITY ASSESSMENT AND GENDER ROLE SOCIALIZATION

As cognitive impairment worsens, an older man and his family may face questions about his ability to independently make appropriate decisions for himself. In most medical settings, this is referred to as "capacity," or one's ability to arrive at appropriate decisions based on the given facts of a situation. Whether an older man has the capacity to make a decision is a context-specific question. That is, "competency," which is a legal term and court judgment, suggests that an individual cannot make decisions in a legal domain and is a global assessment of one's ability to make decisions. However, the aim when considering capacity, which is a medical and clinical judgment, is to determine whether the older man has the cognitive capacity for a particular task or question, asking, "Does this individual have capacity for _____?"

Unfortunately, there is no gold standard or universal criteria for capacity, as capacity is contextual (which does not easily allow for one standard) and can fluctuate over time. There are, however, themes that seem to permeate the extant literature. That is, focus should be directed toward the client's functional ability, rather than a diagnosis, as a diagnosis by itself cannot determine capacity.

In general, capacity can be assessed in four main areas: (a) medical (Is the client able to understand the medical procedure by comprehending risk, benefit, and choice?), (b) financial (What is the client's financial performance in handling change, paying bills, and so on? Is he able to act in his own best interest, having a judgment about financial matters?), (c) contractual (Does he have the ability to comprehend the situation?), and (d) testamentary (Is this individual able to make a will, in that does he have a basic understanding of what a will is, who his heirs are, what his current assets are, and what his plan for distribution is?). The general purpose of such an assessment is to balance the freedom and autonomy of the older man while protecting him from making poor decisions because of cognitive impairment.

Trained psychologists or physicians routinely make capacity decisions. However, the aftermath of such determinations are often explored in psychotherapy given the significant impact results can have on the older man and his family. With a pervasive male gender role socialization to remain in control, be competent, and serve as the head of the family, an older man may interpret the loss of these roles because of cognitive impairment as threatening and distressing. In addition, family members who are accustomed to interacting with the older man as the dominant figure in the family may also experience negative reactions to his cognitive change. For some family members, this can lead to compensation through overreaction by taking full control, stripping the older man of any power. Others, however, may attempt to offset the professional's decision for lack of capacity by adamantly denying difficulties and placing both the older man and themselves at risk by expecting him to function as he once did. For example, an older man who has advancing dementia and no longer believes he is able to maneuver a car safely may continue to drive his wife to her appointments and shopping because of her requests and the socialized male role of the husband driving the car. She may expect him to continue driving when he no longer can remember how to find his way home, rationalizing that she will always be in the car to provide him directions. In a reversed situation, the adult son of an older man recently diagnosed with MCI may use his power of attorney privilege to sell his father's car while the older man is out of the country enjoying a three-week cruise. The son reasons that given the recent diagnosis, his father can no longer drive the car safely, and he believes it will be easier for his father to accept the loss of his driving privileges if the car is no longer in the garage when he returns from his vacation. With good intentions, the son mistakenly believes that he is "protecting" his father's dignity by taking care of this in his absence; thus, the older man will not have to witness the selling of the car.

Unfortunately, the hallmark of many forms of cognitive impairment is limited insight into one's own deficits. Thus, when family members are called on to make a decision out of necessity, the obligation to select the logical choice, albeit an unpopular one from the older man's perspective, has the potential to place strain on family relationships, challenging the comfort level and socialized roles of everyone involved. Older men who strongly adhere to a male gender role may attempt to regain efficacy and control in a gender-role-specific manner that will become increasingly more maladaptive, placing mounting pressure on family members or caregivers. Although perhaps unintentionally, through demanding return to his rightful position as head of the family and being granted full control of all decisions, the older man places others in the difficult situation of either giving in to him, possibly causing detrimental consequences, or having to challenge him for power, an unenviable choice for anyone. Regardless of the specific details of the particular situation, these dynamics can produce intense pressure, conflict, and distress for the older man, as well as his family.

CONCLUSION

Cognitive change for older men occurs across a spectrum, ranging from the normative aging slowing process to the severely impaired, and it impacts not only the older man but also his family. Subtle changes in cognition should be monitored, with assessment regarding the possibility of the cognitive decline being related to depression, normative aging, or emerging dementia. Cognitive decline can influence how older men view themselves in regard to self-worth and masculine identity, their level of functioning and ability to maintain continuity from earlier life, and the role they fill in their family. Older men engaging in psychotherapy to cope with cognitive changes will benefit most from positive directed actions based on flexibility and creativity.

TABLE 9.1   Guidelines for Working With Men Experiencing Cognitive Decline

- Cognitive decline can challenge an older man's sense of worth, masculinity, and perceived role in the family.
- Mild cognitive impairment (MCI) includes a measurable decline in at least one cognitive domain but does not meet criteria for dementia.
  - Some older men with MCI symptoms will progress into dementia.
- The two most common forms of dementia are Alzheimer's disease and vascular.
  - Dementia is often intertwined with depression.
- Older men can be impacted by the interaction between dementia and caregiving either as the caregiver or as the individual requiring care.
  - The impact of caregiving ranges from burdensome to an adaptive way to preserve self-identity (e.g., continuity from previous roles).
- Psychotherapy with older men experiencing cognitive changes should be supportive, strength based, flexible, and creative.
  - Psychotherapy with older adults with moderate to severe dementia is not recommended.

10

Concluding Thoughts on Psychotherapy With Older Men

Much of what has been written in this book addresses ways in which the practice of psychotherapy can provide therapeutic support for older men. However, to ensure optimal benefit, therapists must first make adjustments to overcome older men's potential for negative perceptions of psychotherapy. The competent therapist will meet with the older male client in a manner and place in which he feels as at ease as possible, avoiding elder speak, becoming fluent in the masculine voice, and developing a therapeutic relationship characterized by its complementarity nature. An awareness of the client's context, both as it exists currently and as to how it operated to construct his masculinity and lived life, is critical. Ideally, there will be acceptance of who and where the client is currently in his life span and an understanding of the influences of his age, cohort, and gender.

However, it may be a long process for an older man to accept the offer for assistance and become comfortable with identifying and discussing his emotions; grief and fear, for example, as well as anger at his current situation, may be difficult to admit to himself, let alone verbalize or share with another. The older man may already be feeling vulnerable and perceive that through psychotherapy he surrenders more control, a process he is likely to see as the fault of the therapist. The therapist must be comfortable with the older man's expression of emotion, including blame and anger, or even initial rebuff of the therapeutic relationship and refrain from personalizing his behaviors. Do not give up on the older man; perhaps the more he resorts to male dominant behavior, the more he needs authentic acceptance and understanding of the challenges he faces because of both his age and the socialized masculine role. Trust in him and the strengths he has collected during his many years of living and perhaps remind him and yourself the following: "More powerful than the will to win is the courage to begin" (unknown author).

COMPETENCE IN WORKING WITH OLDER ADULTS

A number of resources have been developed to assist therapists providing psychotherapy to older adults. National organizations such as the American Counseling Association (ACA), National Association of Social Workers (NASW), American Association for Marriage and Family Therapy, and American Psychological Association (APA) offer professional standards and guidelines for working with older adults.

The Association for Adult Development and Aging, a division of the ACA that addresses counseling concerns across the life span, provided one of the earliest documents addressing competence in working with older adults, the *Gerontological Competencies for Counselors and Human Development Specialists* (American Association for Counseling and Development, 1990). These guidelines indicated that therapists working with older adults required specialty training in areas such as the normative experiences of aging, the impaired older adult, techniques for counseling older individuals, and ethics, in addition to normal human development. Focusing on knowledge, skill, and attitudes, examples of competency in working with older adults included the therapist's ability to (a) identify and specify major growth and development needs of older persons; (b) specify major remediation needs of older persons; (c) demonstrate effective communication skills with older persons of both genders and from different racial, social, and economic circumstances; and (d) identify and accurately distinguish between demographic facts and ageist prejudice in statements about older persons and aging.

In response to the expanding older population and the increasing numbers of older adults with chronic illnesses and advances in medical technology that extend life spans, NASW (2004) issued standards for practice in end-of-life care. Eleven basic standards such as knowledge, self-awareness, treatment planning, and ethics were identified regarding clinical work in assessment, treatment, resource linkage, advocacy, and leadership in work with the dying. These guidelines are meant to be applied within the context of an aging population and culturally diverse families and communities that may hold different beliefs about illness, wellness, and medical care. NASW highlighted the culturally related factors involved in working with older adults, including perceptions of illness and death, communication styles, decision making, family support, and use of service delivery system. The recent *Multicultural Competency in Geropsychology* (APA, Committee on Aging, 2009) provides further explorations of key issues regarding the infusion of multicultural competence when working with older adults.

The "Guidelines for Psychological Practice With Older Adults" (APA, 2004) offer therapists a frame of reference for engaging in clinical work with older adults, as well as general information in the areas of attitudes, general aspects of aging, clinical issues, assessment, intervention, and consultation. Building on these guidelines, the Pikes Peak Model (Knight, Karel, Hinrichsen, Qualls, & Duffy, 2009) is the most recent contribution in the area of competence in providing services to an aging population in the areas of attitudes, knowledge, and skills. Key elements include (a) knowledge about the normal aging process, (b) increased self-awareness in the area of human differences, (c) exposure to the variety of settings where older adults are treated (e.g., hospitals, long-term care facilities, client's home), (d) understanding of the interdisciplinary and team approach to treatment necessary when working with older adults, and (e) knowledge of ethical and legal issues unique to working with an older adult population.

FUTURE DIRECTIONS

By definition, addressing the future is speculative in nature. The goal of this book is to move into the next frontier in the understanding of socialized masculinity, cohort, and aging and their connectedness in the manifestations of those older men engaged in psychotherapy. Although extensive research is needed regarding older men and the psychotherapeutic process, certainly much is to be gained by including men of all racial backgrounds and sexual orientations to understand the complexity of aging and gender role conflict.

Many of the linkages offered in the chapters of this book require empirical validation and potential refinement. All components involved in the psychotherapeutic process with older men call for further investigation to be tested and ultimately verified as the extant literatures on aging and the psychology of men continue to collectively grow. Indeed, with careful and determined exploration, there will be discovery of additional questions that lead the literature in new and exciting directions. This is the essence of not only the scientific method but also the psychotherapeutic process.

APPENDIX: RECOMMENDED RESOURCES

American Psychological Association. (2004). Guidelines for psychological practice with older adults. *American Psychologist, 59*(4), 236–260. Retrieved from http://www.apa.org/practice/guidelines/older-adults.pdf

> This document was designed to "assist psychologists in evaluating their own readiness for working clinically with older adults" (p. 237), offering guidance regarding the need for further education, training, and consultation. Twenty guidelines, and their descriptive narrative, are organized under six headings: (a) Attitudes; (b) General Knowledge About Adult Development, Aging, and Older Adults; (c) Clinical Issues; (d) Assessment; (e) Intervention, Consultation, and Other Service Provision; and (f) Education. There is also a significant reference list.

American Psychological Association, Committee on Aging. (2009). *Multicultural competency in geropsychology.* Washington, DC: Author. Retrieved from http://www.apa.org/pi/aging/programs/pipeline/multicultural-competency.pdf

> The purpose of this report is to (a) explore the key issues regarding the infusion of multicultural competence throughout geropsychology; (b) make recommendations for future action addressing practice, research, education and training, and public policy issues; and (c) inform psychologists of existing resources to improve their own multicultural competence in working with older adults. The text is subdivided into five sections, including one devoted specifically to additional resources. Each contains specific recommendations and related discussion; there is also a significant reference list.

Knight, B. G., Karel, M. J., Hinrichsen, G. A., Qualls, S. H., & Duffy, M. (2009). Pikes Peak Model for training in professional geropsychology. *American Psychologist, 64*(3), 205–214.

> The model is an aspirational, competencies-based approach to training professional geropsychologists. The model is presented under the rubric of knowledge, attitudes, and skills with the subsequent competencies described across levels of training. There is an extensive appendix that summarizes the key aspects of each competency and provides specific examples.

National Association of Social Workers. (2004). *NASW standards for palliative and end of life care*. Washington, DC: Author. Retrieved from http://www.socialworkers.org/practice/bereavement/standards/standards0504New.pdf

This document offers 11 standards of care designed to enhance the knowledge of mental health practitioners of the skills, knowledge, values, and methods needed to work effectively with consumers when providing service in both palliative care and end-of-life situations. Each standard is summarized and described, with specific examples provided.

REFERENCES

Addis, M., & Mahalik, J. (2003). Men, masculinity, and the contexts of help seeking. *American Psychologist, 58*(1), 5–14.

Agency for Healthcare Research & Quality. (1992). Acute pain management: Operative or medical procedures and trauma, clinical practice guideline No. 1. *AHCPR Publication No. 92-0032*, 116–117.

Alexopoulos, G. S. (2005). Depression in the elderly. *Lancet, 365*, 1961–1970.

Alexopoulos, G. S., Abrams, R. C., Young, R. C., & Shamoian, C. A. (1988a). Cornell Scale for Depression in Dementia. *Biological Psychiatry, 23*, 271–284.

Alexopoulos, G. S., Abrams, R. C., Young, R. C., & Shamoian, C. A. (1988b). Use of the Cornell scale in nondemented patients. *Journal of the American Geriatric Society, 36*, 230–236.

Alexopoulos, G. S., Meyers, B. S., Young, R. C., Kakuma, T., Silbersweig, D., & Charlson, M. (1997). Clinically defined vascular depression. *American Journal of Psychiatry, 154*, 562–565.

Alpass, F. M., & Neville, S. (2003). Loneliness, health and depression in older males. *Aging and Mental Health, 7*, 212–216.

Ambrose, S. E. (1998). *Citizen soldiers: The U.S. Army from the Normandy beaches to the bulge to the surrender of Germany*. New York: Simon and Schuster.

American Association for Counseling and Development. (1990). *Gerontological competencies for counselors and human development specialists*. Alexandria, VA: Author.

American Cancer Society. (2008). *Cancer facts and figures for African-Americans 2007–2008*. Atlanta, GA: Author.

American Geriatrics Society. (2009, August). *New pain management guidelines issued by the AGS*. Washington, DC: Author.

American Psychiatric Association. (1994). *Diagnostic and statistical manual of mental disorders* (4th ed.). Washington, DC: Author.

American Psychiatric Association. (2000). *Diagnostic and statistical manual of mental disorders* (Text revision). Washington, DC: Author.

American Psychological Association. (2002). Ethical principles of psychologists and code of conduct. *American Psychologist, 57*(12), 1060–1073.

American Psychological Association. (2003). Guidelines on multicultural education, training, research, practice, and organizational change for psychologists. *American Psychologist, 58*, 377–402.

American Psychological Association. (2004). Guidelines for psychological practice with older adults. *American Psychologist, 59*(4), 236–260.

American Psychological Association, Committee on Aging. (2009). *Multicultural competency in geropsychology*. Washington, DC: Author.

American Society of Consultant Pharmacists. (2003). *Seniors at risk: Medication-related problems among older Americans*. Alexandria, VA: Author.

Anton, R., O'Malley, S., Ciraulo, D., Cisler, R., Couper, D., Donovan, D., et al. (2006). Combined Pharmacotherapies and Behavioral Interventions for Alcohol Dependence: The COMBINE Study: A Randomized Controlled Trial. *JAMA: Journal of the American Medical Association, 295*, 2003–2017.

Antonovsky, A., & Sagy, S. (1990). Confronting developmental tasks in the retirement transition. *The Gerontologist, 30*(3), 362–368.

Applegate, J. S. (1997). Theorizing older men. In J. I. Kosberg & L. W. Kaye (Eds.), *Elderly men: Special problems and professional challenges* (pp. 1–15). New York: Springer.

Ashforth, B. (2001). *Role transitions in organizational life: An identity based perspective*. Mahwah, NJ: Lawrence Erlbaum.

Atchley, R. (1976). Selected social and psychological differences between men and women in later life. *Journal of Gerontology, 31*(2), 204–211.

Atchley, R. (1999). *Continuity and adaptation in aging: Creating positive experiences*. Baltimore, MD: Johns Hopkins University Press.

Atchley, R. C. (1989). A continuity theory of normal aging. *The Gerontologist, 29*, 183–190.

Atienza, A. A., Henderson, P. C., Wilcox, S., & King, A. C. (2001). Gender differences in cardiovascular response to dementia caregiving. *The Gerontologist, 41*(4), 490–498.

Atkinson, D. R., Wampold, B. E., Lowe, S. M., Matthews, L., & Ahn, H. N. (1998). Asian American preferences for counselor characteristics: Application of the Bradley–Terry–Luce model to paired data comparison data. *The Counseling Psychologist, 26*, 101–123.

Atkinson, R. M., Tolson, R. L., & Turner, J. A. (1993). Factors affecting outpatient treatment compliance of older male problem drinkers. *Journal of Studies on Alcohol, 54*, 102–106.

Ayers, C., Sorrell, J., Thorp, S., & Wetherell, J. (2007). Evidence-based psychological treatments for late-life anxiety. *Psychology and Aging, 22*(1), 8–17.

Baca-Zinn, M. (1982). Chicano men and masculinity. *Journal of Ethnic Studies, 10*, 20–44.

Baker, K., & Robertson, N. (2008). Coping with caring for someone with dementia: Reviewing the literature about men. *Aging & Mental Health, 12*, 413–422.

Baltes, M. M. (1996). *The many faces of dependency in old age*. New York: Cambridge University Press.

Baltes, P. B. (1997). On the incomplete architecture of human ontogeny: Selection, optimization, and compensation as foundation of developmental theory. *American Psychologist, 52*, 366–380.

Baltes, P. B., & Baltes, M. M. (1990). Psychological perspectives on successful aging: The model of selective optimization with compensation. In P. B. Baltes & M. M. Baltes (Eds.), *Successful aging: Perspectives from the behavioral sciences* (pp. 1–34). New York: Cambridge University Press.

Banks, S. M., Pandiani, J. A., Schacht, L. M., & Gauvin, L. M. (2000). Age and mortality among White male problem drinkers. *Addiction, 95*, 1249–1254.

Barber, J. S., & Mobley, M. (1999). Counseling gay adolescents. In A. M. Horne & M. S. Kiselica (Eds.), *Handbook of counseling boys and adolescent males* (pp. 161–178). Thousand Oaks, CA: Sage.

Barnett, R. C., Marshall, N. L., & Pleck, J. H. (1992). Men's multiple roles and their relationship to men's psychological distress. *Journal of Marriage and the Family, 54,* 358–367.

Barrick, C., & Conners, G. J. (2002). Relapse prevention and maintaining abstinence in older adults with alcohol-use disorders. *Drugs Aging, 19,* 583–594.

Bartels, S. J., Coakley, E. H., Zubritsky, C., Ware, J. H., Miles, K. M., Areán, P. A., Chen, H., Oslin, D. W., Llorente, M. D., Costantino, G., Quijano, L., McIntyre, J. S., Linkins, K. W., Oxman, T. E., Maxwell, J., & Levkoff, S. E. (2004). Improving access to geriatric mental health services: A randomized trial comparing treatment engagement with integrated versus enhanced referral care for depression, anxiety, and at-risk alcohol use. *American Journal of Psychiatry, 161,* 1455–1462.

Barusch, A. S., & Spaid, W. (1989). Gender differences in caregiving: Why do women report greater burden? *The Gerontologist, 29*(5), 667–676.

Batiuchok, D. (2009). An exploratory study of protective factors for individuals at risk for developing anxiety disorders. *Dissertation Abstracts International, 69,* 5011.

Beck, A. T., & Steer, R. A. (1990). *Manual for the Beck Anxiety Inventory.* San Antonio, TX: Psychological Corporation.

Bem, S. L. (1981). Gender schema theory: A cognitive account of sex typing. *Psychological Review, 88,* 354–364.

Bereger, J. M., Levant, R., McMillan, K. K., Kelleher, W., & Sellers, A. (2005). Impact of gender role conflict, traditional masculinity ideology, alexithymia, and age on men's attitudes toward psychological help seeking. *Psychology of Men and Masculinity, 6,* 73–78.

Bergin, A. E., & Garfield, S. L. (1994). *Handbook of psychotherapy and behavior change* (4th ed.). Oxford, UK: John Wiley.

Bernardes, S. F., Keogh, E., & Lima, M. L. (2008). Bridging the gap between pain and gender research: A selective literature review. *European Journal of Pain, 12,* 427–440.

Best, D. (2010). Gender. In M.H. Bornstein (Ed.), *Handbook of cultural developmental science* (pp. 209–222). New York, NY: Psychology Press.

Birren, J. E. (1999). Theories of aging: A personal perspective. In V. L. Bengtson & K. Warner Schaie (Eds.), *Handbook of theories of aging* (pp. 459–572). New York: Springer.

Black, H. K., Schwartz, A. J., Caruso, C. J., & Hannum, S. M. (2008). How personal control mediates suffering: Elderly husbands' narratives of caregiving. *Journal of Men's Studies, 16*(2), 177–192.

Blaine, B. (2000). *The psychology of diversity: Perceiving and experiencing social difference.* Mountain View, CA: Mayfield.

Blazer, D., & Wu, L. (2009). The epidemiology of at-risk and binge drinking among middle-aged and elderly community adults: National Survey on Drug Use and Health. *The American Journal of Psychiatry, 166,* 1162–1169.

Blier, M. J., & Blier-Wilson, L. A. (1989). Gender differences in self-rated emotional expressiveness. *Sex Roles, 7,* 287–295.

Blow, F. C., Brower, K. J., Schulenberg, J. E., Demodananberg, L. M., Young, J. P., & Beresford, T. P. (1992). The Michigan Alcoholism Screening Test–Geriatric Version (MAST-G): A new elderly specific screening instrument. *Alcoholism: Clinical and Experimental Research, 16*, 372.

Blow, F. C., Walton, M. A., Chermack, S. T., Mudd, S. A., & Brower, K. J. (2000). Older adult treatment outcome following elder-specific inpatient alcoholism treatment. *Journal of Substance Abuse Treatment, 19*, 67–75.

Bohlmeijer, E., Smit, F., & Cuijpers, P. (2003). Effects of reminiscence and life review on late-life depression: A meta-analysis. *International Journal of Geriatric Psychiatry, 18*, 1088–1094.

Bookwala, J., & Schulz, R. (2000). A comparison of primary stressors, secondary stressors, and depressive symptoms between elderly caregiving husbands and wives: The Caregiver Health Effects Study. *Psychology and Aging, 15*, 607–616.

Bordin, E. (1979). The generalizability of the psychoanalytic concept of the working alliance. *Psychotherapy: Theory, Research and Practice, 16*(3), 252–260.

Bowen, M. (1978). Family therapy in clinical practice. New York: Jason Aronson.

Breitner, J. C. S., Wyse, B. W., Anthony, J. C., Welsh-Bohmer, K. A., Steffens, D. C., Norton, M. C., et al. (1999). APOE e4 count predicts age when prevalence of AD increases, then declines: The Cache County Study. *Neurology, 53*, 321–331.

Brim, O. G., Ryff, C. D., & Kessler, R. C. (Eds.). (2004). *How healthy are we? A national study of well-being at midlife*. Chicago: University of Chicago Press.

Brody, L. R., & Hall, J. A. (1993). Gender and emotion. In M. Lewis & J. M. Haviland (Eds.), *Handbook of emotions* (pp. 447–460). New York: Guilford.

Brooks, G. R. (1990). Post Vietnam gender role strain: A needed concept? *Professional Psychology: Research and Practice, 21*, 18–25.

Brooks, G. R. (1998). *A new psychotherapy for traditional men*. San Francisco: Jossey-Bass.

Brooks, G. R. (2001). Counseling and psychotherapy for male military veterans. In G. R. Brooks & G. E. Good (Eds.), *A new handbook of counseling and psychotherapy with men* (Vol. 1, pp. 206–226). San Francisco: Jossey-Bass.

Brooks, G. R., & Good, G. E. (Eds.). (2001a). *The new handbook of psychotherapy and counseling with men: A comprehensive guide to settings, problems, and treatment approaches* (Vol. 1). San Francisco: Jossey-Bass.

Brooks, G. R., & Good, G. E. (Eds.). (2001b). *The new handbook of psychotherapy and counseling with men: A comprehensive guide to settings, problems, and treatment approaches* (Vol. 2). San Francisco: Jossey-Bass.

Broverman, I. K., Vogel, S. R., Broverman, D. M., Clarkson, F. E., & Rosenkrantz, P. S. (1972). Sex-role stereotypes: A current appraisal. *Journal of Social Issues, 28*, 59–78.

Brown, T. A., Barlow, D. H., & Liebowitz, M. R. (1994). The empirical basis of generalized anxiety disorder. *American Journal of Psychiatry, 151*, 1272–1280.

Buss, D. M. (1995). Evolutionary psychology: A new paradigm for psychological science. *Psychological Inquiry, 6*, 1–30.

Bye, D., & Pushkar, D. (2009). How need for cognition and perceived control are differentially linked to emotional outcomes in the transition to retirement. *Motivation and Emotion, 33*(3), 320–332.

Calasanti, T., & King, N. (2007). "Beware of the estrogen assault": Ideals of old manhood in anti-aging advertisements. *Journal of Aging Studies, 21*(4), 357–368.

Calvo, E., Haverstick, K., & Sass, S. (2009). Gradual retirement, sense of control, and retirees' happiness. *Research on Aging, 31*(1), 112–135.

Canales, G. (2000). Gender as subculture: The first division of multicultural diversity. In I. Cuéllar & F. A. Paniagua (Eds.), *Handbook of multicultural mental health: Assessment and treatment of diverse populations.* New York: Academic Press.

Canary, D. J., Emmers-Sommer, T. M., & Faulkner, S. (1997). *Sex and gender differences in personal relationships.* New York: Guilford.

Carise, D., Dugosh, K. L., McLellan, A. T., Camilleri, A., Woody, G. E., & Lynch, K. G. (2007). Prescription oxycontin abuse among patients entering addiction treatment. *American Journal of Psychiatry, 164,* 1750–1756.

Carr, D., House, J. S., Kessler, R. C., Nesse, R. M., Sonnega, J., & Wortman, C. (2000). Marital quality and psychological adjustment to widowhood among older adults: A longitudinal analysis. *Journals of Gerontology, 55B*(4), S197–S207.

Casas, J. M., Turner, J. A., & de Esparaza, C. A. R. (2001). Machismo revisited in a time of crisis: Implications for understanding and counseling Hispanic men. In G. R. Brooks & G. E. Good (Eds.), *A new handbook of counseling and psychotherapy with men* (Vol. 2, pp. 754–779). San Francisco: Jossey-Bass.

Center for Substance Abuse Treatment. (1998). *Substance abuse among older adults: Treatment improvement protocol series* (DHHS Pub. No. SMA: 98-3179). Washington, DC: U.S. Government Printing Office.

Centers for Disease Control and Prevention. (2007). *Web-based Injury Statistics Query and Reporting System (WISQARS).* National Center for Injury Prevention and Control, CDC (producer). Retrieved November 1, 2009, from www.cdc.gov/injury/wisqars/index.html.

Charmaz, K. (1991). *Good days, bad days: The self in chronic illness and time.* New Brunswick, NJ: Rutgers University Press.

Charmaz, K. (1994). Identity dilemmas of chronically ill men. *Sociological Quarterly, 35,* 269–288.

Chin, J. L. (1998). Mental health services and treatment. In L. C. Lee & N. W. S. Zane (Eds.), *Handbook of Asian American psychology* (pp. 485–504). Thousand Oaks, CA: Sage.

Chiriboga, D. A., Yee, B. W. K., & Jang, Y. (2005). Minority and cultural issues in late-life depression. *Clinical Psychology: Science and Practice, 12,* 358–363.

Chua, P., & Fujino, D. C. (1999). Negotiating new Asian-American masculinities: Attitudes and gender expectations. *Journal of Men's Studies, 7,* 391–413.

Cialdini, R. B., & Trost, M. R. (1998). Social influence: Social norms, conformity, and compliance. In D. T. Gilbert, S. T. Fiske, & G. Lindzey (Eds.), *The handbook of social psychology* (Vol. 2, pp. 151–192). New York: McGraw-Hill.

Clarke, L. H., & Griffin, M. (2008). Failing bodies: Body image and multiple chronic conditions in later life. *Qualitative Health Research, 18,* 1084–1092.

Clatterbaugh, K. (2001). African American men: The challenge of racism. In T. F. Cohen (Ed.), *Men and masculinity: A text reader* (pp. 409–421). Belmont, CA: Wadsworth.

Cleeland, C. S. (1989). Measurement of pain by subjective report. In C. R. Chapman & J. D. Loeser (Eds.), *Advances in pain research and therapy, Volume 12: Issues in pain measurement* (pp. 391–403). New York: Raven Press.

Cochran, S. V. (2005). Assessing and treating depression in men. In G. E. Good & G. R. Brooks (Eds.), *The new handbook of psychotherapy and counseling with men* (pp. 121–133). San Francisco: Jossey-Bass.

Cochran, S. V., & Rabinowitz, F. (2000). *Men and depression: Clinical and empirical perspectives.* San Diego, CA: Academic Press.

Cohane, G., & Pope, H. (2001). Body image in boys: A review of the literature. *International Journal of Eating Disorders, 29*(4), 373–379.

Collins, A., Goldman, N., & Rodríguez, G. (2008). Is positive well-being protective of mobility limitations among older adults? *Journals of Gerontology: Series B: Psychological Sciences and Social Sciences, 63*(6), P321–P327.

Collins, C., & Jones, R. (1997). Emotional distress and morbidity in dementia carers: A matched comparison of husbands and wives. *International Journal of Geriatric Psychiatry, 12,* 1168–1173.

Collison, B. (1987). *Counseling aging men: Handbook of counseling and psychotherapy with men* (pp. 165–177). Thousand Oaks, CA: Sage.

Comas-Díaz, L., & Jacobsen, F. (1991). Ethnocultural transference and countertransference in the therapeutic dyad. *American Journal of Orthopsychiatry, 61*(3), 392–402.

Comas-Díaz, L., & Jacobsen, F. (1995). The therapist of color and the White patient dyad: Contradictions and recognitions. *Cultural Diversity and Mental Health, 1*(2), 93–106.

Conner, K., & Heesacker, M. (1993, August). Sex and emotional communication accuracy. In M. Wong (Chair), *Celebrating masculinity.* Symposium conducted at the meeting of the American Psychological Association, Toronto, Canada.

Corrigan, P. (2004). How stigma interferes with mental health care. *American Psychologist, 59,* 614–625.

Corrigan, P. W., & Matthews, A. K. (2003). Stigma and disclosure: Implications for coming out of the closet. *Journal of Mental Health, 12,* 235–248.

Courtenay, W. H. (2000). Constructions of masculinity and their influence on men's well-being: A theory of gender and health. *Social Science and Medicine, 50,* 1385–1401.

Courtenay, W. H. (2001). Counseling men in medical settings: The six-point HEALTH plan. In G. R. Brooks & G. E. Good (Eds.), *The new handbook of psychotherapy and counseling with men* (Vol. 1, pp. 59–91). San Francisco: Jossey-Bass.

Courtenay, W. H. (2005). Counseling men in medical settings. In G. E. Good & G. R. Brooks (Eds.), *The new handbook of psychotherapy and counseling with men* (pp. 29–53). San Francisco: Jossey-Bass.

Cross, W. E., Jr. (1995). The psychology of Nigrescence: Revising the Cross model. In J. G. Ponterotto, J. M. Casas, L. A. Suzuki, & C. M. Alexander (Eds.), *Handbook of multicultural counseling* (pp. 93–122). Thousand Oaks, CA: Sage.

Crystal, S., Sambamoorthi, U., Walkup, J., & Akincigil, A. (2003). Diagnosis and treatment of depression in the elderly Medicare population: Predictors, disparities, and trends. *Journal of the American Geriatrics Society, 51*(12), 1718–1728.

Cuijpers, P., Van Straten, A., Smit, F., & Andersson, G. (2009). Is psychotherapy for depression equally effective in younger and older adults? A meta-regression analysis. *International Psychogeriatrics, 21*(1), 16–24.

Cumming, E., Henry, W. E., & Damianopoulos, E. (1961). A formal statement of disengagement theory. In E. Cumming & W. E. Henry (Eds.), *Growing old: The process of disengagement.* New York: Basic Books.

Davis, C., & Nolen-Hoeksema, S. (2001). Loss and meaning: How do people make sense of loss? *American Behavioral Scientist, 44*(5), 726–741.

De la Cancela, V. (1986). A critical analysis of Puerto Rican machismo: Implications for clinical practice. *Psychotherapy, 23,* 291–296.

Deutsch, C., & Gilbert, L. (1976). Sex role stereotypes: Effects on perceptions of self and others and on personal adjustment. *Journal of Counseling Psychology, 23,* 373–379.

Duffy, M. (1999). Using process dimensions in psychotherapy: The case of the older adult. In M. Duffy (Ed.), *Handbook of counseling and psychotherapy with older adults* (pp. 3–20). Hoboken, NJ: John Wiley.

Dupree, L., & Schonfeld, L. (1999). Management of alcohol abuse in older adults. In M. Duffy (Ed.), *Handbook of counseling and psychotherapy with older adults* (pp. 632–649). Hoboken, NJ: John Wiley.

Duran, E. (1990). *Transforming the soul wound.* Berkeley, CA: Folklore Institute.

Duran, E., & Duran, B. (1995). *Native American postcolonial psychology.* Albany: State University of New York Press.

Eisler, R. M. (1995). The relationship between masculine gender role stress and men's health risk. In R. F. Levant & W. S. Pollack (Eds.), *A new psychology of men.* New York: Basic Books.

Eisler, R. M., Skidmore, J. R., & Ward, C. H. (1988). Masculine gender-role stress: Predictor of anger, anxiety, and health risk behaviors. *Journal of Personality Assessment, 52,* 133–141.

Emslie, C., Ridge, D., Ziebland, S., & Hunt, K. (2006). Men's accounts of depression: Reconstructing or resisting hegemonic masculinity? *Social Science and Medicine, 62,* 2246– 2257.

Erikson, E. (1959). Identity and the life cycle: Selected papers. *Psychological Issues,* 11–171.

Ewing, J. A. (1984). Detecting alcoholism: The CAGE Questionaire. *Journal of the American Medical Association, 252,* 1905–1907.

Farrell, W. (1999). *The myth of male power.* New York: Simon and Schuster.

Festinger, L. (1957). *A theory of cognitive dissonance.* Evanston, IL: Row, Peterson.

Festinger, L. (1964). *Conflict, decision, and dissonance.* Stanford, CA: Stanford University Press.

Fielden, M. (1992). Depression in older adults: Psychological and psychosocial approaches. *British Journal of Social Work, 22*(3), 291–307.

Fingerhood, M. (2000). Substance abuse in older people. *Journal of the American Geriatrics Society, 48,* 985–995.

Fischer, E. H., & Farina, A. (1995). Attitudes toward seeking professional psychological help: A shortened form and considerations for research. *Journal of College Student Development, 36*, 368–373.

Fisher, J. D., Nadler, A., & Whitcher-Alagna, S. (1982). Recipient reactions to aid. *Psychological Bulletin, 91*, 27–54.

Fisher, J. D., Nadler, A., & Whitcher-Alagna, S. (1983). Four conceptualizations of reactions to aid. In J. D. Fisher, A. Nadler, & B. M. DePaulo (Eds.), *New directions in helping: Vol. 1. Recipient reactions to aid* (pp. 51–84). San Diego, CA: Academic Press.

Folstein, M. F., Folstein, S. W., & McHugh, P. R. (1975). "Mini mental state": A practical method of grading the cognitive state of patients for the clinician. *Journal of Psychiatric Residence, 12*, 189–198.

Franklin, A. J. (1997). Invisibility syndrome in psychotherapy with African American males. In R. L. Jones (Ed.), *African American mental health*. Hampton, VA: Cobb & Henry.

Franklin, A. J. (1999). Invisibility syndrome and racial identity development in psychotherapy and counseling African American men. *The Counseling Psychologist, 27*, 761–793.

Freysinger, V. J., Alessio, H., & Mehdizadeh, S. (1993). Re-examining the morale-physical health-activity relationship: A longitudinal study of time changes and gender differences. *Activities Adaptation and Aging, 17*, 25–41.

Gallagher-Thompson, D., & Coon, D. (2007). Evidence-based psychological treatments for distress in family caregivers of older adults. *Psychology and Aging, 22*(1), 37–51.

Gallicchio, L., Siddiqi, N., Langenberg, P., & Baumgarten, M. (2002). Gender differences in burden and depression among informal caregivers of demented elders in the community. *International Journal of Geriatric Psychiatry, 17*, 154–163.

Gallo, J. J., Zubritsky, C., Maxwell, J., Nazar, M., Bogner, H. R., Quijano, L. M., Syropoulos, H. J., Cheal, K. L., Chen, H., Sanchez, H., Dodson, J., & Levkoff, S. E. (2004). Primary care clinicians evaluate integrated and referral models of behavioral health care for older adults: Results from a multistate effectiveness trial. *Annals of Family Medicine, 2*, 305–309.

Garand, L., Dew, M. A., Eazor, L. R., DeKosky, S. T., & Reynolds, C. F. (2005). Caregiver burden and psychiatric morbidity in spouses of persons with mild cognitive impairment. *International Journal of Geriatric Psychiatry, 20*, 512–522.

George, L. K., & Gwyther, L. P. (1986). Caregiver well-being: A multidimensional examination of family caregivers of demented adults. *The Gerontologist, 26*(3), 253–259.

Gerschick, T., & Miller, A. (1995). Coming to terms: Masculinity and physical disability. *Men's health and illness: Gender, power, and the body* (pp. 183–204). Thousand Oaks, CA: Sage.

Gibbons, F. X. (1999). Social comparison as a mediator of response shift. *Social Science and Medicine, 48*, 1517–1530.

Gilbert, M. (2004). *The Second World War: A complete history*. New York: Holt.

Goffman, E. (1963). *Stigma: Notes on the management of spoiled identity*. Englewood Cliffs, NJ: Prentice Hall.

Good, G. E., & Sherrod, N. B. (2001). Men's problems and effective treatments: Theory and empirical support. In G. R. Brooks & G. E. Good (Eds.), *A new handbook of counseling and psychotherapy with men* (Vol. 1, pp. 22–40). San Francisco: Jossey-Bass.

Goodwin, S., & Fiske, S. (2001). Power and gender: The double-edged sword of ambivalence. In R. K. Unger (Ed.), *Handbook of the psychology of women and gender* (pp. 358–366). Hoboken, NJ: John Wiley.

Hamilton, M. (1959). The assessment of anxiety states by rating. *British Journal of Medical Psychiatry, 32*, 50–55.

Hamilton, M. (1960). A rating scale for depression. *Journal of Neurology, Neuro-surgery and Psychiatry, 23*, 56–62.

Han, B., Gfroerer, J., Colliver, J., & Penne, M. (2009). Substance use disorder among older adults in the United States in 2020. *Addiction, 104*, 88–96.

Harman, J., Veazie, P., & Lyness, J. (2006). Primary care physician office visits for depression by older Americans. *Journal of General Internal Medicine, 21*(9), 926–930.

Harris, I., Torres, J. B., & Allender, D. (1994). The responses of African American men to dominant norms of masculinity within the United States. *Sex Roles, 31*, 703–719.

Harris, P. (1993). The misunderstood caregiver? A qualitative study of the male caregiver of Alzheimer's disease victims. *The Gerontologist, 33*, 551–556.

Harrison, J. (1995). Roles, identities, and sexual orientation: Homosexuality, heterosexuality, and bisexuality. In R. F. Levant & W. S. Pollack (Eds.), *A new psychology of men* (pp. 359–383). New York: Basic Books.

Hatch, L. (1992). Gender differences in orientation toward retirement from paid labor. *Gender and Society, 6*(1), 66–85.

Heesacker, M., & Bradley, M. M. (1997). Beyond feelings: Psychotherapy and emotion. *The Counseling Psychologist, 25*, 201–219.

Heesacker, M., & Prichard, S. (1992). In a different voice, revisited: Men, women, and emotion. *Journal of Mental Health Counseling, 14*(3), 274–290.

Heesacker, M., Prichard, S., & Socherman, R. (1994). Mythopoetry, antisexism, and the Zax: A reply to Foley, Good and Mintz, and Scher. *Journal of Mental Health Counseling, 16*(2), 245–260.

Heesacker, M., Wester, S. R., Vogel, D. L., Wentzel, J. T., Goodholm, C. R., Jr., & Mejia-Millan, C. M. (1999). Gender-based emotional stereotyping. *Journal of Counseling Psychology, 46*, 417–429.

Helms, J. E. (1990). *Black and white racial identity: Theory, research, and practice.* New York: Greenwood.

Heo, M., Murphy, C. F., Fontaine, K. R., Bruce, M. L., & Alexopoulos, G. S. (2008). Population projection of U.S. adults with lifetime experience of depressive disorder by age and sex from year 2005 to 2050. *International Journal of Geriatric Psychiatry, 23*, 1266–1270.

Heppner, M., & Heppner, P. (2001). Addressing the implications of male social-ization for career counseling. In G. R. Brooks & G. E. Good (Eds.), *The new handbook of psychotherapy and counseling with men: A comprehensive guide to settings, problems, and treatment approaches* (Vols. 1–2, pp. 369–386). San Francisco: Jossey-Bass.

Hill, R. D. (2005). *Positive aging: A guide for mental health professionals and con-sumers.* New York: W. W. Norton.

Hills, H. I., Carlstrom, A., & Evanow, M. (2001). Consulting with men in business and industry. In G. R. Brooks & G. E. Good (Eds.), *The new handbook of psychotherapy and counseling with men* (Vol. 1, pp. 126–145). San Francisco: Jossey-Bass.

Hinrichsen, G. A. (2008). Interpersonal psychotherapy as a treatment for depression in later life. *Professional Psychology: Research and Practice, 3,* 306–312.

Hoffman, B. M., Papas, R. K., Chatkoff, D. K., & Kerns, R. D. (2007). Meta-analysis of psychological interventions for chronic low back pain. *Health Psychology, 26,* 1–9.

Horne, A. M., & Kiselica, M. S. (Eds.). (1999). *Handbook of counseling boys and adolescent males.* Thousand Oaks, CA: Sage.

Horvath, A., & Greenberg, L. (1994). *The working alliance: Theory, research, and practice.* Oxford, UK: John Wiley.

Huyck, M., & Gutmann, D. (1999). Developmental issues in psychotherapy with older men. In M. Duffy (Ed.), *Handbook of counseling and psychotherapy with older adults* (pp. 77–90). Hoboken, NJ: John Wiley.

Isaksson, K., & Gunn, J. (2000). Adaptation to continued work and early retirement following downsizing: Long-term effects and gender differences. *Journal of Occupational and Organizational Psychology, 73*(2), 241–256.

Isaksson, K., & Johansson, G. (2000). Adaptation to continued work and early retirement following downsizing: Long-term effects and gender differences. *Journal of Occupational and Organizational Psychology, 73,* 241–256.

Isenhart, C. (2005). Treating substance abuse in men. In G. E. Good & G. R. Brooks (Eds.), *The new handbook of psychotherapy and counseling with men* (pp. 134–146). San Francisco: Jossey-Bass.

Jack, C. J., Peterson, R. C., Xu, Y. C., O'Brien, P. C., Smith, G. E., Ivnik, R. J., et al. (1999). Prediction of AD with MRI-based hippocampal volume in mild cognitive impairment. *Neurology, 52,* 1397–1403.

Jin, L., & Christakis, N. A. (2009). Investigating the mechanism of marital mortality reduction: The transition to widowhood and quality of health care. *Demography, 46*(3), 605–625.

Jolliff, D., & Horne, A. (1996). Group counseling for middle-class men. In P. Arrendondo (Ed.), *Men in groups: Insights, interventions, and psychoeducational work* (pp. 51–68). Washington, DC: American Psychological Association.

Jones, J., & Pugh, S. (2005). Ageing gay men: Lessons from the sociology of embodiment. *Men and Masculinities, 7*(3), 248–260.

Kamel, H. K., Phlaven, M., Malekgoudarzi, B., et al. (2001). Utilizing pain assessment tools increases the frequency of diagnosing pain among elderly nursing home residents. *Journal of Pain Symptom Management, 21,* 450–455.

Kantarci, K., Jack, C. R., Jr., Xu, Y. C., Campeua, N. G., O'Brien, P. C., Smith, G. E., et al. (2000). Regional metabolic patterns in mild cognitive impairment and Alzheimer's disease: A H-MRS study. *Neurology, 55,* 210–217.

Kantamneni, N., Smothers, M., Christianson, H. F., & Wester, S. R. (in press). Role induction: A potential method for improving men's perceptions of career counseling. *Career Development Quarterly.*

Kao, H. F., & McHugh, M. L. (2004). The role of caregiver gender and caregiver burden in nursing home placements for elderly Taiwanese survivors of stroke. *Research in Nursing and Health, 27*(2), 121–134.

Karel, M. J., Lynch, B., & Moye, J. (2000). Patterns of lifetime alcohol use in a clinical sample of older male veterans. *Clinical Gerontologist, 22*, 55–71.

Katz, S., & Marshall, B. (2003). New sex for old: Lifestyle, consumerism, and the ethics of aging well. *Journal of Aging Studies, 17*, 3–16.

Katz, S., & Marshall, B. (2004). Is the functional 'normal'? Aging, sexuality and the bio-marking of successful living. *History of the Human Sciences, 17*, 53–75.

Kessler, R. C., Brown, R. L., & Broman, C. L. (1981). Sex differences in psychiatric help-seeking: Evidence from four large-scale surveys. *Journal of Health and Social Behavior, 22*, 49–64.

Kilianski, S. E. (2003). Explaining heterosexual men's attitudes toward women and gay men: The theory of exclusively masculine identity. *Psychology of Men and Masculinity, 4*, 37–56.

Kilmartin, C. (2005). Depression in men: Communication, diagnosis and therapy. *Journal of Men's Health and Gender, 2*, 95–99.

Kim, E. J., O'Neil, J. M., & Owen, S. V. (1996). Asian American men's acculturation and gender role conflict. *Psychological Reports, 79*, 95–104.

Kimmel, M. S., & Messner, M. A. (Eds.). (1992). *Men's lives* (2nd ed.). Boston: Pearso.

King, C., Van Hasselt, V., Segal, D., et al. (1994). Diagnosis and assessment of substance abuse in older adults: Current strategies and issues. *Addict Behavior, 19*, 41–55.

Kiselica, M. S. (1999). Avoiding simplistic stereotypes about boys and men and the challenge of thinking complexly: A call to the profession and a farewell address to SPSMM. *SPSMM Bulletin: The Society for the Psychological Study of Men and Masculinity, 4*(1–2), 16.

Kiselica, M. S. (2001). A male-friendly therapeutic process with school-age boys. In G. R. Brooks & G. E. Good (Eds.), *The new handbook of psychotherapy and counseling with men: A comprehensive guide to settings, problems, and treatment approaches* (Vol. 2, pp. 43–58). San Francisco: Jossey-Bass.

Knight, B. G. (2004). *Psychotherapy with older adults* (3rd ed.). New York: Sage.

Knight, B. G., Karel, M. J., Hinrichsen, G. A., Qualls, S. H., & Duffy, M. (2009). Pikes Peak Model for training in professional geropsychology. *American Psychologist, 64*(3), 205–214.

Kochman, T., & Mavrelis, J. (2009). *Corporate tribalism: White men/White women, and cultural diversity at work*. Chicago: University of Chicago Press.

Kogan, J. N., Edlstein, B. A., & McKee, D. R. (2000). Assessment of anxiety in older adults. *Journal of Anxiety Disorder, 14*, 109–132.

Kramarow, E., Lubitz, J., Lentzner, H., & Gorina, Y. (2007). Trends in the health of older Americans, 1970–2005. *Health Affairs, 26*, 1417–1425.

Krasucki, C., Howard, R., & Mann, A. (1999). Anxiety and its treatment in the elderly. *International Psychogeriatrics, 11*, 25–45.

Krein, S. L., Heisler, M., Piette, J. D., Butchart, A., & Kerr, E. A. (2007). Overcoming the influence of chronic pain on older patients' difficulty with recommended self-management activities. *The Gerontologist, 47*, 61–68.

Kroenke, K., Spitzer, R. L., & Williams, J. B. (2001). The PHQ-9: Validity of a brief depression severity measure. *Journal of General Internal Medicine, 169*, 606–613.

Kupers, T. A. (2001). Psychotherapy with men in prison. In G. R. Brooks & G. E. Good (Eds.), *The new handbook of psychotherapy and counseling with men* (Vol. 1, pp. 170–184). San Francisco: Jossey-Bass.

Kuruvilla, T., Fenwich, C. D., Haque, M. S., & Vassilas, C. A. (2006). Elderly depressed patients: What are their views on treatment options? *Aging and Mental Health, 10,* 204–206.

LaFrance, M., & Banaji, M. (1992). Toward a reconsideration of the gender–emotion relationship. In M. S. Clark (Ed.), *Review of personality and social psychology* (Vol. 14, pp. 178–201). Newbury Park, CA: Sage.

Lazarus, R., & Folkman, S. (1986). Cognitive theories of stress and the issue of circularity. In M.H. Appley & R. Trumbell (Eds.), *Dynamics of stress: Physiological, psychological, and social perspectives* (pp. 63–80). New York, NY: Plenum Press.

Lazur, R. F. (1998). Men in the family: A family system approach to treating men. In W. S. Pollack & R. F. Levant (Eds.), *A new psychotherapy for men.* Hoboken, NJ: John Wiley.

Lazur, R., & Majors, R. (1995). Men of color: Ethnocultural variations of male gender role strain. In R. Levant & W.S. Pollack (Eds.), *A new psychology of men* (pp. 337–358). New York, NY: Basic Books.

Leach, L. S., Christensen, H., Mackinnon, A. J., Windsor, T. D., & Butterworth, P. (2008). Gender differences in depression and anxiety across the adult lifespan: The role of psychosocial mediators. *Social Psychiatry and Psychiatric Epidemiology, 43,* 983–998.

Lebowitz, B., Pearson, J., Schneider, L., Reynolds, C., Alexopoulos, G., Bruce, M., et al. (1997). Diagnosis and treatment of depression in late life: Consensus statement update. *JAMA: Journal of the American Medical Association, 278*(14), 1186–1190.

Leit, R., Pope, H., & Gray, J. (2001). Cultural expectations of muscularity in men: The evolution of Playgirl centerfolds. *International Journal of Eating Disorders, 29*(1), 90–93.

Levant, R. F. (1995). Toward the reconstruction of masculinity. In R. F. Levant & W. S. Pollack (Eds.), *The new psychology of men.* New York: Basic Books.

Levant, R. F. (1996). A new psychology of men. *Professional Psychology: Research and Practice, 27,* 259–265.

Levant, R. (2001a). Desperately seeking language: Understanding, assessing, and treating normative male alexithymia. In G. R. Brooks & G. E. Good (Eds.), *The new handbook of psychotherapy and counseling with men: A comprehensive guide to settings, problems, and treatment approaches* (Vols. 1–2, pp. 424–443). San Francisco: Jossey-Bass.

Levant, R. (2001b). The crises of boyhood. In G. R. Brooks & G. E. Good (Eds.), *The new handbook of psychotherapy and counseling with men: A comprehensive guide to settings, problems, and treatment approaches* (Vols. 1–2, pp. 355–368). San Francisco: Jossey-Bass.

Levant, R. F., & Brooks, G. R. (1997). *Men and sex: New psychological perspectives.* New York: Wiley.

Levant, R. F., Hall, R. J., Williams, C. M., & Hasan, N. T. (2009). Gender differences in alexithymia. *Psychology of Men and Masculinity, 10,* 190–203.

Levant, R. F., & Pollack, W. S. (Eds.). (1995). *A new psychology of men.* New York: Basic Books.

Levine, S. B. (2000). *Father courage: What happens when men put family first.* New York: Harcourt.

Levinson, D. J. (1978). *The seasons of a man's life.* New York: Knopf.

Lindesay, J., Briggs, K., & Murphy, E. (1989). The guy's/age concern survey: Prevalence rates of cognitive impairment, depression and anxiety in an urban elderly community. *British Journal of Psychiatry, 155,* 317–329.

Lips, H. M. (2007). *Sex and gender: An introduction* (6th ed.). Mountain View, CA: Mayfield.

Little, J., Reynolds, C., III, Dew, M., Frank, E., Begley, A., Miller, M., et al. (1998). How common is resistance to treatment in recurrent, nonpsychotic geriatric depression? *American Journal of Psychiatry, 155*(8), 1035–1038.

Liu, W. M. (2003). Exploring the lives of Asian American men: Racial identity, male role norms, gender role conflict, and prejudicial attitudes. *Psychology of Men and Masculinity, 3,* 107–118.

Livneh, H. (1991). A unified approach to exiting models of adaptation to disability: A model of adaptation. In R. P. Marinelli & A. E. Dell Orto (Eds.), *The psychological and social impact of disability* (3rd ed., pp. 111–138). New York: Springer.

Logsdon, R., McCurry, S., & Teri, L. (2007). Evidence-based psychological treatments for disruptive behaviors in individuals with dementia. *Psychology and Aging, 22*(1), 28–36.

Lorenz, K., Rosenfeld, K., & Wenger, N. (2007). Quality indicators for palliative and end-of-life: A quantitative review. *Journal of Clinical Psychology in Medical Settings, 16,* 254–262.

Lukassen, J., & Beaudet, M. P. (2005). Alcohol dependence and depression among heavy drinkers in Canada. *Social Science and Medicine, 61,* 1658–1667.

Lunde, L., Nordhus, I. H., & Pallesen, S. (2009). The effectiveness of cognitive and behavioural treatment of chronic pain in the elderly. *Journal of the American Geriatrics Society, 55*(2), S318–S326.

Mackenzie, C. S., Gekoski, W. L., & Knox, V. J. (2006). Age, gender, and the underutilization of mental health services: The influence of help-seeking attitudes. *Aging and Mental Health, 10,* 574–582.

Mahalik, J. R. (2005). Cognitive therapy for men. In G. E. Good & G. R. Brooks (Eds.), *The new handbook of psychotherapy and counseling with men* (pp. 217–233). San Francisco: Jossey-Bass.

Mahalik, J. R., Good, G. E., & Englar-Carlson, M. (2003). Masculinity scripts, presenting concerns, and help seeking: Implications for practice and training. *Professional Psychology: Research and Practice, 34*(2), 123–131.

Majors, R. (1986). Cool pose: The proud signature of Black survival. *Changing Men: Issues in Gender, Sex, and Politics, 17,* 5–6.

Majors, R. (1991). Nonverbal behavior and communication styles among African Americans. In R. Jones (Ed.), *Black psychology* (3rd ed., pp. 269–294). Berkeley, CA: Cobb & Henry.

Majors, R. (1994). *The American Black male: His present status and future.* Chicago: Nelson and Hall.

Majors, R., & Mancini Billson, J. (1992). *Cool pose: The dilemmas of Black manhood in America.* New York: Lexington Books.

Manstead, A. S. R. (1998). Gender differences in emotion. In B. M. Clinchy & J. K. Norem (Eds.), *The gender and psychology reader* (pp. 236–264). New York: New York University Press.

Markowitz, J. D. (2007). Post-traumatic stress disorder in an elderly combat veteran: A case report. *Military Medicine, 172*(6), 659.

Marks, I. M., & Mathews, A. M. (1979). Brief standardized self-rating for phobic patients. *Behaviour Research and Therapy, 17*, 263–267.

Mathew, L. J., Mattocks, K., & Slatt, L. M. (1990). Exploring the roles of men: Caring for demented relatives. *Journal of Gerontological Nursing, 16*(10), 20–25.

Matthews, J. T., Dunbar-Jacob, J., Sereika, S., Schulz, R., & McDowell, B. J. (2004). Preventive health practices: Comparison of family caregivers 50 and older. *Journal of Gerontological Nursing, 30*(2), 46–54.

McCarthy, J., & Holliday, E. (2004). Help-seeking and counseling within a traditional male gender role: An examination from a multicultural perspective. *Journal of Counseling and Development, 82*(1), 25–30.

McCreary, D., & Sasse, D. (2000). An exploration of the drive for muscularity in adolescent boys and girls. *Journal of American College Health, 48*(6), 297–304.

McCurry, S., Logsdon, R., Teri, L., & Vitiello, M. (2007). Sleep disturbances in caregivers of persons with dementia: Contributing factors and treatment implications. *Sleep Medicine Reviews, 11*(2), 143–153.

McDougall, F., & Brayne, C. (2007). Systematic review of the depressive symptoms associated with vascular conditions. *Journal of Affective Disorders, 104*, 25–35.

Menninger, J. A. (2002). Assessment and treatment of alcoholism and substance related disorders in the elderly. *Bull Menninger Clinic, 66*(2), 166–183.

Menza, M. A., & Liberatore, B. L. (1998). Psychiatry in geriatric neurology practice. *Neurologic Clinics, 16*, 611–633.

Merrick, E. L., Horgan, C. M., Hodgkin, D., Garnick, D. W., Houghton, S. F., Panas, L., Saltz, R., & Blow, F. C. (2008). Unhealthy drinking patterns in older adults: Prevalence and associated characteristics. *Journal of the American Geriatrics Society, 58*, 214–223.

Meyer, N., & Nimoy, L. (Writers/Directors). (1991). *Star Trek VI: The undiscovered country* [Motion picture]. United States: Paramount Pictures.

Meyer, T., Miller, M., Metzger, R., & Borkovec, T. D. (1990). Development and validity of the Penn State Worry Scale. *Behavior Research and Therapy, 28*, 487–495.

Milberg, D. (2010). *World War II on the big screen: 450+ Hollywood films.* Jefferson, NC: McFarland.

Miller, A. M., & Iris, M. (2002). Health promotion attitudes and strategies in older adults. *Health Education and Behavior, 29*, 249–267.

Miller, P., Brown, T., DiNardo, P., & Barlow, D. (1994). The experimental induction of depersonalization and derealization in panic disorder and nonanxious subjects. *Behaviour Research and Therapy, 32*(5), 511–519.

Miller, W. R. (1985). Motivation for treatment: A review with special emphasis on alcoholism. *Psychological Bulletin, 98*, 84–107.

Miller, W. R., Villanueva, M., Tonigan, J. S., & Cuzmar, I. (2007). Are special treatments needed for special populations? *Alcoholism Treatment Quarterly, 25*, 63–78.

Mohlman, J. (2004). Psychosocial treatment of late-life generalized anxiety disorder: Current status and future directions. *Clinical Psychology Review, 24,* 149–169.

Moore, A., & Stratton, D. (2002). *Resilient widowers: Older men speak for themselves.* New York: Springer.

Morley, J. (2003). *New dementia screening tool: SLUMS.* St. Louis, MO: St. Louis University.

Nadler, A., & Fisher, J. D. (1986). The role of threat to self-esteem and perceived control in recipient reaction to help: Theory development and empirical validation. In L. Berkowitz (Ed.), *Advances in experimental social psychology* (Vol. 19, pp. 81–122). San Diego, CA: Academic Press.

National Association of Social Workers. (2001). *NASW standards for cultural competence in social work practice.* Washington, DC: Author.

National Association of Social Workers. (2004). *NASW standards for palliative and end of life care.* Washington, DC: Author.

National Center for Health Statistics. (2009). *Health, United States, 2008* (with chartbook). Hyattsville, MD: Author. Retrieved November 22, 2009, from http://www.cdc.gov/nchs/data/hus/hus08.pdf#001

National Institute of Aging. (2009). Talking with your older patient: A clinician's handbook. Retrieved from http://www.nia.nih.gov/HealthInformation/Publications/ClinicianHB.

Nemes, S., Rao, P. A., Zeiler, C., Munly, K., Holtz, K. D., & Hoffman, J. (2004). Computerized screening of substance abuse problems in a primary care setting: Older vs. younger adults. *American Journal of Drug and Alcohol Abuse, 30,* 627–642.

Nolen-Hoeksema, S. (1987). Sex differences in unipolar depression: Evidence and theory. *Psychological Bulletin, 101,* 259–282.

Nolen-Hoeksema, S. (2001). Ruminative coping and adjustment to bereavement. In M. Stroebe, R. O. Hansson, W. Stroebe, & H. Schut (Eds.), *Handbook of bereavement research: Consequences, coping, and care* (pp. 545–562). Washington, DC: American Psychological Association Press.

O'Brien, R., Hunt, K., & Hart, G. (2005). "It's caveman stuff, but that is to a certain extent how guys still operate": Men's accounts of masculinity and help seeking. *Social Science and Medicine, 61,* 503–516.

Office of Applied Studies. (2004). Results from the 2003 National Survey on Drug Use and Health: National findings (DHHS Publication No. SMA 04-3964, NSDUH Series H-25). Rockville, MD: Substance Abuse and Mental Health Services Administration.

Okuda, M., Okuda, D., & Mirek, D. (1994). *The Star Trek encyclopedia: A reference guide to the future.* New York: Pocket Books.

O'Neil, J. M. (1981a). Male sex-role conflict, sexism, and masculinity: Implications for men, women, and the counseling psychologist. *The Counseling Psychologist, 9,* 61–80.

O'Neil, J. M. (1981b). Patterns of gender role conflict and strain: Sexism and fear of femininity in men's lives. *Personnel Guidance Journal, 60,* 203–210.

O'Neil, J. M. (1995). The gender role journey workshop: Exploring sexism and gender role conflict in a coeducational setting. In M. Andronico (Ed.), *Men in groups: Insights, interventions, and psychoeducational work.* Washington, DC: APA Books.

O'Neil, J. M. (2008). Summarizing twenty-five years of research on men's gender-role conflict using the gender role conflict scale: New research paradigms and clinical implications. *The Counseling Psychologist, 36,* 358–445.

O'Neil, J. M., Good, G. E., & Holmes, S. (1995). Fifteen years of theory and research on men's gender role conflict. In R. F. Levant & W. S. Pollack (Eds.), *The new psychology of men* (pp. 164–206). New York: Basic Books.

O'Neil, J. M., Helms, B., Gable, R., David, L., & Wrightsman, L. (1986). Gender role conflict scale: College men's fear of femininity. *Sex Roles, 14,* 335–350.

Oslin, D. W. (2005). Treatment of late-life depression complicated by alcohol dependence. *Journal of the American Geriatrics Society, 13,* 491–500.

Owens, G. P., Baker, D. G., Kasckow, J., Ciesla, J. A., & Mohamed, S. (2005). Review of assessment and treatment of PTSD among elderly American armed forces veterans. *International Journal of Geriatric Psychiatry, 20,* 1118–1130.

Paterniti, S., Verdier-Taillefer, M. H., Dufouil, C., & Alpérovitch, A. (2002). Depressive symptoms and cognitive decline in elderly people. *British Journal of Psychiatry, 181,* 406–410.

Pederson, E. L., & Vogel, D. L. (2007). Male gender role conflict and willingness to seek counseling: Testing a mediation model on college-aged men. *Journal of Counseling Psychology, 54,* 373–384.

Peretti, P., & Wilson, C. (1975). Voluntary and involuntary retirement of aged males and their effect on emotional satisfaction, usefulness, self-image, emotional stability, and interpersonal relationships. *International Journal of Aging and Human Development, 6*(2), 131–138.

Petersen, R. C., Smith, G. E., Waring, S. C., Ivnik, R. J., Kokmen, E., & Tangalos, E. G. (1997). Aging, memory, and mild cognitive impairment. *International Psychogeriatrics, 9,* 65–69.

Petersen, R. C., Stevens, J. C., Ganguli, M., Tangalos, E. G., Cummings, J. L., & DeKosky, S. T. (2001). Practice parameter: Early detection of dementia; mild cognitive impairment (an evidence-based review). Report of the Quality Standards Subcommittee of the American Academy of Neurology. *Neurology, 8,* 1133–1142.

Pinquart, M., & Schindler, I. (2007). Changes of life satisfaction in the transition to retirement: A latent-class approach. *Psychology and Aging, 22,* 442–455.

Pinquart, M., & Sorensen, S. (2003). Differences between caregivers and non-caregives in psychological health and physical health: A meta-analysis. *Psychology and Aging, 18*(2), 250–267.

Pinquart, M., & Sörensen, S. (2006). Gender Differences in Caregiver Stressors, Social Resources, and Health: An Updated Meta-Analysis. *The Journals of Gerontology: Series B: Psychological Sciences and Social Sciences, 61B,* 33–45.

Plant, E. A., Hyde, J. S., Keltner, D., & Devine, P. G. (2000). The gender stereotyping of emotions. *Psychology of Women Quarterly, 24,* 81–92.

Pleck, J. H. (1981). *The myth of masculinity.* Cambridge, MA: MIT Press.

Pleck, J. H. (1995). The gender role strain paradigm: An update. In R. F. Levant & W. S. Pollack (Eds.), *The new psychology of men* (pp. 11–32). New York: Basic Books.

Pollack, W. (1992). Should men treat women? Dilemmas for the male psychotherapist: Psychoanalytic and developmental perspectives. *Ethics & Behavior, 2,* 39–49.

Pollack, W. (1998). The trauma of Oedipus: Toward a new psychoanalytic psychotherapy for men. In W. Pollack & R. Levant (Eds.), *New psychotherapy for men* (pp. 13–34). Hoboken, NJ: John Wiley.

Pollack, W., & Levant, R. (1998). *New psychotherapy for men.* Hoboken, NJ: John Wiley.

Quintana, S., Troyano, N., & Taylor, G. (2001). Cultural validity and inherent challenges in quantitative methods for multicultural research. In J. G. Ponterotto, J. M. Casas, L. A. Suzuki, & C. M. Alexander (Eds.), *Handbook of multicultural counseling* (2nd ed., pp. 604–630). Thousand Oaks, CA: Sage.

Rabinowitz, F. E., & Cochran, S. V. (2002). *Deepening psychotherapy with men.* Washington, DC: American Psychological Association.

Rabinowitz, F. E., & Cochran, S. V. (2008). Men and therapy: A case of masked male depression clinical case studies. Clinical Case Studies, 7, 575–591.

Raschko, R. (1990). The gatekeeper model or the isolated, at-risk elderly. In N. L. Cohen (Ed.), *Psychiatry takes to the street* (pp. 195–209). New York: Guilford.

Reynolds, C., Frank, E., Dew, M., Houck, P., Miller, M., Mazumdar, S.,Perel, J.M., & Kupfer, D.J. (1999). Treatment of 70+-year-olds with recurrent major depression: Excellent short-term but brittle long-term response. *The American Journal of Geriatric Psychiatry,* 7, 64–69.

Reynolds, S. L., Hayley, W. E., & Kozlenko, N. (2008). The impact of depressive symptoms and chronic diseases on active life expectancy in older Americans. *American Journal of Geriatric Psychiatry,* 16, 425–432.

Robertson, J. M., & Fitzgerald, L. F. (1992). Overcoming the masculine mystique: Preferences for alternative forms of assistance among men who avoid counseling. *Journal of Counseling Psychology,* 39, 240–246.

Robertson, J. M., & Newton, F. B. (2001). Working with men in sports settings. In G. R. Brooks & G. E. Good (Eds.), *The new handbook of psychotherapy and counseling with men* (Vol. 1, pp. 92–125). San Francisco: Jossey-Bass.

Rochlen, A. B., Blazina, C., & Raghunathan, R. (2002). Gender role conflict, attitudes toward career counseling, career decision-making, and perceptions of career counseling advertising brochures. *Psychology of Men and Masculinity,* 3, 127.

Rochlen, A. B., & Hoyer, W. D. (2005). Marketing mental health to men: Theoretical and practical considerations. *Journal of Clinical Psychology,* 61, 675–684.

Rochlen, A. B., Mohr, J. J., & Hargrove, B. K. (1999). Development of the attitudes toward career counseling scale. *Journal of Counseling Psychology,* 46, 196–206.

Rochlen, A. B., & O'Brien, K. M. (2002a). Men's reasons for and against seeking help for career-related concerns. *Journal of Men's Studies, 11,* 55–63.

Rochlen, A. B., & O'Brien, K. M. (2002b). The relation of male gender role conflict and attitudes toward career counseling to interest in and preferences for different career counseling styles. *Psychology of Men and Masculinity,* 3, 9–21.

Rogers, C. R. (1966). *On becoming a person: A therapist's view of psychotherapy.* Boston: Houghton Mifflin.

Rojas-Fernandez, C. H., & Moorhouse, P. (2009). Current concepts in vascular cognitive impairment and pharmacotherapeutic implications. *The Annals of Pharmacotherapy, 43,* 1310–1323.

Ryan, E., Giles, H., Bartolucci, G., & Henwood, K. (1986). Psycholinguistic and social psychological components of communication by and with the elderly. *Language and Communication, 6*(1), 1–24.

Ryan, E., Hummert, M., & Boich, L. (1995). Communication predicaments of aging: Patronizing behavior toward older adults. *Journal of Language and Social Psychology, 14*(1), 144–166.

Saleh, S. S., & Szebenyi, S. E. (2005). Resource use of elderly emergency department patients with alcohol-related diagnoses. *Journal of Substance Abuse Treatment, 29,* 313– 319.

Salthouse, T. A. (1996). The processing-speed theory of adult age differences in cognition. *Psychological Review, 103,* 403–428.

Sanavio, E. (1988). Obsessions and compulsions: The Padua Inventory. *Behaviour Research and Therapy, 26,* 169–177.

Satre, D., Knight, B., & David, S. (2006). Cognitive-behavioral interventions with older adults: Integrating clinical and gerontological research. *Professional Psychology: Research and Practice, 37*(5), 489–498.

Satre, D., Knight, B., & Steven, D. (2006). Cognitive behavioral interventions with older adults: Integrating clinical and gerontological research. *Professional Psychology: Research and Practice, 37,* 489–498.

Satre, D., Knight, B., Dickson-Fuhrmann, E., & Jarvik, L. (2004). Substance abuse treatment initiation among older adults in the GET SMART program: Effects of depression and cognitive status. *Aging & Mental Health, 8,* 346–354.

Satre, D. D., Mertens, J., Areán, P. A., & Weisner, C. (2003). Contrasting outcomes of older versus middle aged and younger adult chemical dependency patients in a managed care program. *Journal of Studies on Alcohol, 64,* 520–530.

Sattar, S., Petty, F., & Burke, W. (2003). Diagnosis and treatment of alcohol dependence in older alcoholics. *Clinics in Geriatric Medicine, 19,* 743–761.

Schaie, K. W. (1994). The course of adult intellectual development. *American Psychologist, 49,* 304–313.

Schulz, R., Heckhausen, J., & O'Brien, A. (1994). Control and the disablement process in the elderly. *Journal of Social Behavior and Personality, 9*(5), 139–152.

Schwartzberg, S., & Rosenberg, L. G. (1998). Being gay and being male: Psychotherapy with gay and bisexual men. In W. S. Pollack & R. F. Levant (Eds.), *New psychotherapy for men* (pp. 259–281). New York: Wiley.

Scogin, F. (2007). Introduction to the special section on evidence-based psychological treatments for older adults. *Psychology and Aging, 22*(1), 1–3.

Scogin, F., & McElreath, L. (1994). Efficacy of psychosocial treatments for geriatric depression: A quantitative review. *Journal of Consulting and Clinical Psychology, 62*(1), 69–74.

Scogin, F., Welsh, D., Hanson, A., Stump, J., & Coates, A. (2005). Evidence-based psychotherapies for depression in older adults. *Clinical Psychology: Science and Practice, 12*(3), 222–237.

Scott, K., Von Korff, M., Alonso, J., Angermeyer, M., Bromet, E., Bruffaert, R., et al. (2008). Age patterns in the prevalence of *DSM-IV* depressive/anxiety disorders with and without physical co-morbidity. *Psychological Medicine, 38*(11), 1659–1669.

Shapiro, C. E. L. (2001, May). High-risk sexual behavior in the context of alcohol use: An intervention for college students. *Dissertation Abstracts International: Section B: The Sciences and Engineering, 61*(11-B), 6149.

Shapiro, D., Schwartz, C., & Astin, J. (1996). Controlling ourselves, controlling our world: Psychology's role in understanding positive and negative consequences of seeking and gaining control. *American Psychologist, 51*(12), 1213–1230.

Sharp, L. C., & Vacha-Haase, T. (2010, February). Physician attitudes regarding alcohol use screening in older adult patients. *Journal of Applied Gerontology.*

Shear, K., Frank, E., Houck, P. R., & Reynolds, C. F. (2005). Treatment of complicated grief: A randomized controlled trial. *JAMA: Journal of the American Medical Association, 293,* 2601–2608.

Sheng, B., Cheng, L. F., Law, C. B., Li, H. L., Yeung, K. M., & Lau, K. K. (2007). Coexisting cerebral infarction in Alzheimer's disease is associated with fast dementia progression: Applying the National Institution for Neurological Disorders and Stroke. *Journal of American Geriatric Society, 55,* 918–922.

Simoni-Wastila, L., & Yang, H. K. (2006). Psychoactive drug abuse in older adults. *American Journal of Geriatric Pharmacotherapy, 4,* 380–394.

Simonsen, G., Blazina, C., & Watkins, C. E., Jr. (2000). Gender role conflict and psychological well-being among gay men. *Journal of Counseling Psychology, 47,* 85–89.

Singer, E. (1981). Reference groups and social evaluations. In M. Rosenberg & R. H. Turner (Eds.), *Social psychology: Sociological perspectives* (pp. 66–93). New York: Basic.

Sirey, J. A., Bruce, M. L., Carpenter, M., Booker, D., Reid, M. C., Newell, K., & Alexopoulos, G. S. (2008). Depressive symptoms and suicidal ideation among older adults receiving home delivered meals. *International Journal of Geriatric Psychiatry, 23,* 1306–1311.

Smiler, A. (2004). Thirty years after the discovery of gender: Psychological concepts and measures of masculinity. *Sex Roles, 50*(1), 15–26.

Smith, B. (1999). The abyss: Exploring depression through a narrative of the self. *Qualitative Inquiry, 5,* 264–279.

Smith, G., & Rush, B. K. (2006). Normal aging and mild cognitive impairment. In D. K. Attix & K. A. Welsh-Bohmer (Eds.), *Geriatric neuropsychology: Assessment and intervention* (pp. 27–55). New York: Guilford.

Snarey, J. (Ed.). (1993). *How fathers care for the next generation.* Cambridge, MA: Harvard University Press.

Solomon, K. (1981). The masculine gender role and its implications for the life expectancy of older men. *Journal of the American Geriatrics Society, 29,* 297–301.

Sperry, L. (1995). *Psychopharmacology and psychotherapy: Strategies for maximizing treatment outcomes.* Philadelphia: Brunner/Mazel.

Spiegel, E. (1965). *Progress in neurology and psychiatry: An annual review.* Oxford, UK: Grune & Stratton.

Spitzer, B., Henderson, K., & Zivian, M. (1999). Gender differences in population versus media body sizes: A comparison over four decades. *Sex Roles, 40*(7), 545–565.

Sprenkel, D. (1999). Therapeutic issues and strategies in group therapy with older men. In M. Duffy (Ed.), *Handbook of counseling and psychotherapy with older adults* (pp. 214–227). Hoboken, NJ: John Wiley.

Stanley, M., Beck, J., & Glassco, J. (1996). Treatment of generalized anxiety in older adults: A preliminary comparison of cognitive-behavioral and supportive approaches. *Behavior Therapy, 27*(4), 565–581.

Steinhauser, K., Christakis, N., Clipp, E., McNeilly, M., McIntyre, L., & Tulsky, J. (2000). Factors considered important at the end of life by patients, family, physicians, and other care providers. *JAMA: Journal of the American Medical Association, 284*(19), 2476–2482.

Sternbach, J. (2001). Psychotherapy with the young older man. In G. E. Good & G. R. Brooks (Eds.), *The new handbook of psychotherapy and counseling with men: A comprehensive guide to settings, problems, and treatment approaches* (Vols. 1–2, pp. 464–480). San Francisco: Jossey-Bass.

Stice, E., Schupak-Neuberg, E., Shaw, H., & Stein, R. (1994). Relation of media exposure to eating disorder symptomatology: An examination of mediating mechanisms. *Journal of Abnormal Psychology, 103*(4), 836–840.

Stroebe, M., Boelen, P., van den Hout, M., Stroebe, W., Salemink, E., & van den Bout, J. (2007). Ruminative coping as avoidance: A reinterpretation of its function in adjustment to bereavement. *European Archives of Psychiatry and Clinical Neuroscience, 257*(8), 462–472.

Stroebe, M., Hansson, R., Schut, H., Stroebe, W., & Van den Blink, E. (2008). *Handbook of bereavement research and practice: Advances in theory and intervention.* Washington, DC: American Psychological Association.

Stroebe, M., & Schut, H. (2005). To continue or relinquish bonds: A review of consequences for the bereaved. *Death Studies, 29*, 477–494.

Stroebe, M., Hansson, R., Stroebe, W., & Schut, H. (2001). Introduction: Concepts and issues in contemporary research on bereavement. In M.S. Stroebe, R.O Hansson, W. Stroebe, & H. Schut (Eds.), *Handbook of bereavement research: Consequences, coping, and care* (pp. 3–22). Washington, DC: American Psychological Association.

Stroebe, M., Schut, H., & Stroebe, W. (2007). Health outcomes of bereavement. *The Lancet, 370*(9603), 1960–1973.

Stroebe, W., & Stroebe, M. S. (1987). *Bereavement and health: The psychological and physical consequences of partner loss.* Cambridge, UK: Cambridge University Press.

Substance Abuse and Mental Health Services Administration. (1998). *Substance abuse among older adults: Treatment improvement protocol (TIP)* (Series 26). Rockville, MD: U.S. Department of Health and Human Services.

Substance Abuse and Mental Health Services Administration (SAMHSA). (2009). *National survey on drug use and health.* Rockville, MD: U.S. Department of Health and Human Services.

Sue, D. (2005). Asian American Masculinity and Therapy: The Concept of Masculinity in Asian American Males. In G. Brooks & G.E. Good (Eds.), *The new handbook of psychotherapy and counseling with men: A comprehensive guide to settings, problems, and treatment approaches (Rev. & abridged ed.)* (pp. 357–368). San Francisco, CA: Jossey-Bass.

Sue, D. W., Arrendondo, P., & McDavis, R. J. (1992). Multicultural counseling competencies and standards: A call to the profession. *Journal of Counseling and Development, 70,* 477–486.

Tamir, L. M. (1982). *Men in their forties: The transition to middle age.* New York: Springer.

Thompson, E. H., Jr. (1994). Older men as invisible men in contemporary society. In E. H. Thompson, Jr. (Ed.), *Older men's lives* (pp. 1–21). Thousand Oaks, CA: Sage.

Thompson, L., Gallagher-Thompson, D., & Dick, L. P. (1996). *Cognitive-behavioral therapy for late-life depression: A therapist's manual.* Stanford, CA: VA Palo Alto Health Care System and Stanford University.

Thompson, L. W., Gallagher-Thompson, D., Futterman, A., Gilewski, M. J., & Peterson, J. (1991). The effects of late-life spousal bereavement over a 30-month interval. *Psychology and Aging, 6*(3), 434–441.

Torges, C. M., Stewart, A. J., & Nolen-Hoeksema, S. (2008). Regret resolution, aging, and adapting to loss. *Psychology and Aging, 23*(1), 169–180.

U.S. Department of Health and Human Services. (2006). *The road ahead: Research partnerships to transform services. A report by the National Advisory Mental Health Council's Workgroup on Services and Clinical Epidemiology Research.* Bethesda, MD: National Institutes of Health, National Institute of Mental Health.

U.S. Preventive Services Task Force. (2004). Screening and behavioral counseling interventions in primary care to reduce alcohol misuse: Recommendation statement. *Annals of Internal Medicine, 40,* 554–556.

Vacha-Haase, T. (2010). Consultation and training competency. In V. Molinari (Ed.), *Gerontological psychology.* New York: Oxford.

Van den Berg, P., Thompson, J., Obremski-Brandon, K., & Coovert, M. (2002). The tripartite influence model of body image and eating disturbance: A covariance structure modeling investigation testing the meditational role of appearance comparison. *Journal of Psychosomatic Research, 53*(5), 1007–1020.

Vesga-Lopez, O., Schneier, F. R., Wang, S., Heimberg, R. G., Liu, S., Hasin, D. S., & Blanco, C. (2008). Gender differences in generalized anxiety disorder: Results from the National Epidemiologic Survey on Alcohol and Related Conditions (NESARC). *Journal of Clinical Psychiatry, 69,* 1606–1616.

Vogel, D. L., Wade, N. G., & Haake, S. (2006). Measuring the self-stigma associated with seeking psychological help. *Journal of Counseling Psychology, 53,* 325–337.

Vogel, D. L., Wester, S. R., Larson, L. M., & Wade, N. G. (2006). An information-processing model of the decision to seek professional help. *Professional Psychology: Research and Practice, 37,* 398–406.

Wade, J. C. (1996). African American men's gender role conflict: The significance of racial identity. *Sex Roles, 34*, 17–34.

Wade, J. C. (1998). Male reference group identity dependence: A theory of male identity. *The Counseling Psychologist, 26*, 349–383.

Welsh-Bohmer, K. A., & Warren, L. H. (2006). Neurodegenerative dementias. In D. K. Attix & K. A. Welsh-Bohmer (Eds.), *Geriatric neuropsychology: Assessment and intervention* (pp. 56–88). New York: Guilford Press.

Wester, S. R. (2008). Multicultural advances in the psychology of men: Implications for counseling psychology. *The Counseling Psychologist, 36*(3), 294–394.

Wester, S. R., Arndt, D., Arndt, L., & Sedivy, S. K. (in press). Male police officers and stigma associated with counseling: The role of anticipated risk, anticipated benefit, and gender role conflict. *Psychology of Men and Masculinity*.

Wester, S. R., & Lyubelsky, J. (2005). Supporting the thin blue line: Gender sensitive therapy with male police officers. *Professional Psychology: Research and Practice, 36*, 51–58.

Wester, S. R., Pionke, D., & Vogel, D. L. (2005). Male gender role conflict, gay men, and same-sex romantic relationships. *Psychology of Men and Masculinity, 6*, 195–208.

Wester, S. R., & Vogel, D. L. (2002). Working with the masculine mystique: Male gender role conflict, counseling self-efficacy, and the training of male psychologists. *Professional Psychology: Research and Practice, 33*, 370–376.

Wester, S. R., Vogel, D. L., Pressly, P. K., & Heesacker, M. (2002). Sex differences in emotion: A critical review of the literature and implications for counseling psychology. *The Counseling Psychologist, 30*, 629–651.

Wester, S. R., Vogel, D. L., Wei, M., & McLain, R. (2006). African-American men, gender role conflict, and psychological distress: The role of racial identity. *Journal of Counseling and Development, 84*, 419–429.

Williams, J. B. W. (1988). A structured interview guide for the Hamilton Depression Rating Scale. *Archives of General Psychiatry, 45*, 742–747.

Wilson, D. (2000). End-of-life care preferences of Canadian senior citizens with caregiving experience. *Journal of Advanced Nursing, 31*(6), 1416–1421.

Winter, L., & Parker, B. (2007). Current health and preferences for life-prolonging treatments: An application of prospect theory to end-of-life decision making. *Social Science and Medicine, 65*, 1695–1707.

Winters, D. (2006). *Beyond band of brothers: The war memoirs of Major Dick Winters*. New York: Berkley Caliber.

Wisocki, P. A., Handen, B., & Morse, C. (1986). The Worry Scale as a measure of anxiety among home bound and community active elderly. *Behavior Therapist, 9*, 91–95.

Worden, J., & Monahan, J. (2001). *Caring for bereaved parents. Hospice care for children* (2nd ed., pp. 137–156). New York: Oxford University Press.

Yalom, I. (2008). *Staring at the sun: Overcoming the terror of death*. San Francisco: Jossey-Bass.

Yancura, L. A., Adlwin, C. M., Levenson, M. R., & Spiro, A. (2006). Coping, affect, and the metabolic syndrome in older men: How does coping get under the skin? *Journal of Gerontology: Psychological Sciences, 61B*, 295–303.

Yang, J., & Jackson, C. (1998). Overcoming obstacles in providing mental health treatment to older adults: Getting in the door. *Psychotherapy: Theory, Research, Practice, Training, 35*(4), 498–505.

Yang, Y. (2008). Social inequalities in happiness in the U.S. 1972–2004: An age-period-cohort analysis. *American Sociological Review, 73*, 204–226.

Yesavage, J. A. (1988). Geriatric depression scale. *Psychopharmacology Bulletin, 24*, 709–710.

Zeidan, F., Gordon, N. S., Merchant, J., & Goolkasian, P. (2009). The effects of brief mindfulness meditation training on experimentally induced pain. *Journal of Pain, 11*(3), 199–209.

Zung, W. W. K. (1965). A self-rating depression scale. *Archives of General Psychiatry, 12*, 63–70.

INDEX

A

ACA. *See* American Counseling
    Association
Acamprosate, 131
Accidental addiction to medication, 119
Active adult communities, 67
Addiction. *See also* Alcoholism;
    Substance use, abuse
    to medication, 114, 119
Adjustment to loss, meaning making in,
    72–73
Adult children, siblings, inclusion of, 37
African American men, 43–44
Ageism, 4–7
Alcohol-Related Problems Survey, 126
Alcohol treatment programs, 129–130
Alcohol use, 12, 118–119
    binge drinking, 120
    early-onset, *vs.* late-onset, 120–121
    prevalence of, 118
Alcohol Use Disorders Identification
    Test, 125
Alcoholism, 120. *See also* Alcohol use
    risk factors, 121–122
Alexithymic vascular presentation with
    dementia, 142
Alliance with client, 38–39
Alprazolan, 102
Alzheimer's disease, 137–138
American Association for Marriage and
    Family Therapy, 150
American Counseling Association, 150
American Indian men, 46
American Psychological Association,
    150, 153
Antabuse, 130

Anti-aging marketing, 6–7
Antidepressants, 86, 89, 101, 114
Antiepileptics, 114–115
Anxiety, 12, 72, 91–102
    Anxiety Disorders Interview
        Schedule, 97
    assessment, 95–98
    assessment measures, 97–98
    Beck Anxiety Inventory, 97
    clinical interview, 95–97
    cognitive behavioral therapy,
        98–100
    description, 94–95
    generalized anxiety disorder, 92–94
    Generalized Anxiety Scale, 97
    Hamilton Anxiety Rating Scale, 97
    pharmacological treatment, 101–102
    psychotherapy, 98–102
    screening, 95–98
    stress reduction interventions,
        100–101
    treatment options, 98–102
APA. *See* American Psychological
    Association
Appetite changes, 108
ARPS. *See* Alcohol-Related Problems
    Survey
Arthritis, 106
Asian American men, 44–45
Aspirin, 114
Assisted living, 67
Association for Adult Development and
    Aging, 150
Ativan, 102
AUDIT. *See* Alcohol Use Disorders
    Identification Test
Avolition, with dementia, 142